Worse Than You Think

Worse Than You Think

The Mostly True Story of Two Teachers
Running for Congress Deep in the
Heart of Texas

Todd Allen and Heath Hamrick

Fort Worth, Texas

Library of Congress Cataloging-in-Publication Data

Names: Allen, Todd, author. | Hamrick, Heath, author.
Title: Worse than you think : the mostly true story of two teachers running
    for Congress deep in the heart of Texas / Todd Allen and Heath Hamrick.
Description: Fort Worth, Texas : TCU Press, [2024] | Summary: "In
    contemporary American politics, where absurdity often overshadows
    reality, Worse Than You Think emerges as a refreshingly candid and witty
    account of what happens when ordinary individuals, fueled by a blend of
    idealism and frustration, leap into the political arena. This narrative
    dives into the real-life journey of a high school teacher, Edward "Todd"
    Allen, who took the bold step of running for Congress in 2018. Along for
    the ride was his best friend and fellow educator, Heath Hamrick, who had
    a simple job: make everything work out in the end. Todd and Heath embark
    on a quest to fix the "crazy circus" of our partisan divide, only to
    find themselves in a series of comical and eye-opening situations,
    encountering bizarre characters that could only arise deep in the heart
    of American politics. Worse Than You Think offers laughter, surprises,
    and perhaps a spark of inspiration to those contemplating their role in
    democracy. Whether you're seeking validation for your political
    cynicism, a guide on what not to do in a political campaign, or just a
    good laugh, this book promises to be an engaging read"-- Provided by
    publisher.
Identifiers: LCCN 2024033004 (print) | LCCN 2024033005 (ebook) | ISBN
    9780875658858 (paperback) | ISBN 9780875658964 (ebook)
Subjects: LCSH: Allen, Todd--Political activity. | Hamrick,
    Heath--Political activity. | United States. Congress--Elections,
    2018--Biography. | Political campaigns--Texas--History--21st century. |
    Campaign management--Texas--History--21st century. | High school
    teachers--Political activity--Texas. | United States--Politics and
    government--2017-2021.
Classification: LCC F391.3 .A55 2024 (print) | LCC F391.3 (ebook) | DDC
    324.9764/093--dc23/eng/20240801
LC record available at https://lccn.loc.gov/2024033004
LC ebook record available at https://lccn.loc.gov/2024033005

Illustrations and cover art by Heath Hamrick.
All photos are from authors' collection.

TCU Box 298300
Fort Worth, Texas 76129
www.tcupress.com

Design by Bill Brammer

For my children, Harper and Sam. Do big, bold, impossible things, take chances, and remember risk is worth experience.

To Lauren, forever.

—TODD ALLEN

To my wife Liz, whose sweetness, patience, understanding, and support were the truest things in this mostly true tale.

To Ethan and Abigail, who will one day ask about this book with Daddy's name on it, and after reading it maybe, just maybe, will decide that reaching for the stars without a safety net is okay.

And to Diana, who smiled and was kind at the right time to make a difference.

—HEATH HAMRICK

. . . faith in the face of doubt.

Contents

Two Idiots in the Rain
(An Introduction of Sorts)

It's been said that the best stories start off with the slaughter of a sleeping village by rampaging barbarians, or maybe the breakup of a romantic relationship. Unfortunately, the time I spent trying to get my friend Todd Allen elected to Congress could never be described as romantic (and pillaging the suburbs of a voting district isn't exactly on the table until *after* one gets elected). So, unlike the best of stories, *our* story starts with two idiots in the rain. It should go without saying that Todd and I were the idiots in question. I should warn you right away that this is not the kind of story where the scrappy underdogs win the championship, or the upright outsiders clean up the town by spin-kicking corrupt assholes through plate glass windows. If it helps, though, think of Todd Allen as Patrick Swayze in *Road House*, only with better hair (if possible). I'd like to think that makes *me* Sam Elliott.

I'd like to think that.

Back to those idiots in the rain: it was a few weeks before the primary elections in March of 2018, just after midnight on the first day political signs were allowed to be installed at polling places. Todd was a political neophyte and a congressional candidate that almost everyone thought was going to get his ass kicked in the primary; I was his friend and campaign manager and spent most of my time telling myself that he wasn't going to get his ass kicked in the primary. Neither of us knew much about what we were doing, and that was true whether that encompassed setting up campaign signs or running for political office. About all I thought I knew for certain that night was that Edward "Todd" Allen was *not* going to the US House of Representatives outside of a tour group or watching C-Span. And yet, despite what I suspected was sure and certain knowledge of impending defeat and embarrassment, we were hauling campaign signs from polling place to polling place in the freezing rain, hoping to get at least a couple hours of sleep in before we had to get up and go teach our respective classes at metroplex-area high schools.

That's right: we were and are teachers, not political operatives, not crusading attorneys, and not fighter pilots (although I have watched *Top Gun* more times than I can count). We were two average, apathetic, everyday Americans, finally driven off our respective couches by a desire to get involved and make a difference. It was 2018, and your average, apathetic, everyday American had plenty of motivation to get off the couch if they were so inclined and of a certain disposition. Our welcome in the world of politics had been less open arms and more middle finger. For two naïve, idealistic teachers who spent each weekday lecturing on the ideals of American democracy, the reality of a couple of months in the political trenches had been the spiritual equivalent of a throat punch.

At the best of times, the Allen for Congress political machine had maybe four or five cogs to move it along, and rainy nights in February did not qualify as the best of times. Thus, we were alone that night, hauling signs in the back of Todd's SUV. The signs were massive, the largest the counties would allow. They were also expensive as hell, and we could only afford about a dozen of them. I was eager to see what the largest single expense of the campaign looked like, so when I met up with Todd that night, I was a little anxious.

Todd popped the trunk door open and there they were: big blue signs with the name TODD ALLEN in a bold white font, the "O" forming a stylized, snarling bear for reasons best summed up as *reasons*. They were

How does that sentence go? "It was a dark and stormy night . . . when we put up signs."

big. They were expensive. They were creased.

I frowned.

"Hey, what the fuck, man?" I said, showcasing the wit and vocabulary for which I am well known.

Todd shrugged.

"We're not gonna lose the election because of a crease," he said irritably.

"We might," I shot back, although I knew he was right. I liked things to look *just so*, and, for that matter, so did Todd, which accounted for his irritation.

"This is what we get for ordering the biggest signs possible and never considering how to get them to polling locations." Todd has his own proclivity for post hoc wisdom. He usually got away with it.

It was a fair point.

"The signs are too big and the car is too small," I said, pointing out the obvious.

"The car is too small," he confirmed. "So I stuffed the signs in here however I could because it was that or leave them with the printer."

"And now they're creased," I said.

"Yeah," Todd affirmed. "Now they're creased."

Shakespeare would swoon at our dialogue, swear to God.

Anyway, the signs *were* big, and now they were creased. A few months past, that kind of thing would have driven us crazy. We'd have been embarrassed that we had overlooked something simple, like how the hell we were going to transport a dozen huge billboards with Todd's name on them. We'd have MacGyvered the shit out of the situation before we'd show the public anything with creases, misspellings, or horrible graphic design. But by that night, neither one of us thought anything we did on the campaign really mattered. Truth is, we'd have put those signs up if they had called for voters to send *Toad* Allen to Congress on a platform of equality for all amphibians.

Had running for Congress burned us out on solving exasperating problems of our own making and on humanity in general? You could say that, and I had, at an increasing volume and rate. It was a surprising condition to find myself in, since I'd previously considered myself immune to burnout. After all, I've been a teacher for twenty years now without ever burning out on my job. Despite all the issues that go hand in hand with public education, and all the hurdles teachers face, and the mounting evidence that an educator's worth in society's eyes is about nil, I still approach each day with energy and enthusiasm. Politics, however, was a whole 'nother beast. Politics, as you'll discover, is a daily gut punch. Politics sucked my soul in six months flat. By that night in February, I had hit the stage where I was actively rooting for Todd to give a speech that started, "Well, I'd like to thank all you assholes for ruining the political process, the ideals of the Founding Fathers, and my life, not necessarily in that order. Enjoy the General Tso's chicken on the buffet and go fuck yourselves."

Missed opportunities.

I noticed that the sharp edges of the signs had actually gouged out scratches in the interior paneling of Todd's SUV. Nervously, I asked, "Ummm . . . has Lauren seen those?"

"I'm saving that surprise for tomorrow," Todd responded.

"Awesome," I said as we set off for the first polling location. "You

Yup, the signs were big . . . and creased.

know, that'll work out really well for everyone involved. I can sense it. She's not gonna be pissed at all."

Sarcasm. Of course Lauren was going to be pissed, and I was certain I was gonna be the pissee.

Lauren, as you might have guessed from context clues, is Todd's wife. She's brilliant, beautiful, and somehow was raising two small children, teaching, and getting a doctorate in statistics all while Todd was running for Congress (if I had enough time and a phone handy, I could spell *statistics*). At this point in the campaign, she also hated the sound of my voice, possibly my mere existence, and almost everything to do with politics in general. I very much did not want her to see those scratches in her car. I cannot tell you how much I did not want her to see them. The only reason I feel even remotely safe writing it down now is because I feel an hour's drive through Metroplex traffic is a long way to go just to murder someone.

By the time we got to the first polling location, a small forest of yard signs had sprouted in various combinations of red, white, and blue. I felt a small pang of accomplishment: our giant billboards would stand out, and maybe people wouldn't notice that we had just *one* sign while other campaigns had littered the ground with them like trash under the stands at a football game.

Then I felt a slightly more robust pang when the sign whipped around in the wind like a sail and slapped me in the face.

When you read it, it sounds like a clever metaphor for what some average Joes ran up against when they tried to get into politics. Small accomplishments, mostly personal, followed by surprising bouts of pain and suffering. At the time, I wasn't looking at my life script as a metaphor, so mostly I was just annoyed that I was out in the rain wrestling a piece of plastic that was getting the best of the encounter.

Meanwhile, Todd was staring at the metal stake in his hands as if it were a complicated math problem.

"What?" I asked.

"You know what would've made this a lot easier?" Todd asked.

"This is one of those questions you want to answer yourself," I pointed out, finally getting the sign under something approaching control. I wasn't in much of a mood to indulge rhetorical questions. "So tell me what I missed. Enlighten me."

So he did. "It occurs to me that we probably needed *something* to hammer these stakes into the ground. You know, like a post driver or a sledgehammer, maybe a shovel."

Moments like these are meant to test us.

I exhaled slowly and when the crimson veil of self-rage had subsided, the sky was still above and the earth was still below and both were still spinning. "Okay," I said, "we forgot to buy a post driver. It's not the end of the world. Let's just look around and find a rock."

"A rock," Todd repeated tonelessly. "We're idiots."

It was hard to argue. We were, after all, standing in the rain for reasons that were becoming increasingly hard to fathom or justify. Worse yet, neither one of us even brought up the possibility of going to the nearest Walmart to get the aforementioned post driver, sledgehammer, or shovel. I can't say we even spent much time looking around for a handy rock. Nope, instead we decided to brute force those fuckers into the ground because we had started the job and we weren't going to stop, even if stopping made sense. I improvised a sophisticated technique that involved jumping up and down on the posts with my feet. At times, that

Todd poses beside one of the big signs on the rainy night when we both ruined our shoes.

would drive the post into the ground a half inch or so; other times, no amount of hopping and cussing would work, and we'd move the sign five or six feet away and try again. The rubber soles of my shoes were so sliced up by the end of the night that they went straight into the garbage.

Maybe that is a metaphor, too.

The thing I remember most about that night occurred just as we were beginning our futile struggle with the signs, the posts, the rain, and all that jazz. As Todd and I struggled with a sign outside a local library, a big pickup truck, the kind you might use to invade a small landlocked nation, rolled up with a massive flat-bed trailer in tow. Five or six high-school- or college-age boys piled out. While Todd and I watched, dumb-founded, they set about putting up campaign signs left and right. They were like a well-oiled machine, driving in stakes with a few pounding blows from a sledgehammer.

Wam, Wam. There was a conservative candidate for judge.

Wam, Wam. There was the Republican nominee for county commis-sioner.

It was dizzying.

"Ah," I said, nudging Todd and gesturing, "you were right. A sledge-hammer would make it easier."

Todd jumped one more time on a stake and wiped the rain from his face. "I'm starting to feel like we're doing this wrong."

A couple of five- or six-year-old kids were running around, laughing in the rain, setting up the smaller yard signs while their brothers were pounding in the giant billboards. I never saw an adult; maybe they stayed in the cab of the truck while the youngsters did all the dirty work. Within five minutes, the crew was gone, heading for the next polling place, leaving in their wake freshly planted signs for conservative candidates and Republican officeholders across the spectrum of public offices up for grabs. Todd and I hadn't put up one sign. Not one. We had, however, managed to make a fair start on fucking up two perfectly good pairs of shoes.

Looking back on it, that small encounter summed up the differences between the two major political parties, at least in Texas. The Republicans were organized, efficient, and mobilized energetic youth to get things done. Meanwhile, as a Democrat, I often felt like Todd and I were on some kind of political version of the *Titanic*, post-iceberg, sinking into freezing waters while panic and chaos erupted around us. At times that night, over the sound of Todd cussing and the freezing drizzle, I often thought I heard the strains of a band playing "Nearer, My God, to Thee" (which, to be honest, is a catchy tune).

"Stop humming that," Todd said, shaking his head. "And give me a hand with this sign."

The whole night, we saw only one other group of Democrats. They were better prepared than us. They had brought tools. They had a post driver. One of them eyed our signs appreciatively. "Nice wolf," he commented. I didn't bother to correct him; I was too tired. Besides, Todd's logo kinda did look like a wolf.

We chatted for a moment, and when he saw that we were trying to force the posts in by hand, he handed us his post driver. "Here," he said with a look of absolute sympathy, "you need it more than Home Depot does."

That is why I got home at 4 a.m. instead of two hours or so later.

So how did the election turn out? Did anyone vote for the guy who could barely put up campaign signs in the rain? Did we contribute to society one bit? Did we make the world a smidge better? Well, since you've never heard of Todd Allen or Heath Hamrick, you've probably made a few shrewd guesses about how an ordinary guy fared once he fell down the rabbit hole of American politics. If we're not spinning a rah-rah, feel-good tale of the triumph of the average Joe (and we're not) and we're not crying sour grapes (and the grape flavor is hopefully marginal), what kind of story is this?

What kind of story are we telling? One that is mostly true, sometimes frustrating, hopefully entertaining, perhaps infuriating or annoying, maybe even inspiring. How funny you think it is might depend on how much you appreciate dry humor as an appropriate, if inadequate, response to the ever-escalating shit show that is American politics. Take it from an expert: humor might be the only weapon an average, everyday, formerly apathetic but increasingly worried American has when they turn on the television, scroll through Twitter, or make the mistake of looking up old high-school friends on Facebook. It's okay to laugh, folks, and if you want to get a little angry, that's okay, too. When you set this book down, if you feel like doing more for the first time, then just know there are at least two guys out there who know the feeling. We'll be rooting for you.

For everyone else reading, we promise we'll say *fuck* only when absolutely fucking necessary.

So what is this story? It's the answer to a pretty good question for any American to ask in today's topsy-turvy world: What happened when two average, apathetic, everyday Americans ran for Congress?

Why don't you join a couple of idiots in the rain and find out?

PART I

Everyone Has a Plan Until They've Been to the Burger Barn

Margaritaville

If you had the ability, the inclination, and the requisite plutonium-powered vehicle (preferably with gull-wing doors), you could travel back in time to the winter of 2017 and witness the inception of the Todd Allen for Congress campaign. I have no idea why you'd want to do that, but, hey, some people think spending every weekend of their lives protesting in front of City Hall is fun, so . . . different strokes. If you did travel back to that February day in the dim and distant past, you could witness a political campaign being born while enjoying a plate of nachos and an adult beverage or two. It is a truth universally acknowledged that most worthwhile events in life revolve around Mexican food and margaritas, and this was no exception, even if you want to argue about the exact definition of what makes something worthwhile.

The first time I seriously tried to persuade Todd to run for Congress, we met at a Mexican restaurant just off Main Street in Grapevine, Texas. I was there early.

"Table for two," I told the hostess. "And if you have a table ready, I'm ready. My buddy won't mind if I have a margarita while I wait."

I knew Todd wouldn't care if I started the festivities a bit early. He was used to walking into restaurants and finding me looking bored, drumming my fingers on the table with an empty plate of appetizers in front of me. Besides, I was ready to get the night's conversation started, and melted cheese and carbohydrates took the edge off my impatience. The previous day I'd sent Todd a Facebook message suggesting that we should get together to talk about how the hell Donald Trump won the 2016 presidential election, the fall of American democracy, the general shittiness of politics, and Todd running for Congress. Maybe not in that particular order.

His reply was classic Todd Allen.

"Well," he wrote back, "let's meet over by that Mexican-food place off Main. If we're going to discuss the fall of the republic and seeking an office we can't win, then we might as well have a few margaritas."

To be clear, I wasn't going to be seeking any office, winnable or not. You weren't going to find the name Heath Hamrick anywhere near a ballot, even if I didn't think twice about volunteering my friend for that honor and all the headaches it entailed. Running for office just wasn't my bag: I had been one of those insanely socially awkward teenagers and time hadn't improved my general dislike of human beings since then. The only place I was comfortable around people was standing in a classroom, lecturing on the elitism of Alexander Hamilton or Macedonian tactics at the Battle of Gaugamela; in all other cases, I much preferred the company of classic movies on the DVD player to actual people.

Besides, I didn't have the fashion sense to be a political candidate. In fact, I have been reliably informed that I have no fashion sense at all. As I sat down at a booth that night, I was wearing a pullover and a go-to-hell cap, my traditional look.[1]

"What can I get you?" the waitress asked after I had made it clear that I had no intention of waiting on Todd to start stuffing my face with both cheese and alcohol.

"Frozen margarita," I told her, then clarified, "but I need you to do me a favor. Can you have them put it in a regular glass or maybe a beer mug for me?"

---

[1] The flat cap, or go-to-hell cap, gained its charming name by being most likely worn by irritable old men who were, as a rule, inclined to tell people to "go to hell." Yeah, I was in character.

The scene of many a campaign meeting: a table and a bowl of queso.

She looked confused. "You mean you don't want it in the cocktail glass?"

"Nope," I said. "Just a personal preference."

"Okay," she said, clearly convinced that I was both wasting her time and an asshole. I hated those comical cocktail glasses most restaurants serve margaritas in. Unless I was on a beach, I wanted something easy to hold, easy to drink, and nondependent upon a straw.

I was well on my way to downing that first margarita by the time Todd showed up (which was, incidentally, right on time). He was wearing what I call "white guy casual": jeans, untucked button-up, sandals. I hadn't seen him in a couple of years—years he had spent getting re-married and having kids and that I spent getting divorced and collecting swords and armor (the latter not necessarily related to the former). We'd basically been keeping touch solely through snippets of mutually beloved movie dialogue we posted on each other's timelines on Facebook.

Todd's a central-casting stereotype of a potential young politico, right down to the faux-Kennedy haircut. It was one of the reasons I had been bugging him, off and on over the last decade, about running for office. The dude *looked* the part, which, as I soon came to find out, was actually going to do him no favors as a Democratic candidate.

"Doctor," he said by way of a hello, sliding into the booth. That has been his habitual greeting for years, and I still have no clue what it means.

I slid a napkin across the table. On it, I had written three words in felt-tip marker: Allen for America. I felt no shame, then or now, in stealing from Aaron Sorkin. I've heard it is the sincerest form of flattery. Regardless, I knew Todd would understand the reference and draw the obviously appropriate conclusion: *Hey, maybe I can be the next statesman played by Martin Sheen who serves as a force for good will and acerbic wit.*

Todd squinted at the napkin, picked at something in the corner, and wondered aloud, "Is this queso?"

"Yeah," I said.

"So we had queso at one point?"

"Fifteen minutes ago," I said, motioning back to the napkin. "I need you to focus. They'll bring more queso."

He was frowning as he looked at the bowl in the middle of the table. "And you ate most of the chips," he said.

"I also drank a margarita," I said. We take our Mexican food seriously. In college, we cast our amateur film productions with actors who auditioned by answering a single, searing question: *what kind of Mexican food would you be, and why?*[2]

I leaned across the table and tapped the napkin. "What do you think?"

"I think *The West Wing* is a great show," Todd answered. "And I think that if we're gonna have the conversation I think we're gonna have, I need to go ahead and get a drink order in."

I got the feeling that the waitress didn't think Todd was an asshole as she took his order, but then, he made no odd demands about stemware. He got the comical glass, complete with an umbrella. He frowned,

---

[2] I've since used the same question in a frankly embarrassing number of professional development icebreakers and random employment interviews.

removed the umbrella and the straw, and muttered, "Who can drink out of these things, anyway?"

"My point exactly," I said dryly. "I think it should be your major policy platform. Fuck those funny glasses, anyway."

"Sounds like you've got the slogan all figured out." He laughed. "Put that shit on a T-shirt."

Then he leaned forward, and we started talking seriously about two ordinary, average, working Americans taking a shot at politics.

"Look," he said, "you teach the same classes I teach, so I know *you know* what an uphill battle this is. Americans fucking hate Congress. If Congress could poll in negative numbers, it would. If Congress had a face, America would punch it, maybe rip its throat out like in *Road House*."

"Love that movie," I said between bites.

"Everyone does, it's a brilliant film," Todd agreed. "But here's the thing, *Road House* is basically the inverse of Congress. People love *Road House*. People hate Congress. Except, and this is where it gets tricky, everyone loves their congressman. So, once you're in Congress, you've got something like a ten percent chance of getting voted out."

"Less than ten percent," I said, mostly 'cause I felt I needed to say something.

"Right." Todd reached over for another nacho. "An incumbent has an ungodly advantage. It's a job for life."

I nodded. Todd was on a roll. I didn't want to interrupt. It's often best that way.

He tapped the napkin and said, "So, knowing that, and knowing we don't know shit about running for office, you want to challenge an incumbent? A guy who has been re-elected every two years without rolling out of bed in the morning? We'd have, maybe, a one percent chance of winning. And that's probably too high."

It was too high, and I can't even say we didn't know it then.

Todd paused, bit into the chip. "And we're just regular guys. We got no money, no friends, no connections. I'm not a lesbian ex–fighter pilot turned crusading district attorney. I'm a teacher. People hate teachers."

"They really do," I said, holding up my end of the dialogue. It was true, or at least I thought it was: people might say they respect and honor teachers as the stewards of the next generation, but not-so-deep down most folks aren't big fans of professional educators. Don't believe me? Try this stat on for size: in a recent study, over 60 percent of Americans reported that they did not want their children to be teachers.[3]

If you were a time-traveling observer of this little scene, you'd probably sum up the conversation as two people talking about the impossible. That isn't the medical definition of crazy, but it probably isn't far from it.

Then I saw Todd's eyes fall on that napkin again, and I knew he was just playing devil's advocate.

"What do you really think?" I asked, even though I knew exactly what was running through his head. We had been friends and creative partners for too long for me not to. As he sat there trying not to stare at the napkin with his name on it, he was hearing a voice that sounded a hell of a lot like Burgess Meredith whisper, Why can't you run? What if you're different? What if you're the one that'll break the cycle? What if you can do the impossible just this once?

"I think I need to go home and watch *Rocky*," Todd said wistfully. I knew exactly what he meant.

He looked up from the napkin, finally, and said, "The underdog wins in the end, right? A guy that is nothing more than ordinary? That's the story you're trying to pitch me on?"

I shrugged. "I've always liked that story."

He grinned, ordered another margarita, and changed the subject, but I could tell that the idea lingered, like a line from a song.[4]

Todd wasn't wrong: we were and are just ordinary guys. We were too damn ordinary. Todd didn't have an inspirational story about overcoming odds. He hadn't grown up in a dumpster or been awarded medals for storming a Nazi-held beach, or even won a state championship while coaching football. He was just an average American, right down to the fact that he hadn't voted in most elections. He was part of that 46.9 percent of Americans who don't vote in presidential contests, and who feel like politics is for someone else—someone with more wealth, someone with a cause or a crusade, someone with a lot more free time

---

[3]Tim Walker, "NEA: Real Solutions, Not Band-Aids, Will Fix Educator Shortage," *NEA Today*, October 4, 2022, https://www.nea.org/nea-today/all-news-articles/nea-real-solutions-not-band-aids-will-fix-educator-shortage.

[4]I'll say this, I don't miss politics, but I sure as hell miss the dream that two regular guys could get off their couch and make a difference. I miss that a lot.

on their hands than a teacher raising two small children in Texas. That was all before 2016, of course. The '16 election shook both of us, and we weren't alone. It motivated a Democratic base to mobilize in a way they never had before. It brought Todd to that restaurant (along with the tequila) and set us on the merry little path that leads right to this page in your hands.

Lucky you.

Reaching for the *damn-near* or *for-fucking-certain* impossible was something we did fairly often, to be honest. Todd Allen has been my best friend since my freshman year at Trinity University in San Antonio, where we both found ourselves playing football. Neither one of us was anything but a decent high school player, so we spent most of our time re-enacting the most grueling scenes of *Rudy* while All-Americans took turns running over us on the scout team. We both graduated with political science degrees, ostensibly because we wanted to be lawyers, a job that is respected and pays well. Instead, we racked up massive amounts of private school debt to become teachers, a job that isn't and doesn't. In the fifteen years or so since we graduated, we had been through life's rough patches in similar doses, including a failed marriage for each of us.

Todd brought up our various domestic and professional failures somewhere around our third round of margaritas. He had a theory, which, like the best theories, only got better under the influence of alcohol. "Sometimes," he said, absently swirling the dregs of his glass, "it feels like we are always trying to prove we're good enough. You name it, man: college football, making films, being a husband and dad—"

"And politician?"

"Maybe," he said. "Maybe we find ourselves taking those long shots because we have something to prove." After a moment's reflection, he added, "Or maybe it's because it feels like our generation never had a beach to storm."

I saluted him with my own empty glass and said, "Profound."

We'd spent most of our college years running around with video cameras and scripts, pretending to be filmmakers when we should have been studying constitutional law.[5] We were, and remain, *storytellers*, which

---

[5] Sorry, Dr. Hermann.

is probably why we both wound up being teachers. In my history classes, I found the perfect vehicle to tell stories and bring characters to life for students. I won't speak for Todd, but I'd hazard a guess that his choice of profession follows similar logic, even if, as he often claims, he never learned to read.

That night, over nachos and margaritas, Todd and I ignored the practicalities and spun a fairytale for ourselves. We talked about telling voters a story about a guy frustrated by what he saw on the nightly news, an ordinary teacher with no money or connections who could run for office on the promise that things could be better. We threw out a lot of words that night that we believed were missing from politics—words like *civility*, *compassion*, *conversation*, and *compromise*. Boiled down, our dialogue revolved around a single, simple question: What if someone ran for office who wasn't batshit insane?

Now, of course, we know better. Insane politicians aren't a bug of modern American politics, they're a feature. Only crazy fuckers, ego-maniacs, and the wealthy run for office more than once; being batshit is basically a prerequisite.

I sometimes wonder how often ordinary Americans think about just how crazy politics has become. Do two nurses sometimes stop, wipe their brows, and wonder if one of them could run for Congress? Does a post-al worker meet up with a construction foreman and talk about how they could get votes from other Americans just like them? Does a steelworker in Pennsylvania or an oil hand in Texas ever show up at a meeting of a local political activist group and say, "Hey, I'm not fucking crazy, and I think a lot of folks out there are willing to vote for someone, anyone, who *isn't* fucking crazy"?

I was willing to bet there were enough Americans out there like me. Americans who were sick and tired of political theater, golden escalators, and elections that felt meaningless. I was willing to bet those Americans were out there, waiting on their couches and scrolling through Twitter looking for someone worth voting for. I was also betting that I could make Todd Allen believe those Americans were waiting for *him*.

With enough margaritas, maybe I could pull it off.

Get Back in the Car
'Cause You Are About to Die

You might have caught on by now that Todd and I share a certain affection for the *Rocky* films, maybe because we both connected with the plight of a seemingly regular, down-on-his-luck guy going the distance in a fight against impossible odds. He might never have gotten the chance to take a literal punch to the face, but I still say that Todd Allen deserves a lot of credit for going the distance in politics, from those nachos all the way through to the beer we drank as we watched the numbers come in on election day. You might be wondering why he did it, why he jumped into something he knew to be impossible, and what the fuck I was doing helping.

The answer lies in California.

Or, more accurately, in a trip the two of us had taken to California during our college years. We spent a lot of time at Trinity University running around campus with a video camera and bulky Hi8 tapes, trying to make movies. This was just before the digital revolution, so the quality of the cameras we checked out from the library was super low.

The only way we could edit the footage was in darkened editing bays in the Communications Department, waiting five hours for three seconds of footage to render, with nothing to do but drink caffeine and talk. Our real friendship probably dates back to those editing bays, come to think of it.

One night, Michael Moore walked through those editing bays, maybe looking for a bathroom. He was speaking that night at Trinity, but, tellingly, this particular political science major had no idea who he was.

That, ladies and gentlemen, is what we call an indicator.

Anyway, Todd and I quickly realized a life truth that we nonetheless spent years trying to ignore: namely, that the only people we could rely on to act in our films were the two of us, and as thespians we were just goddamn awful. "We're not Jake Lloyd in *Phantom Menace* awful," Todd would sometimes say, "but we rival Hayden Christensen in *Attack of the Clones* awful."

Our writing, though . . . we thought our writing, particularly our sense of dialogue, was pretty decent. Good, even. And from that tiny little germ of an idea (*hey, our writing isn't nearly as shitty as our acting*), a plan blossomed that was equal parts naïvete, arrogance, and straight-up head-scratching *What the shit, son?* nonsense.

The plan, in its glorious simplicity (and lunacy), involved printing off two dozen copies of our latest script, tossing them in the back seat of my Mustang, driving down I-10 from Todd's parent's house in Iraan, Texas (which is just south of nowhere in a part of Texas that can only be described as hellish), to Los Angeles, all basically overnight. Once there, somehow we'd deliver said scripts to agents who would make us famous before we had to drive back home on Sunday. Sleep didn't seem to be built into the schedule, but that was fine, because we forgot sense along with it. Anyone with any familiarity or involvement with the entertainment industry probably is already rolling on the floor in hysterical convulsions after reading that paragraph. Impossible doesn't begin to describe what we intended with our forty-eight-hour California adventure.

And yet, we almost pulled it off.

Things started off well enough as we went tearing off across West Texas for what seemed like hours, listening to CDs I had burned especially for the trip, and daydreaming about Hollywood fame and fortune. That night, somewhere around the Arizona line, we pulled over at a truck stop. This is where the plot thickens, so pay attention. I want to be clear that I wasn't tired at that point. Sure, we'd been driving for ten hours or so, and sure, it was pitch black, and sure, the fetid, overhanging feedlot stink that is the state of New Mexico didn't exactly encourage a condition of restful zen, but I wasn't tired. I was self-medicating with enough caffeinated beverages to wake the dead, at speeds considerably over the speed limit, even for the American West.

Seriously, back in those days, I was fond of Dr Pepper to the point of overindulgence. Back, in other words, before the ravages of my aging, slowing, back-stabbing bastard of a metabolism forced me to rethink my calorie intake. I had left empty bottles of Dr Pepper over the better part of two states by the time we pulled into that truck stop, so, again, for the record, I wasn't tired.

In what had to have been an abundance of caution (always a laudable motive, I think), I decided to hedge my bets against encroaching fatigue. I bought a bottle of caffeine pills known as Yellow Jackets, though the bottle might as well have been labeled Tic Tac, 'cause that is how I treated them. Off we drove into the dark of the Southwest, my foot heavy on the gas pedal of the Mustang, popping caffeine pills like Chiclets and chasing them down with Dr Pepper. I felt good, if a bit disappointed in the lack of effect from those Yellow Jackets. I didn't feel a damn thing. No rush of energy, no spark in the soul or fire in the gut, no superpowers or the ability to use 100 percent of my brain's potential, nothing. Annoyed, I popped another pill, hoping for a rush of energy. Then another.

Then another.

And another. *Ad infinitum* or *ad nauseum*, whichever came first, and I'm guessing you know which that was. Somewhere around the California border, those Yellow Jackets finally bit me. The little fuckers.

Todd has forever after referred to the events of the night as "the pukening." I'm not sure *pukening* is an actual word, and Google's spell checker seems to agree, but you know what? Let's forget that squiggly red line for a moment and reflect on how awesome a title Todd found for the movie they will base on this trip: *The Pukening*. I like it. It sums up the next events perfectly.

Which events, you ask? Well, to start, my stomach leapt into my throat, and I suddenly swerved across three lanes of traffic and parked beside a ditch. Five seconds later I was on my knees, upchucking the better part of a six pack of Dr Pepper and a Big Mac into the desert dust. I heard the passenger door open, and Todd ask sleepily, "Hey, what the fuck, dude? You alright?"

Funnily enough, after a moment, I thought I was. I even got back into the driver's seat and pulled back into traffic. *That was weird*, I remember thinking. I blinked hard, took a swig of flat Dr Pepper to rinse out the vomit flavor in my mouth, and tried to focus on the road.

Minutes later, I was back in the ditch, convinced I was dying. It was the only reasonable explanation. Symptoms I had only been vaguely aware of were making themselves known. No, scratch that: those fuckers weren't just introducing themselves, they were walking into my house, kicking my dog, violating my possessions, and pissing on my rug.[1] The vomit wasn't the worst, but it was bad, uncontrollable, like my stomach was locked on the *spasm* setting. Everything I'd eaten for a week was winding up in the ditch.

"Just like that scene from *Jaws*," I heard Todd say.

By way of a response, I vomited some more.

Todd took it as an invitation to expand upon the theme. "You know the scene I mean," he said conversationally, "the one where they catch that shark that *isn't* Jaws and they cut it open and all that shit spills out on the dock? Any minute you are gonna puke up a license plate."

I had no immediate comeback, just vomit and an increasing awareness that I was, medically speaking, not okay. My heart was slamming against my ribs like I was in the middle of running wind sprints, and the horrid, terrible, awful cherry on that shit sundae was that it wasn't just *not* slowing down . . . it was speeding up. Every minute, just when I didn't think my heart could beat any faster, some biological overseer in my body clamped down on a cigar and was like, "Whelp, the boss says faster, we're gonna go faster!" It was an out-of-body experience: my heart was outside my body, sprinting Usain Bolt–style down the highway, and I was trailing behind, begging it to slow the fuck down.

Meanwhile, Todd had picked up the bottle of Yellow Jackets and was studying it with a look on his face that was a cross between disgust and panic. Later on, he'd tell me what was on the label in clear, truck-stop language: *Do not take more than two (2) in a 24-hour period. Side effects may*

---

[1] The latter, as you might have heard, really tied the room together

include heart attack, chest pain, stroke, and a bunch of other really bad shit.

I might have made the last bit up, but you get the picture.

"Hey, Heath," Todd said. "Just how many of these did you take?"

I sputtered out some version of the truth. I told him that five or ten wasn't out of the question, but I had lost count. In response, there was a deep sigh, like a student finally realizing they don't know the answer to those con law questions and fuck this exam anyway.

It was at this point, with me on my knees in the middle of the California desert, that I heard the words that have been etched in my memory ever since. When he dies, I will make sure Todd has these words engraved on his tombstone and published in his obituary.

"Okay," he said bitterly, "I'm gonna need you to get back in the car, 'cause I think you are about to die."

I've kinda blocked out the rest of the night, but Todd assures me that I didn't seek out additional clarification or even get really upset when he told me that I was on death's door. Apparently, I just crawled over to the car and climbed into the passenger seat in what was the saddest fucking thing he'd seen up to that point in his life, which included at least one theatre viewing of a *Star Wars* prequel. I do vaguely remember the roar of the Mustang's engine as Todd pulled back into traffic and the irritation in his voice as he said, "Fasten your seat belt. Roll down the window. Puke as needed, but we're gonna keep moving." Off we went across the California desert, me puking out the window of the speeding Mustang, leaving vomit to dry on the paint job in long strings.

Some of you may be wondering why we didn't just pull over when I needed to hurl. Well, when you are retching up last week's breakfast every five minutes for a few hours, pulling over puts a little dent in your ability to get anywhere (namely, a hospital). We stopped pulling over; it wasn't going to help, and my stomach wasn't going to cease and desist. We drove across Southern California in the early morning darkness, realizing there is absolutely nothing between the border and Los Angeles but desert, dust, more desert, and, of course, my vomit. A hospital, you ask? Fat chance: there was road and more road, and let me just take a moment here to point out that the California highway system can go fuck itself with a sharp, rusty stick, preferably one with some kind of ninety-degree bend in it.

"Goddamnit," Todd said at one point. "Is Texas the only state with a functional highway system?"

Maybe. Regardless, I might have some lingering bitterness concerning California.

Five hours later, after vomiting all over Southern California and, I'm proud to say, a good part of Beverly Hills, I was no longer puking up anything but bile (cheerier words have rarely been spoken, I know). Todd found a clinic that didn't make either of us feel we might be robbed, beaten, or raped in the waiting room, and I saw some medical professionals who seemed disappointed that I had overdosed on something as banal as caffeine pills.

Todd was out in the hallway, reaching out to people who needed to know that somehow I had wound up in a California hospital due to an overdose of stupidity. I remember hearing him call my fiancée and leading off with the kind of golden wordplay that made me think he was a born politician. "So," he began, "don't freak out. Heath is in the hospital, and he overdosed. No, on caffeine pills." He paused then yelled out, "Yeah, he's a fucking idiot."

I think Todd called my parents, too, if only to ask them for their insurance information.

After about six IV bags of fluids to replace everything I'd lost on our little jaunt to California, and a strong anti-nausea drug to get my stomach to stand the fuck down, Todd and I were set loose on an unsuspecting Tinseltown to make our fortunes in the thirty hours or so of the weekend that remained.

Here's one thing you need to know about us: we're not quitters.

We put on dress shirts and ties (in my case, both extremely wrinkled), grabbed scripts, and started walking into every talent agency we could find. Keep in mind that I had just driven across most of the Southwest, overdosed on pills that would soon be banned from sale, spent at least six hours hurling the contents of my stomach out the window of my Mustang, and another six hours in a hospital bed, wondering just how much a typical IV bag costs and whether six of them were really necessary. In other words, I was in what we might politely term *a condition*.

"You look like shit," Todd said before we shouldered through the doors of the first agency.

He wasn't wrong. My sleeves were rolled up, revealing the blood-stained bandages wrapped around both arms where the nurse had stuck the IVs in and apparently had some trouble getting them out (her exclamation of "oops" was telling). I was white as a sheet and looked like I'd just walked off the set of *The Walking Dead*, which was impressive given that show was over a decade away from being produced.

I got even paler as we quickly faced reality: for an agent to see you or read your material, it really requires that you've *done something* to assure them that they aren't wasting their time. This made sense. After all, you don't want to read scripts from every asshole who shows up after driving cross-country through a haze of caffeine pills and vomit. The problem is, in order to do something in Hollywood, you have to have an agent. It was a circle that seemed impossible to break into, which didn't keep us from trying. Todd laid the charm on several secretaries, only to be politely but firmly shown the door.

Then, God bless him, Todd Allen changed tactics and showed why years later I thought he'd take Congress by storm. He had realized that our only option was to create a story so plausible that a secretary might just fear for her job if she didn't take our script. All he needed was an opening, which the next secretary provided in spades.

"Is your friend okay?"

We were in our third or fourth agency lobby, facing our third or fourth incredulous secretary. This particular one had seen me looking like death warmed over and was concerned. Todd swung into action. He leaned his elbows up against her desk, smiled, and said something along the lines of, "Yeah, he's had a bit of a rough day. Our friend Carl Bowman over at Showtime thought we had something Paul should look at, so we drove from Texas last night. Thought we'd deliver the script and maybe do some sightseeing; you know how it is."

It was like throwing a switch. As soon as Todd said we were from Texas, the woman mentioned she was from Texas and suddenly Todd was her new best friend. I tried not to vomit or pass out as they chitchatted about the Lone Star State, how she had recently ended up in California, and of course how important Carl thought it was for us to deliver this script.

I like to think of it as a completely necessary lie.

"Is he going to be okay?" the secretary asked again, looking my way. I can't tell you how many times people have asked Todd that very same question about me over the years.

I was a bit shocked by Todd's audacity: our friend Carl was barely our friend, knew nothing about what we were doing, and was employed at Showtime as something akin to a coffee fetcher.

"He's gonna be fine," Todd continued, "he just took some expired caffeine pills that really messed him up, so we spent the last twelve hours or so in the hospital."

Then he launched into an abbreviated, if exaggerated, version of our last twenty-four hours. I found myself thinking the whole story would make a good script. I also found myself wondering if the secretary would mind if I lay down on the lobby's couch or, failing that, just passed out on the floor.

"Oh, wow," the secretary said. "He does look like he just got out of the hospital."

"He literally just walked out about twenty minutes ago," Todd agreed. "So much for our sightseeing, right? We have to head on back to Texas, but need to drop off a few copies of the script around town first. It's been a hell of a trip."

"Sounds like it," she said, shaking her head.

"So," Todd said, "would you mind delivering this for me, or should I just drop it outside Paul's office, or . . . ?"

Holy shit. *Holy fucking shit.* She promptly directed him to the agent's office, where Todd dropped off the script (and a few more copies at other doors along the way). He winked at me as we left, and suddenly, we had a game plan. It didn't work everywhere, but damned if my zombielike appearance and Todd's charm (not to mention name-dropping a non-name) didn't work! By the end of the afternoon, every script was delivered somewhere, even if it was only a dumpster, and we were on our way back to Texas.

What is the moral of this particular tale? Simply this: four weeks later, I got a call from a Hollywood talent agency, asking about the script and wondering what else we had to offer. This, as folks can tell you, was impossible. It never happens. Legit agents like the one who rang us up just don't make cold calls. And yet, there I was, on the phone with an agent at 8:00 on a Monday morning. I proceeded to blow that once-in-a-lifetime chance with astonishing speed, but that's not the moral of this fable.

The lesson is what you learn about Todd Allen and Heath Hamrick through this little adventure to California. Are they naïve to the point of idiocy? Absolutely. Audacious and willing to risk big chunks of time and effort on the slimmest of possibilities, certainly. Painfully prone to self-sabotage if given half a chance, embarrassingly so.

But we were also willing to stare straight into the face of doubt and have faith that we could succeed, regardless of the impossibilities. Ninety-nine percent of people out there wouldn't have gotten in that Mustang and driven to California for what amounted to a glorified delivery run. Heck, 99.9 percent of people wouldn't have a script to deliver in the first place. I'm not saying we're especially talented, but we are, in a way, especially stubborn. Once we decide we're gonna go, then we *go*, and we do it with an intensity that can be called zealous; occasionally, we do it while popping caffeine pills, vomiting, winding up on a hospital bed, and manipulating our way into talent agencies.

Knowing that puts a whole 'nother slant on our meeting in a Mexican restaurant in February 2017. We weren't deciding if we could run a campaign for Congress; we both knew we could before we ever picked up a nacho. We were trying to decide whether we wanted to commit to this idea. Could an average Joe run for office? I was betting so, but what the hell do I know? The answer is next to nothing *now*, and that's after running a congressional campaign and producing media for everything from the Texas Democratic Party (I know) to statewide candidates to congressional wannabes to folks running for local dogcatcher. Back then, as I tackled a third margarita, I knew less than nothing. Neither did Todd. But what I did know was this: once Todd Allen said he was gonna run, then come election day, his name would be on that ballot. He wouldn't quit, and he'd do the best job he could.

I was convinced he could do it. I wanted him to get in that Mustang and take a trip all the way to Washington, DC. Now I just needed to convince him.

Faith in the face of doubt.

Fix All The Shit

I f I've learned one thing from the cinematic characters of Alec Baldwin, and I'd like to think that I have, it's be careful what you shoot at
aboard a Russian nuclear submarine, because some things don't react
well to bullets. If I've learned two things, it's that I should *Always Be
Closing*, because it's fuck or walk. By that measure I guess I was walking,
because when Todd and I wrapped up dinner at that Mexican restaurant
back in 2017, I hadn't closed the deal and he was far from convinced
that running for Congress was a good idea (or even remotely possible).
All I had really accomplished so far was to polish off a plate of fully
loaded nachos while Todd pointed out just how much of a waste of time
an Allen for Congress campaign would be.

"Scale of one to ten," I asked, fishing through the chip bowl for
anything larger than a grain of sand. "One to ten, how close are you to
actually running for US Congress?"

He motioned for the check. "It's not as easy as that. It's not like I'll
say *yes*, order a celebratory round, and down tequila shots while the

other folks in here slowly rise to their feet while clapping and thanking us for saving democracy."

"No shit," I said, exasperated (or maybe just slightly drunk). "That's because you're not a *jump-right-in* kind of guy, and you're certainly not a *round-of-shots* kind of guy. You hate shots. You're a *worst-case-scenario* kind of guy."

"I really am," he said reflectively. "Just ask Lauren. She'll tell you straight up that I'm no fun. I call it being a realist."

"So? Shots aside, are we gonna do this or not?"

Todd is pretty invulnerable to peer pressure. Pressing him to make a decision he's not ready to make just isn't going to work. It wasn't like he feared taking on a political run because it was obviously impossible. Neither one of us was scared of the impossible, but the impossible, coupled with the exhausting going hand in hand with the expensive, was bordering on too much, even for two guys who bluffed their way into a Hollywood callback on nothing but vomit and charm.

As he stood up from the table, Todd said, "I've got a hunch a decision like this requires a bit of thought, okay? Putting myself forward as a candidate for US Congress needs to be fully thought out for longer than the space of time it takes you to eat a plate of nachos—"

"I also had a piece of *tres leches*," I pointed out.

He was undeterred. "Not to mention that something with the potential to bring the normal flow of my life to a grinding halt needs total team support at Casa Allen. I've got to talk to Lauren. I've got to think about things. So don't go mocking up my campaign posters just yet."

By the time we hit the parking lot, I felt the idea of a Todd Allen candidacy was probably buried alongside some of my more improbable schemes. I was certain the dinner was a bust and that Todd was gonna shrug off the pipe dream of a congressional run. I wasn't even sure if I could blame him. We stood by our cars in the parking lot and moved on to discussing what had really brought us to the table that winter, and it wasn't the impossibility of taking on an entrenched Republican incumbent in Texas and winning. Given the year and the situational awareness of any functioning human not living under a rock, I'd bet you already know what inspired a couple of apathetic government teachers to get off the couch, start slamming tequila, and contemplate something as crazy as a run for Congress, and it wasn't the fucking deficit.

In February 2017, Donald John Trump had been president of the United States for about three weeks.

Love him or hate him (and there seems to be no in-between), you must admit that Trump shook up the country in a way that terrorist attacks, economic depressions, and failed Middle Eastern regime changes never did. Twenty years ago, if you had told me that the guy I only knew from a scene in *Home Alone 2* would occupy some permanent real estate in my daily mental space, I'd have wondered what kind of drug you were on. Now, I don't hesitate to say that the single most important person in American history in the last century is Donald Trump, and if you've got a visceral, gut-level negative reaction to that statement, well . . . now you know how I felt that February.

Those three weeks felt like an eternity. Every day was a shit storm of tweets and Trump campaign surrogates spewing mind-numbing nonsense and frankly admirable levels of total bullshit on cable TV. Every morning I'd call Todd, or he'd call me, and we'd talk about the dumpster fire being passed off as presidential policy the night before. For a while, each morning ended with a mutual sense of worry that America had hit rock bottom. By the time of that dinner at the Mexican restaurant, we each had realized there was no bottom.

So, obviously, Todd and I had some strong opinions as regards Mr. Trump and his ability to walk in straight lines, talk in complete sentences, and finish (or have) a coherent thought. In this, we weren't alone—conservative or liberal, Democrat or Republican or politically apathetic, your life changed with the political ascendancy of Donald Trump, whether you want to admit it or not. I firmly believe that historians will divide American history into two periods: *before* Donald Trump came down a golden escalator like something out of a *Saturday Night Live* skit, and *after*, when alternative facts became a real thing. No one really got through the 2016 election season without somehow facing up to the new reality that was Donald Trump, not even two high school government teachers like Todd and me.

I woke up on the morning of September 11, 2001, just in time to watch a jumbo jet crash into the side of one of the World Trade Center towers, a tragedy that my current students weren't even alive for. At the time, I thought the 9/11 attacks were going to be the event that shaped my life, but now I can honestly say that my world changed more because a guy with orange-tinged skin managed to become a cult-like icon in American politics. Go figure.

The good news is that I don't have to describe how or why Donald Trump's existence changed things. Red or blue, you already know because you experienced it. I can just skip to the good parts, beginning in that Mexican restaurant parking lot with Todd as I was trying to convince him that the country was in a flat spin, heading out to sea with both engines flamed out.

"Wait," he said. "Am I Goose in this scenario or—"

"Jesus, no," I responded. "Maverick. Come on, man. Try to keep up."

Todd was naturally skeptical of the doom and gloom prophecies I weaved around Trump's sudden rise to the White House. "Look," he said, "it's not like the guardrails of democracy are gonna crumple like tinfoil. We've got checks and balances, constitutional norms, shit like that. You know, the things we lecture on in class every semester."

Todd's a remarkably even-keeled dude, all told. He doesn't get mad or worked up about life's little things. It wasn't just hubris or ego that pushed me to push *him* into running for Congress. I thought, if anyone was built to listen and interact with people of all shapes, sizes, creeds, and colors, it was Todd Allen. He didn't hold grudges, and he wasn't prone to exaggeration or flights of fancy.

It could be irritating.

"I'm talking about a fucking dystopia!" I said, gesturing wildly.

"You're talking about a Stephen King movie," he replied, unfazed.

"No, no," I said, having a brainstorm. "I'm talking about your first political ad."

He chuckled. "Jesus Christ. Okay."

So I pitched him on what I thought his first political ad should be. It would be brilliant, I told him, because it would play off the same fears that had prodded us into action (or, you know, eating nachos and bitching about the election, which was pretty much the same thing).

"Picture this," I said, going into full-on Spielberg mode. "Blighted urban landscape—"

"That's how I know you're serious," he said. "That word right there. Blighted. No one in the history of storytelling has opened with a word like blighted and not been serious."

"Massive storm clouds," I continued, warming to the pitch. "Thunder rolls. A man in a pea coat walks down a dark alley, hands in his pockets, all hunched over 'cause this version of the near-future is cold 24-7, 365 days a year. We see his face: grizzled, bearded, old before his time—"

"You know, Bobby could play that guy," Todd said, leaning against the door of his car. "He pretty much constantly looks disheveled. Or like a guy who has decided beard maintenance and caloric intake just don't matter anymore."

"Your brother is exactly who I was picturing," I said, "especially since he's still rocking that *Jeremiah Johnson* beard. I was driving up here thinking, 'We really need someone to play stoic and suffering and bearded in a political ad, and that someone is Bobby Allen.' "[1]

Rabbit trail. I pulled the conversation back onto the road by saying, "Okay, so the wind blows a newspaper across the alley right under his feet, along with a bunch of garbage. He looks down at a headline that says, I dunno, 'Third Term in a Landslide!' He scowls and keeps walking—"

"That's not gonna happen," Todd said, shaking his head. "You'd need a constitutional amendment at minimum or a court willing to ignore a violation of the Twenty-Second Amendment. Basically impossible."

"People don't *know* that," I shot back, "so let me set the fucking scene, alright? Not everyone teaches AP Government. So, anyway . . . Bobby keeps walking. He comes up on a dilapidated building all boarded up and padlocked. Big yellow sign on the door. Lots of seals. And it says, 'This newspaper closed by order of the President of the United States'. He shakes his head and—"

"Dude." Todd rolled his eyes.

"I know, you don't think it's gonna happen." I could sense a theme developing. The government teacher in me wanted to launch into a nuanced discussion on the Espionage Act of 1917, but it was cold out, and I was in a hurry. Anyway, I talked about our grizzled and weary point-of-view character walking past faded propaganda posters featuring a

---

[1]This was, more or less, one of Todd's first political ads, and Bobby Allen did indeed play the grizzled Jeremiah Johnson stand-in. Like, maybe a hundred people saw it.

familiar silhouette and the words Believe Me in big letters. I talked about how this character would feel beat down by the oppressive environment, but just when the viewer would feel depressed enough to start thinking about pounding straight vodka, good ole grizzled Bobby would suddenly stop. His face would take on a determined look. He'd walk back up to one of those totalitarian-esque posters and take a can of blue spray paint out of his jacket pocket.

"Yep," Todd interrupted with a laugh. "No, that makes perfect sense. Everyone carries a can of spray paint at all times. That's why they make pockets so big."

I frowned. "Okay, stepped on the climax a bit, but here it goes. Bobby walks up to that sign, shaking the can, and BAM! He spray-paints your campaign slogan across the poster in bright blue letters."

"We don't have a slogan." Todd paused and added, "Or a candidate. Yet."

"Yet," I repeated, with emphasis.

"Right. Yet," he echoed. "You know, I don't like Trump any more than you do, but I just don't see it."

"See what?" Irritation might have been creeping ever so slightly into my voice. Or, and I suspect this is increasingly true, I might just always sound like Richard Schiff forced to lecture fucking morons.

Todd gestured around us, said, "All this devolving into a fascist hellscape just because of Donald Trump. People don't want that. They want McDonald's and ballgames and Amazon delivering everything you could ever want overnight. No one wants to fuck that up so we can start goose-stepping around Papa Don. We're too fucking lazy to be fascists."[2]

He paused for a second. "Don't get me wrong, just because I don't think we're gonna be living out the worst chapters of the fucking *Hunger Games* doesn't mean I'd want my son to be like him or my daughter to date him."

"That's a good line," I said, and we used it in the campaign (minus the *Hunger Games* reference). I didn't have kids in 2017. Today, as I write these words, I have a son and a daughter and frequently wonder about New Zealand's immigration laws.

—————————————————

[2]It remains to be seen if Americans are, in fact, too lazy to be fascists.

I found myself thinking about my first government class, back in the halcyon days of 2007. I was teaching at a small rural school, so there were maybe eight seniors in the classroom, sitting in a half circle as we talked about what American government was and what it was intended to be. Those were the days when Hillary Clinton and Barack Obama were battling it out in the Democratic primaries, so I brought up for discussion that there was a chance that the next president would be either African American or a woman, both firsts in American history. I asked the students to respond to that (something I'd never do today, mostly because I enjoy being employed). Finally, a petite white girl we'll call Courtney raised her hand.

"Black people shouldn't lead," she said matter-of-factly. "They are the color of dirt."

BOOM. That is the sound of your entire life outlook shifting on its axis.

They are the color of dirt. Until that point, I was aware of racism only as something vaguely movie-like, with racists always being the Snidely Whiplash villains who are both readily recognizable and easily condemned because they are Hollywood-style evil caricatures. That day, in that class, with that comment, uttered so calmly, I realized that I was living in a different world from the one I had occupied up until then.

Suddenly, I was confronted with the fact that there were people, normal people, who saw things, everyday things, through a lens so distorted that I'd never be able to understand their motives. Years later, Donald Trump's rise to power added to that revelation with the horrifying realization that the Courtneys of the world didn't just *exist* but were *plentiful* and maybe even in the majority. I don't think Courtney ever realized that she had impacted me in such a profound way. She wasn't angry, bitter, or even passionate about her opinion because, to her, it wasn't an opinion. She had stated a fact, and when was the bell going to ring?

That was my "Courtney Moment," and I am pretty sure it is when I first started paying attention—*really* paying attention—to my government. Sure, I had sat in a series of Con Law classes and sweated over the obscure phrasing of Supreme Court dissents. And yeah, I spent a good deal of my time explaining the concept of checks and balances to high school seniors who'd rather be somewhere else, but I had never heard a student sum up why government ought to matter to our lives in so few words. Sometimes the words that matter to our lives aren't inspirational, and they're not Shakespeare. Sometimes they are ugly and hateful, but that doesn't mean they can't be eye-opening. So, yeah, I got up off the couch and sent a buddy of mine a Facebook message insinuating he needed to run for Congress and *fix all the shit*.

By February 2017, it felt like maybe the whole country had gone through a "Courtney Moment." I knew Todd had; it was why he was there that night. What I didn't know, for either of us, was what would result. When Todd drove off that night, I was left with some unanswered questions. I went home to pound some Tums and wonder how we'd start a campaign if he called me up in a few weeks and told me to saddle up. I was already working on the slogan that we didn't have. Somehow, I didn't think Fix All The Shit[3] would work.

---

[3]I've since come around to the idea that we probably should have gone with it.

The Kitchen Table

If Aaron Sorkin were writing this script, the next scene would take place in a mom-and-pop diner somewhere in suburban America. Todd would be standing at the front of a tiny room, looking awkward and nervous in a suit and tie. He would certainly be wearing the glasses I've only ever seen him wear once, when he was trying to set himself apart from the other thirty-something white guy in the race. Having introduced our awkward hero, the camera would pan just enough for us to see that the meeting is sparsely attended and that the attendees are bored out of their minds with both Todd and the chicken-fried steak on their plates. In the back, we'd see the gruff but lovable and witty campaign manager, watching the train wreck of a speech with increasing amounts of sheer irritation and no small measure of annoyance.

Then, after stumbling over lines of cookie-cutter stump speech and watching one or two potential voters walk out, something miraculous happens: Todd suddenly becomes *good at this*. He finds his inner soul and speaks from the heart, reaching out and grabbing attention by being plainspoken and obviously well-intentioned. He ditches the prepared speech and goes full-on populist, the music rising, the audience responding with increasing ardor . . . and then we'd cut to the next scene, Todd's political viability established, his underdog campaign well underway.

Basically, that scene from *All the King's Men* (either version). You know the scene I mean: the good one.

Well, take it from me: that Sorkin[1] script skips several of the steps facing a potential political candidate, starting with the most obvious, which is "How the hell do I go about running for Congress, anyway?"

Which is exactly the question Todd called to ask me not too many days later.

"I mean, I assume you'll figure it all out," he said. "I just have a lot of questions."

So I set about trying to figure it out while he spent a month or so pondering his willingness to be the face of a political campaign. It didn't take long for me to realize that the American political system isn't really set up to encourage the average citizen to put themselves on a ballot. I spent way too much time reading poorly written self-published books on Amazon and looking up how-to videos on YouTube, just to get some sense of what Todd and I would be in for.

If Todd had been a traditional candidate, he'd have spent at least one previous election cycle volunteering, blockwalking, and hobnobbing with the local activist groups (or he'd have had the good fortune to be born independently wealthy). He'd have reached out to local Democrats of influence and broached the subject of running. They'd have offered muted words of support or politely encouraged him to forget it and get his ass back in the classroom where he belonged. Knowledgeable political operatives would have taken him in hand and walked him through all the boring shit that I was trying to decipher using YouTube and Google. He'd have flown to Washington to speak to leaders in the Democratic establishment, maybe even met some consultants who could do everything I was trying to do but quicker and for the small, small price of a couple grand a month.

----

[1] Mr. Sorkin, we love your work and think you'd have a ball adapting this story. It wouldn't even take a lot of work on your part since half our day-to-day dialogue consists of *West Wing* quotes. Todd's basically like Jeff Daniels in *Newsroom*, only with less extemporaneous speaking talent or on-air charisma.

Todd wasn't a traditional candidate, though. Activists in our district didn't know him from Adam. No one was going to take him by the hand; if he wanted to run, it would be on his own until he convinced folks that he was worth taking a look at. Until then, resources were slim. As an example, the only training the Texas Democratic Party offered in our area came about six weeks after Todd announced his candidacy. We showed up to a small classroom in a National Guard barracks with two other people and tried to hide our dismay as three septuagenarians read off a PowerPoint slideshow in a voice that wavered between bored and comatose. The classroom decor and the political advice were straight out of the 1970s. The most often cited political figure was Ronald Reagan. So, yeah . . . not exactly cutting edge.

I remember Todd leaned over once and whispered, "Do you get the sense these guys don't really care if we run or not?"

As it turns out, they really didn't. In fact, I was certain all they really cared about was getting to Luby's before the rush. I remember thinking that the Democratic Party treated candidate recruitment and training like they had no idea they should be involved in the process at all.

I'm a teacher, so if there is one thing I know (other than Alec Baldwin quotes) it is soul-crushing bureaucracy. That means I have a healthy fear of the form that I *didn't* fill out. Trust me, it exists somewhere, the form that stands between you and what you want, the form you didn't even know to look for, and it's always *that* form that gets you in trouble. I knew that running for office wouldn't be as simple as declaring a candidacy. I knew that the Federal Elections Commission, among others, would have reams, possibly even entire galaxies, of forms waiting to be filled out, and woe to the campaign that missed a box or failed to sign on the dotted line on page ten. While Todd was busy wondering if he was ready for the spotlight, I was trying to figure out what forms needed to be signed and by when. By April, Todd was ready to get serious about exploring a candidacy. We set a meeting at his house so that we could review everything we knew, ponder the things we didn't, and somehow reach an informed decision (or even a gut-level one) about a Todd Allen candidacy.

I was ready to do my part in that meeting. A month spent with the infallible information source known as the internet had produced a bunch of material that I printed off and placed in a fancy binder with a nice cover. Have you ever noticed how putting something into a binder automatically increases the importance and potential worth of whatever it is you're presenting? Well, it does, which is why you should never leave home without at least one three-ring binder.

Todd seemed impressed. He opened the front door, said hello, and nodded at the binders. "Nice," he said. "When a guy shows up with a binder, you know he means business. This is great. Really sets the tone of the meeting."

"Sure," I said, shouldering past him into the house. "I am not to be trifled with. That's the tone."

This was an all-hands-on-deck situation, which meant that my fiancée Liz and I sat at Todd's kitchen table while I tried to convince Todd and his wife Lauren that running for office was a bad, possibly *historically bad*, idea. I hadn't seen Lauren since their wedding, and neither one of them had met Liz before that night. Liz and I had just moved in together, and we were planning a wedding that summer, so naturally here I was, plotting an all-consuming time suck like a political campaign. I don't deserve her, but she's still here, and exactly that much is right with the world on any given day. It kinda goes without saying that both Todd and I had very special women in our lives. We took on the impossible because they said *go try*. I didn't know Lauren, but I knew that she was open to Todd jumping into a congressional campaign while she managed her job, their two children, and a freaking doctoral program.

Todd seemed excited as he sat down at the kitchen table, handing Liz and me cups of coffee. "This is like something out of a movie," he said with a knowing grin. "Four friends around a table, discussing plans to storm the castle. Anyone bring a black cloak and a wheelbarrow?"

"Listing our assets comes later tonight." I began to hand out the binders which, if I can say so again, looked pretty spiffy. "I'm going to go through all this," I said, "but I can sum it up quickly: Todd is almost guaranteed to lose, and spend a lot of money and time, particularly *my* time, losing. We're not talking about the impossible, but we're not *not* talking about it either."

"Seems like an awfully thick binder if we're talking about a waste of time." Todd flipped idly through the impressive packet of information. Binders, man.

"Good color choice," Lauren mentioned, motioning to the wordmark emblazoned on the binder covers. It read *All-In for Allen* in bright crimson. Lauren went to the University of Alabama which, I later learned, meant anything crimson was just fine.[2]

"In there," I said, tapping that crimson cover, "is a summary of all the pertinent data I can find. The district, demographics and industry, political opponents, election history, and, most importantly, all the reasons why someone like you really shouldn't do this."

I paused, then dropped the hammer, "Not without everyone being on board and ready for what's coming."

This was the key point, really. The impossible, I've found, often fails in the face of brute force persistence. Put another way, the only way to do what can't be done is to exhaust reality with balls-to-the-wall fanatic energy. Then, when the motherfucker is on the ropes wondering just how long you can keep up the onslaught in the face of the impossible, you double down. That kind of energy is basically the norm for Todd and me on our little passion projects, whether it be a script or coaching football or running for Congress, but for others it can be off-putting, annoying, or downright infuriating.

I just wanted to be sure Lauren and Liz knew what we were in store for and were ready for it.

"Alright," Todd said after a moment, "why don't you walk us through this?"

"Sweet." I flipped the binder open to the first pages. "First up, your congressional district, CD-24. To make things as complicated as fucking possible, the district sprawls over nearly a dozen communities in three counties. The bad news is that you're looking at one of the most affluent districts in Texas. We're not looking at a district that's hurting, man. People weren't washed out of their homes by a fucking hurricane. The schools aren't falling apart. Gangs aren't selling drugs on every street corner. The economy is booming. It's the kind of place people move to because it's the poster child for the American Dream."

"No wonder we can barely afford to live here," Todd muttered.

"Right," I said. "People here don't have needs, they just have wants, and what they want is not the kind of thing we say out loud, if you get

---

[2] As an aside, did you know people who attended Alabama will yell out "Roll Tide!" to strangers on the street?

my drift. So you're not gonna be able to run on saving this district from anything but itself, and that ain't gonna fly."

"Agreed," Todd said. "What's next?"

"Santa Claus in the offseason," I said, turning to the dossier I had compiled on the incumbent Republican representative from Texas CD-24.

"Santa Claus?" Lauren asked, puzzled.

I nodded. "A charming description your husband used to describe the current representative of CD-24, the honorable Kenny Marchant."

Todd looked at Lauren, said "He's the incumbent that we can't beat."

"Good," I said. "I'm glad to see you've been paying attention to what I've been telling you. This guy is one of the richest congressmen in Washington, which is probably saying something. Kenny hasn't lost by less than twenty percentage points in this district, ever. He also votes slightly to the right of Attila the Hun, when he bothers to vote at all."

Todd looked up. "So you're telling me this guy barely does his job?"

I tipped my coffee cup his way by way of a salute and said "That's one way of saying it. Another is to say he has one of the highest absentee rates in the House."

"People aren't going to like that much," Liz offered. "Isn't getting something for nothing basically what most people hate? Especially conservatives?"

"It gets better. Guy hasn't had a town hall in the district in five years, maybe longer." I paused, took a drink of my ever-present coffee, continued, "You know, when he was in the Texas legislature, Kenny was on the committee that gerrymandered this district, basically carving himself out a nice, fat, permanent job in Washington. Look up *political sleaze* in the dictionary, I'd bet you'd find this asshole's picture."

There was something else, something that both Todd and I felt had been overlooked by the geniuses known as Texas Democrats. Marchant's margin of victory had been shrinking over the last few cycles, and the demographics of the once reliably red CD-24 were trending in a way that made the honchos in the Democratic Party figure that the district would be in play in 2020. Todd and I thought differently. We thought there was an outside chance that Marchant would be vulnerable in 2018 for someone willing to take a chance.

Somewhere in there, with half of the binder flipped through and the other half remaining, I saw Lauren pull a face. Concerned, she finally said, "Okay, this seems like a lot to take on. Should you guys wait until 2020 when our lives aren't as crazy?"

"Waiting until 2020 is out," Todd explained. "By then, everyone will know the district is realistically up for grabs. The Democrats will find some district attorney or astronaut to run, and we can't compete with that."

"I know that this is a really cool thing to do, but . . . " Lauren trailed off thoughtfully. She was still concerned, as any functioning human being, wife, and mother would be. "But . . . we have a lot going on in our lives and this . . . this doesn't seem like it's going to be something you can just do on the weekends."

"You're absolutely right," I said, "This is going to consume our lives. That's why if we're gonna go, we've gotta *go*. Right now everyone thinks this is a pointless race. No one is paying attention. Kenny's not worried, 'cause all he thinks is coming for him is an old lady with a squeaky voice."

The Old Lady with a Squeaky Voice. As appellations go, it didn't exactly strike fear into the heart; if it had, I might have shown more respect . . . but probably not. Call her The Old Lady with a Squeaky Voice or Political Death Incarnate on Dread Wings, it wouldn't have mattered: I was going to overlook Jan McDowell, mostly because it seemed like everyone did, including the Republicans. Jan was the perennial Democratic candidate in the district, and she was, as mentioned, an older woman with a squeaky voice. Kenny had hardly bothered to campaign against her in 2016.

"And I can't blame him," I said dismissively. "As far as I can tell, this is the kind of candidate that you get when you're in a gerrymandered district without a prayer of a chance of winning. The only reason people vote for her in a primary is because she's the only one willing to show up year after year and lose big in the general. She's got no media presence, no voice, no money, and a question mark where her inspiring backstory should be." I paused, added, "Folks, her big selling point is that she's an accountant. She's got the letters *CPA* emblazoned on all her campaign materials. I shit you not."

"So you're not worried about her?" Todd asked.

"No," I said, sipping at my coffee. "As far as I can tell, she's the candidate because no one cares who the loser is."

And that, ladies and gentlemen, is what my professors back at school would refer to as *hubris*. Much later, I realized Jan had more than a few tricks up her sleeve, and when she called the banners, there would be a sizable horde ready to bend the knee and kiss the ring. A more experienced (or humble) rookie to politics might have paused to wonder why, but I was green as grass, cocky, and willing to bet that The Old Lady with the Squeaky Voice was going to be a pushover. What I didn't know then was that Jan was like the Great Pyramids—weathered, sure, showing the years, but not even Napoleon was able to knock those fuckers down. They are one determined set of historical landmarks, and that was Jan in a nutshell. Determined. Persistent.

Idiot that I was and occasionally still am, I turned the page on Jan McDowell and drained the coffee cup. "If you run," I said, shaking the empty cup, "we're gonna need a lot more of this."

Todd took the hint and refilled the cup. He shook his head, said, "Your ability to consume caffeine in copious amounts is awe-inspiring. Seriously."

I ignored him, held up a hand, and started counting on my fingers. "Let's talk about why you *shouldn't* run," I said. "You don't know what you're doing, you don't know anything about politics, you don't know anyone *in* politics, you have zero name recognition, you're a fucking teacher and everyone hates teachers, you've got no money, you're probably not going to raise any money, you've got a primary opponent who is the presumptive nominee already, an entrenched incumbent with over a million dollars in a war chest he hasn't had to dip into for a decade, a gerrymandered district, and the only staff you can count on are the four people sitting at this table."

"And I never learned to read," Todd added.

"And you never learned to read," I confirmed.

Liz looked puzzled and Lauren looked annoyed; sometimes, most times, our banter isn't appreciated by those around us.

"So . . . *if* you run," I said, "the campaign needs to start up by July 4th, because Jan is already raising money and hitting events every week as the presumptive nominee. People are getting used to the idea that she is *it*. Every week that goes by hurts your chances. If we don't know if you're running by June 1st, then, shit . . . you aren't running."

Lauren got excited. "Oh, we could have a launch party at our house!" Almost immediately, she began writing down things in her binder, notes that I could only assume read something like, *Need political decorations, preferably in crimson.*

Roll Tide.

"Well, let's decide we're doing this thing first," Todd said.

We talked some more about the wonderful stuff in the binder, then started regaling the ladies with tales from our college years neither had ever heard. It was late, but not too late, when we left. I caught Todd and Lauren exchanging a look before the door closed.

In the car, Liz yawned. "I can see why you are friends. He's funny. Why haven't we seen them more?"

"Because neither of us are *people* people," I told her truthfully. Todd hid it better, and there are times he genuinely seems to like hanging out with someone other than himself, but for me, fuck no. I hate people. Truth be told, we could go long stretches without meeting up because, in the end, we were basically loners. So, naturally, Todd was thinking about running for political office, a job that almost entirely consisted of talking to other people. Better him than me, that's all I can say.

"He's going to run," Liz said with certainty. "You sold him."

I chuckled and said, "I spent all night telling him how horrible an idea it was."

She shrugged. "Sounds like a genius strategy. Hey, can we stop by Starbucks on our way home?"

"Sure," I answered, flipping on the turn signal and trying to hide a smug grin.

Coffee's for closers.

The Long Shot

The first thing Liz said to me after we left Todd's house that April night was, "You know, I think what you're doing is really noble." The second thing she said, almost immediately afterward, was, "Hey, are we still going to grab that coffee on the way home or what?"

I nodded as I tried to process her first statement. Noble? Folks that know me have often called me *ambitious*, and some have shaded that characteristic over into *arrogant* nudging up against *asshole*, but *noble*? Yeah, that was a whole new bag demanding some clarification, which I asked for as soon as we had our white chocolate mochas in hand.

Liz didn't disappoint. "Well," she said, sipping her coffee, "you basically just spent two hours telling Todd all the reasons he's going to lose, and the best-case scenario is y'all will work real hard and lose by a bit less. Right?"

"That about sums it up," I confirmed. "I'm beginning to think I didn't need all those pages in that binder after all."

"Well, but they were awesome binders," Liz admitted. "But, back to the point: knowing the futility of it all, you're still willing to drop everything and do it if he says *yes*. For no tangible benefit that I can see other than you think you should. That's noble."

"Huh," I said, struck by the thought. To be fair, she was only about *half* right. I was willing to jump into the race swinging, but it wasn't due to nobility. It was because, deep down, I thought there was a slim, infinitesimal, virtually nonexistent sliver of a chance that Todd Allen could win a seat in the US Congress. A long shot, a Hail Mary pass, a prayer to Crom, call it what you will, but my blood was pumping at the idea of taking that chance. Was it noble? Well, here I was, on the precipice of taking a risk just because I thought it was the right thing to do. And Liz thought it was noble.

The drive home felt a bit warmer because of it.

Coffee in hand, Liz and I drove home from that meeting at Todd's kitchen table wondering which way he'd jump and when the call would come. I wasn't so sure where Todd was going to land, even after months of our back-and-forth conversations. Yes, we had a track record of attempting the impossible, but that was before stable marriages and kids and cozy homes in the Dallas suburbs. Before we became old, in other words, or, to phrase it a trifle more delicately, before we became functioning and reasonably mature adults. Jumping into a political campaign as an average American sounds like a good idea when you're sitting in a recliner rage scrolling through Twitter, but after a kitchen table ego pounding delivered by your best friend, that good idea probably seems more like a waste of time.

After a while, her coffee nearly gone, Liz asked the ten-million-dollar question: "So, what do you *want* him to say?"

I'd been pondering the same thing. A *yes* would mean an adventure. It would mean a chance to do something special by anyone's reckoning, utter failure notwithstanding. It would mean having an easier time looking in the mirror each morning, knowing that I wasn't just lobbing bombs into the void of social media, but was actually *doing* something. It would mean doing something big, even if the campaign and everyone involved in it was little.

"I want to do it," I finally told Liz. "Yeah, I want him to run."

Liz looked worried, said, "I love that you are even talking about doing this. But if I were him, I wouldn't do it. And if I were *her*, I'd wonder if he'd lost his mind."

"Valid," I said.

But had he lost his mind? Or at least enough of it to ignore everything I had laid out in that fancy binder and take a long-shot chance? I'll admit it: all the work and stress and the absolute metric ton of bullshit of a no-shot congressional campaign would be worth it if Todd gave me the nod. It would be worth it because when that nod came, it would mean that Todd knew the odds and was in it for the right reasons, or maybe just reasons I could understand. It would be Rocky the night before the big fight, admitting that he couldn't win but that wasn't what mattered anyway.

I wanted Todd to call me up and say, "All I wanna do is go the distance."

Liz stared out the window at the Metroplex traffic. "What do you think he'll say?"

I shifted in my seat. "Well, here's the funny thing about Todd: you can always tell how interested he is about something by how long it takes him to start the next conversation about it. So if he grasped the big takeaway from that meeting, which was that he'd be absolutely *fucking crazy* to run for Congress, he might send me a text or something a few days from now. If he's interested despite his better judgment, he might give me a shout tomorrow just to talk about how crazy it is."

I thought for a second. "Of course, if he *is* crazy, he'll call before we get home just hoping I'll tell him it's not a waste of time."

"That would make two of you," Liz said. I raised my eyebrow. Seeing the look, she clarified, "Crazy."

"Yeah," I admitted.

That's when the phone rang.

Liz shot me a look. "You're kind of a freak sometimes. You know that, right?"

"I think it's come up once or twice," I said, then picked up the phone.

It was Todd, sounding upbeat and energetic. "I thought that went well," he said without preamble or greeting, which was a habit of his whenever he really wanted to dig into a conversation.

"Sure," I confirmed. "I mean, Lauren didn't hit me with a frying pan or anything, so, yeah, it went well."

"Exactly," he said, then paused. "She's not sure about this."

Liz waits with petition documents in hand as Todd greets voters at table-level in the background

"I gathered that," I said. "She's not wrong."

"You made it real for her," Todd said. "Up until now, running for office was just kind of a neat idea, you know? Something that was fun to talk about at dinner. Then you show up with binders and stats and strategy and this deadline of paperwork that has to be filed and suddenly it isn't just daydreams anymore. Now she's thinking about taking care of the kids and doing her doctorate and working her day job, all with no backup 'cause I'm off running for Congress."

"I guess she was paying attention," I said.

"Binders," Liz whispered from the passenger seat. She got it.

Todd didn't say anything for a second. I thought maybe he was disappointed I hadn't provided some kind of argument he could use to refute Lauren's ironclad logic that his run for Congress equated to handing her a concrete block when what she really needed was a float and a helping hand back to shore. I even had a counterargument ready, tenuously based though it may be. I barely knew Lauren, but what I knew confirmed that she and Todd shared at least one key trait. They were both ambitious. They both had something to prove, if only to themselves. Lauren hadn't hit me with a frying pan that night precisely *because* something about her husband running for Congress tickled a competitive nerve in her.

That was my theory, anyway, but what did I know? I wasn't married to her.

Todd finally said something, and it wasn't what I was expecting. Quietly, he asked, "Do you think I can win?"

I snorted a little and said, "I get it. Lauren was paying attention, but you weren't, right?"

"No, no," he said, "I was hooked on every word. The binders were really impressive. I especially liked point three in the 'Why Todd Shouldn't Do This' list."

Liz was already flipping through her copy of the binder, looking for a section I'd included near the back that cataloged what I thought Todd's various strengths and weaknesses were as a candidate. One list took up about half a page, double-spaced. The other I could have rolled up and used as a club in case of a sudden zombie apocalypse. I'll let you puzzle out which was which.

"Point three," Liz recited. "Mr. Allen has never served in public office or been elected by his peers, while his anticipated opponent has been in office since January of 2005. His primary opponent has been a member of the local activist community for years, with all the relationships that implies. When it comes to the nuts and bolts, Mr. Allen is in danger of being made to look ignorant or incapable simply because he has *not* been a legislator day in and day out for over a decade. Mr. Marchant and Ms. McDowell have been amassing political contacts and political favors since 2005. Mr. Allen will not be able to overcome, equal, or even come within hailing distance of his opponents in that category. For instance, in a close race, Mr. Marchant can, very likely, call upon the president of the United States to support him via a scathing tweet. Mr. Allen has his adoring wife and children."

Liz paused and asked, "Does Lauren use Twitter?"

"Not sure that would matter, honey," I said. I continued on the phone, "And that's not even the first on the list of your weaknesses, dude."

"As a man or a candidate," Todd confirmed. He paused, asked again,

"But . . . do you think I can win?"

Silence in the car.

"Fuck yeah," I finally said.

It wasn't just ego, although neither Todd nor I have ever lacked for ego. We have a healthy respect for our own talents. Truth was, I *did* think Todd could win. There was a perfect storm of conditions that we both thought were being ignored by the Democratic Party, conditions that the right candidate could exploit to squeak out a surprise victory. It started with a race that was coming at the tail end of a decade, when all the gerrymandering done after the last census was starting to grow stale and losing its iron crimson grip. What had been a safe district was shifting under the GOP's feet, only they weren't sensing it. The demographics were growing exponentially more diverse, trending in a direction that didn't typically favor Republicans. Kenny Marchant had avoided a town hall for five years, and there was a bipartisan feeling in the district that he was taking the seat for granted. Donald Trump's ascendency to the White House had jolted Democrats to the core, along with no small amount of otherwise reliably conservative voters, so turnout in 2018, I predicted, would be much larger than a traditional midterm election.

And there was one more point. A few cycles before, the Democrats hadn't even bothered to put up a candidate to run against Marchant. The candidate who had run and been defeated in 2016, Jan McDowell, the presumptive nominee in 2018, had campaigned with piss-poor media presence and zero money. Unless Todd Allen ran, it looked like Democrats were all set to run with her again. Kenny Marchant was showing every sign of ignoring the contest while he sleepwalked his way to another election victory.

But what if the Democrats ran someone *new*? Someone young, energetic, and charismatic? Someone who could run a social media campaign that hit voters like a ton of bricks, day in and day out? Someone that could surprise sleepy Kenny and take advantage of unprecedented motivation and enthusiasm among voters looking to respond to the rise of Donald Trump? Someone who could appeal to everyone who was sick and tired of how goddamn crazy politics had gotten and just wanted to see a regular American take a shot at fixing things?

None of it was hard data. None of it added up to a guaranteed win; if it did, the Democrats would have imported a candidate that checked more boxes, and Kenny would have found himself running against an ex-astronaut single mom who looked like a cast member from *Armageddon* and introduced her candidacy with a video produced by Stephen Spielberg. That candidate wasn't out there. The Democrats weren't looking at the Twenty-Fourth District in 2018. Neither were the Republicans. No one really seemed to think the district was up for grabs.

But I did.

"Fuck yeah," I said again. "Yeah, you can win."

I could tell, somehow, that Todd was smiling on the other end of the line.

"Okay," he chuckled. "I'll talk to Lauren and think about it. Good work tonight."

"Adios," I said, and hung up. Then I took a deep breath.

Liz was flipping through the binder, puzzled. "I think my copy is missing a few pages," she said.

"What you're looking for isn't in there," I said. Liz shot me a speculative glance before shutting the binder. We drove the rest of the way home in silence, listening to the music on the radio as a soft rain began to fall. I was smiling in the darkness, maybe even smirking.

"He's gonna run," I said, the grin widening as the storm worsened and the taillights on Highway 121 began to light the night up in shades of red. I tightened my grip on the steering wheel. "He's gonna fucking run."

Milkshake

When Todd walked into my kitchen a few days later, he was carrying a milkshake from Whataburger. That's when I knew that he'd decided to run for Congress. For as long as I've known him, Todd has had a fondness for a good milkshake. They were his way of rewarding himself for a job well done, a lesson well taught, a game superbly coached, or any kind of life victory that was best celebrated with sugar in copious amounts. Personally, I've never been big into self-denial, especially when it comes to food, so I've never quite understood his relationship with milkshakes. I've never needed the permission of a celebratory life event to have a milkshake; I've just needed my debit card. Regardless, milkshakes were a good barometer of Todd's mood on any given day, so when he walked in carrying that Whataburger cup, I knew he was feeling just fine.

I also wouldn't have minded a milkshake of my own.

"Doctor," Todd said, taking a seat at my kitchen table—slurping the last dregs of the milkshake. "Have you finished that *Rocky* movie marathon you were gonna make Liz sit through?"

"Yeah," I said, grabbing a Dr Pepper from the fridge. Then I hastily clarified, "Except for *Rocky V*. Life's too short for that shit."

He nodded. "So she gets it now?"

It's a measure of how long we've been friends that I instantly understood what *it* was.[1] I shrugged. "More or less. She never knew that 50 percent of a movie's run time could be taken up by montage or that the Cold War ended with a boxing match."

Todd put down the cup. "What, did she grow up under a rock? Everyone knows that. Next, you're gonna tell me that she doesn't know that there's no shortcut home."

"Or an easy way out," I said dryly. "She probably needs some time to absorb that one."

He leaned forward. "So she's gonna get it when you tell her that we're gonna beat the Russian, right?"

"She might get it," I confirmed. "Then again, maybe not. It's possible she didn't internalize the intricacies of the *Rocky* franchise to the extent that you and I have." I paused. "So . . . *are* we going to beat the Russian?"

"How do we start?" Todd said after a moment.

"I've had a lot of time to think about how we'd get started," I said, leaning forward eagerly. "First, we need somewhere isolated to train. Lots of snow. Preferably mountainous."

"Sounds like this might involve a lot of free weights," Todd said.

"Absolutely," I confirmed. "Not to mention jogging up mountains."

I sat back. "I'm gonna need you to grow a beard, too." I cracked open the can of soda and thought about all the things I'd *really* need to do in order to kickstart a congressional campaign. Unfortunately, none of the things on the list involved an extensive knowledge of Stallone movies or song lyrics by Survivor. Most of the immediate steps involved registering with various federal agencies, setting up bank accounts, and signing my name on a lot of official-looking documents that threatened some really bad shit if the campaign so much as stepped one toe out of line or filled out a form in the wrong order. It was a big ask. It was as intimidating as a seven-foot-tall blonde Russian with limited English skills

---

[1] The question is, do you? Go watch *Rocky IV* again.

promising to break me.

Luckily, I'm cocky as shit, otherwise I'd have told Todd where he could put that milkshake.

Todd was fiddling with his empty cup. Thoughtfully, he said, "I know what I want to do. I've always known. I've known I was going to run ever since we met at that Mexican resteraunt."

"Really?" I asked. "That was months ago."

"I don't know if you've realized this," Todd said, "but deciding to run for Congress is kinda a big fucking deal." He paused. "I just needed some time. Lauren's starting a doctorate program. I've got a four-year-old and a two-year-old. I have a full-time job. Nothing about my life says that running for Congress makes any sense."

"I've been saying that for weeks," I pointed out. "We've got a whole binder that says that. So why today?"

"A song I keep hearing when I'm driving the kids to daycare in the morning. Song called 'Head Full of Doubt' by the Avett Brothers. You heard it?"

"Nope," I said, shaking my head. Todd knew that, musically speaking, I was always at least thirty years behind the times. A turntable sits in my office and Miles Davis and Glen Miller play each morning. I am decades past being able to recognize the names of trendy pop singers. There are massive hits with a shit ton of radio play that have never penetrated the bubble that is my little pop-culture consciousness. So, no, I was not familiar with the Avett Brothers.

"The kids love 'em. Especially their cover of 'How I Got to Memphis,' which is weird, considering Harper's four years old."

"Not exactly *Sesame Street*," I said, wondering what kind of music I had liked when I was four.

"Anyway," Todd continued, "there's a line that's stuck in my head."
I had to ask.

"What was the line?"

He looked up at me. "Decide what to be and go be it."

There it was. I didn't need him to say anything else. He didn't need to confirm the decision he'd made that morning in explicit terms. He didn't need to say, "Okay, Heath, I'm going to run for Congress, now get to fucking work."

All he needed to do was repeat the line from a song. *Decide what to be and go be it.*

Yeah, I thought, that's a good line.[2]

"That's a good line," I said.

"I know," he said. "So, I'm driving over here, and I play it again and all I can think about are all the folks who ignore that line in their life, you know? They paint over it. They block it out because it's too hard, or too expensive, or they're just too afraid. So somewhere on Highway 121 heading north to your house I decided it was okay to go ahead and just be it."

I grinned. "And that's when you bought a milkshake, right?"

"And that's when I bought a milkshake. I figured it was time to make it official."

I understood his decision-making process completely. After all, I was the guy who made a mixtape soundtrack for our drive to California to find fame and fortune (or nausea and disappointment) in the movie business. Music, movies, books, these things matter, and if Todd was inspired by a long drive listening to tunes, all I really wanted to know was which tunes so I could make a CD for the campaign.

Todd tossed his empty cup in the trash can and said, "So now that I've decided what to be, do you have any clue how to *go be it*? Setting aside for a moment the question of cardio training, you know, free weights, beards, and shit."

"I like how you assume I've got it all figured out," I said.

"Don't you?" he asked.

"Well, yeah," I admitted. "Of course I have."

"Thought so," he said with a smug smile, settling back in his chair and waiting to hear the word. What was our first move? How were we going to kick off a long-shot campaign of two political underdogs trying to stick up for all the everyday Americans out there? Unfortunately, I did have it figured out, and it wasn't going to be anywhere near as stirring as Todd might have expected.

I told him what our first decision was going to need to be, knowing it was something he'd never thought about or remotely expected. He

_____

[2]By the way, that song, "Head Full of Doubt"? There is an alternate title, and that title speaks volumes. It's called "Road Full of Promise." Seems appropriate.

My favorite ad that the campaign ran on social media, hopefully inspiring others to give politics a shot.

frowned, his eyebrows knitting together, leaned forward again as if getting physically closer was going to help him understand what he just heard.

"I'm gonna need you to repeat that," he said.

"I said that you're going to have to figure out what your name is," I repeated.

Silence. Todd was nodding as if his body was mechanically trying to get his mind on board with this line of thinking. "Right," he mumbled. "Right. Okay. I thought maybe we'd be a bit further along than that."

I could see I was going to have to walk him through it.

"Look, your real name isn't Todd," I reminded him, as if he needed a reminder. "It's Edward. Your name is Edward Allen. But no one knows that but your family. I barely know it. State law says your real name needs to be on the ballot. Now, I've read the statute a dozen times and even though I'd like to think I'm pretty smart, it's still as clear as mud. I don't think we can put 'Todd Allen' on the ballot, but I do think we can put it in quotation marks."

"Quotation marks?" Todd asked.

"Yeah," I said. "Around your nickname. So the ballot would read 'Edward "Todd" Allen.' We just gotta decide if all your campaign stuff needs to use the same, or just say 'Todd' and risk confusion, or we just go with 'Edward' and make it easy."

He was shaking his head. "Jesus," he said, "isn't this a bit ridiculous? Like, you actually are having to spend time thinking about it? We have to spend time *talking* about my fucking name?"

"Welcome to politics," I said.

"My name is Todd Allen," he said firmly. "Do what you have to on the ballot, but I'm not gonna campaign as anyone but myself."

There it was: our first campaign decision. In a way, it was symbolic of what was coming, with Todd reaffirming that he was going to run as himself despite the pressure to do otherwise. I wish I could say it was the most eye-rolling moment of ridiculousness in the campaign, but that would make me a liar, and while I'm not afraid to embellish, exaggerate, or even stretch the truth out thin, I'm not a liar. I looked down at my notepad and scrawled, "Todd is Todd."

It *was* ridiculous. But I couldn't help but wonder if those quote marks were going to cost Edward "Todd" Allen some votes.

I also wondered if it was too early in the day for a drink of something a lot stronger than a milkshake.

I Like Dwight

I had a feeling very early on that the campaign would be measured not by volunteers pounding the pavement or dollars donated or endorsements accumulated, but in calories packed on. Dieting is all well and good, and maybe exercise is a balm for the soul, but politics demands a more robust kind of comfort, found only in carbohydrates and caffeine and occasionally in a *churrascaria* steakhouse. By the time I felt we were ready for our big campaign launch, I'd gotten intimately familiar with the special late-night menu at Jack in the Box. I'm especially fond of any establishment that takes a plain-Jane menu item, like a taco, and serves it deep-fried and two for a dollar. If you don't like calories and heart attacks served up cheap, you probably shouldn't consider running for office (or managing a political campaign best classified as existing on a wing and a prayer).

I deserved a few misspent calories. I'd been in a virtual cave for most of June, wrestling a US congressional campaign into some form of Frankenstein-ish life, a month that had taken me way out of my comfort zone. At the end of it, Todd Allen had a campaign committee, a treasurer, and a tax ID number. "It" was also registered with umpteen federal and state agencies. We might not have had a clue about what we were doing, but we were officially *official*. I'd even come to a bit of peace with quotation marks.

"How's it feel to be running an actual political campaign?" Todd asked me on one of our hundreds of calls that month.

Numb, I responded, "Great. Ask me again when I can feel anything below the neck."

"Awh, that's just the lack of sleep talking," he shot back, laughing. "Now all we gotta do is figure out what to do next." He paused. "You know, there's something comforting about not knowing what the hell we're doing. Dangerous, but comforting. Pete Mitchell–style dangerous. What do you think?"

"I think I might need the number to that truck-driving school," I said, and hung up.

It was a busy month. Not only were we figuring out all the paperwork bullshit behind running for office, but, miracle of miracles, the Todd Allen for Congress campaign was no longer just a two-man operation because we had a newly hired social media director. People might have asked me if I was worried about running a congressional campaign with zero political experience, and all arrogance and self-confidence aside, I'd have answered, "Hell no, I'm not worried. I've got Dwight."

And, at least for a while, I could honestly say, "I like Dwight."

Dwight was a young man who had once, in the not-so-distant past, been one of Todd's government students. Apparently, he'd gone out into the world and eschewed the life of a college undergrad for a career as some kind of social media guru/consultant. Todd assured me that the kid had done more than well for himself, and now he was willing to bring his talents, and the talents of his firm, to work for the campaign *pro bono*, *gratis*, for absolutely free. It hadn't taken us long to discover that other candidates and politicos are deeply impressed by the size of a campaign staff. Having Dwight on our team somehow made our campaign feel more official, which is a strange truth that says so much about the bullshit optics of campaigning.

We met for the first time as a campaign staff in June, sitting in my living room with Todd's temporary logo cast onto my television's paltry forty-two inches. I liked what I saw in Dwight at that first meeting: he

An early campaign meeting, perhaps discussing keychains.

was young, eager, and confident. We have a media team, I thought with something approaching giddiness. Holy shit, things are getting real.

Media was going to be a big deal. Media was where I was putting all my hopes for the Todd Allen campaign. I wasn't counting on donations because, in my life, people don't just hand you money. I was thinking about media, and about how everyone in my world walked around with their eyes on the little magic box in their hands.

Todd's candidacy was still something known only to our friends and family at that point. I was keeping Todd's candidacy under wraps until the time came when all our ducks were in a row, and we could announce in something approaching style. A first impression, I'd always thought, was the most important thing in the establishment of a new relationship—something that maybe went double for political candidates. I wanted Todd to explode onto the scene on July 4 looking like a star-spangled savior with more money than God and a brand that made McDonald's executives green with envy. I knew what the Democratic primary voters in the Twenty-Fourth District were used to in Jan McDowell (or I thought I did), and I wanted it to be immediately apparent that she was outclassed. I wanted everyone who had ever voted Democrat within fifteen square miles to see quality media that screamed out that Todd was a legitimate candidate. I wanted Jan to see our website and cry herself to sleep before tearfully conceding that she didn't have a prayer with Todd in the game.

People in hell want ice water, too, or so I've heard.

"We're gonna be like McDonald's," I told Dwight as we settled into a long meeting.

He looked puzzled. "McDonald's?"

Todd nodded. "People might not like us, but they are damn sure gonna know we exist and we're offering to supersize their fries."

I added, "Dwight, our goal is simple: you're not going to be able to pull out your phone and scroll through your social media of choice without seeing Todd's logo."

Dwight looked apprehensive, and it was no wonder. I was talking about ten grand worth of media each month, a mountain of work that was, to Dwight, a whole lot of effort for nothing but a campaign title. For me, it was Thursday. I didn't particularly care, because that's what I do: I work harder, longer, faster than anyone around me, so I didn't think twice about laying assignments down on Dwight that probably weren't his best introduction to the world of politics.

"Copy for posts," I said, ticking items off on my fingers, "graphic memes, sharing across platforms, a website, pictures and videos from events, digital fundraising, ad buys, data analysis . . . all yours, buddy. We are gonna bury folks in our digital media 'cause Jan McDowell can't afford to match what we can do *for free* and Kenny won't want to until it is too late. Someone searches Google for the Twenty-Fourth Congressional District, they're gonna see Todd's name along with quality media that speaks of money in big, fat piles."

"Which we don't actually have," Todd pointed out.

"Which we don't actually have," I confirmed. I locked eyes with Dwight, leaned forward, and delivered the sledgehammer blow. "I'm counting on you and your team, man. I'm not gonna say the fate of the campaign is in your hands, but . . . the fate of the campaign is in your hands."

Did I say Dwight looked apprehensive? He looked downright panicked, like I was calling in a loan while suggestively punctuating my statements with a baseball bat.

Dwight had been handed a laundry list of what I considered to be some of the most important things about the campaign: a website, producing and running social media, and drafting up a logo that would jump out at voters and practically drag them into a voting booth to cast a ballot for Todd Allen. I'll say this: Dwight was game. Sure, I expected him to do a shit ton of work for nothing but my heartfelt thanks, but he seemed to swallow that pill and rally. Before we got too far into our vision for the campaign's social media, he dropped the bombshell idea that he thought would make Todd Allen a household name. Like I said, he was eager, and couldn't contain his excitement about what was, he guaranteed, the greatest fucking thing since sliced bread or margarita machines.

I wasn't sure I had heard correctly.

Frowning, I leaned forward. "Keychains?"

Dwight nodded enthusiastically. "Absolutely, man," he said. "Absolutely. You give them something in return for checking out your content. Something for nothing, right? Someone likes a post on Facebook, boom, they get a sticker. Someone visits your website, bam, they get a Todd Allen keychain in their mailbox."

Todd tried valiantly to get on board with this idea. He nodded slowly and mechanically. "Right. Right. Keychains."

"Keychains," I said thoughtfully.

I risked looking over at Todd, who looked over at me with a raised eyebrow. "Keychains," he repeated to me, as if I hadn't heard it the first fucking time.

"Keychains," Dwight said, pleased with himself.

Neither Todd nor I said anything in response, much less what we were actually thinking. That was going to become the norm for a while, and I blame it on the sheer size of what we were attempting. Running for Congress was so big, involving so many things that we were so unfamiliar with, it negated our customary confidence in our own judgment. For a month or two, we took advice from damn near anyone as political gospel, tapping down our own instincts in favor of what we were assured was the right way of doing things. Dwight, for instance, surely he knew what he was doing, right? Surely, he had thought of all the cynical thoughts swirling around in my head and he had an answer for them . . . right?

After Dwight left, I turned to Todd and said, "So, yeah . . . I have questions."

Todd held up a hand. "I know, I know. Like . . . where the hell is all this money for keychains and stickers coming from?"

I nodded vigorously. "Or, you know, who is paying for postage? Or, fuck, who is sitting around stuffing envelopes all day? Is that something Lauren wants to do when she's not busy raising two kids and studying for her doctorate? 'Cause that sounds like something Lauren would *love* to do."

"Hey," Todd said, trying to ignore my sarcasm while simultaneously keeping an open mind. "It's not a bad idea, really. We just can't make it work . . . you know, probably ever. Still, it's not a bad idea." After a moment he added, "And that is absolutely the last fucking thing Lauren would love to do."

It seemed like a pretty bad idea to me, so I couldn't help but ask, "Dwight's people are going to be able to produce for us, aren't they?"

Todd shrugged. "A former student I barely know with a team of people we've never met working for absolutely nothing on a list of complicated tasks that demand both quality and quantity, over and over again for months? Yeah, sure. What's the problem?"

Fucking sarcasm. Double-edged sword.

"I already need a vacation," I said.

You Gotta Have a System

"You gotta have a system," the old man said with the same kind of conviction that most people reserve for religious beliefs or their opinion on that last season of *Game of Thrones*. I nodded to show my grudging acceptance of his basic premise, if only to forestall further conversation. Conversation with strangers was not my forte or my preference, and it was nowhere near my list of acceptable things to engage in when on vacation. I was taking two days away from the campaign in late June to sit in a casino in Louisiana, watching a little silver ball spin and gambling on the result while sipping on complimentary margaritas. My parents preferred spending these days at the slot machines, but I wasn't quite old enough for that shit yet. I was young. I was alive. I wanted to risk my money on a fucking marble.

"You gotta have a system," the old man sitting next to me repeated, chuckling a little as his numbers came up. My best guess, he was a shrimp boat captain spending an off day amidst bright lights and noise instead of warm seas and crustaceans. If Forrest Gump had never gone on to bump into more historical figures after striking it rich in the shrimping business, he'd have looked like this guy, right down to the red hat with a cartoon picture of a grinning shrimp. "You got a system?" Captain Gump asked, chewing on the end of a pencil as if it were a cigar.

"Sure," I said after a moment. "Mostly I try to bet small and bet safe for as long as I can before I lose my patience and bet it all on black."

Captain Gump looked at me as if I had lost my mind (a fair guess at any time) shrugged, and growled, "Well, whatever works, right, bud? As long as you enjoy yourself."

I *was* enjoying myself. Liz and I were having a few days without stress, dining out with my parents, enjoying each other and the scenery as we spent money teachers didn't really have to spend. It might sound strange, but it was fun to gamble with money instead of with my time for a change, even if my new life as a campaign manager kept intruding. Speaking of . . .

I looked down. Sure enough, there was a new text message on my phone from Todd.

I read it, then took a deep breath to try to find my center before I lost my shit on the casino floor and got dragged off into the bayou by security. I motioned at the cocktail waitress who had been keeping me in drinks all night, and instead of ordering a fresh margarita, I asked her to please find me a pen or pencil.

And, while she was at it, she might as well bring me a fresh margarita.

The message from Todd was succinct: Dwight doesn't get it.

Few things could have shocked me less. I went on to set up a conference call among Todd, myself, and Dwight's team of graphic designers, all so we could rehash something we'd been kicking around since day one: the campaign logo. Almost from the jump, I'd had this image in my head of using a dialogue bubble as an integral part of Todd's logo, mostly because I felt it sent the right message about who Todd was and what he wanted his campaign to accomplish. He wanted to *talk* to people. He wanted to *listen*. He wanted to reset political discourse in this country so the most frequent reaction a politician had was no longer the legislative equivalent of throwing a temper tantrum.

"Everybody just yells nowadays," Todd had complained to me recently. "They hear something they don't like, or can't get exactly what they want, they have a hissy fit and pound the table and threaten to take their ball and go home. It's bullshit; nothing gets done if we're all behaving like three-year-olds on a playground."

The campaign was coalescing around three words that encompassed what we felt politics needed: *civility*, *conversation*, and *change*. What better symbol for all three, and for the campaign, than a dialogue bubble? It certainly beat using an eagle, or a star, or a flag, or a bunch of wavy stripes blowing in the imaginary breeze common to campaign posters. I thought a dialogue bubble was modern, different, and perfectly symbolic of what Todd Allen was all about (or, at the very least, what we were saying Todd Allen was all about). Instantly recognizable but totally unique.

So, naturally, neither Dwight nor his team could produce a single mock-up for Todd's campaign logo because they just didn't get it.

What the fuck's not to get? I wondered.

"Here you go, honey," the cocktail waitress said when she returned, offering up a battered Bic and a margarita. For a moment, I wondered what the oddest thing she'd been asked to provide on that casino floor was. I was sure it wasn't a pen, but I've been wrong before.

Then I bet a hundred bucks on black and lost.

"Gotta have a system," Captain Gump pointed out in his best I-told-you-so voice, shaking his head.

Irritated at the world, I took the proffered pen and alcohol from the cocktail waitress, tried to ignore the roulette advice of Captain Gump, and quickly sketched out what I was thinking on a drink napkin. Naturally, it caught his attention, so I wasn't surprised when he leaned over between spins of the wheel and grunted out, "What's the Q stand for, anyway?"

I looked over at him, exasperated. "It's not a Q. It's a dialogue bubble."

He looked down at the napkin, then up at me, then back to the napkin.

"Kinda looks like a Q to me,"

"It's not," I assured him.

"If you say so, bud," he said. Then, "Who's Todd Allen?"

"Guy running for Congress in Texas."

He recoiled a bit, as if he'd just gotten a whiff of a pungent cheese, a toddler's diaper, or maybe some fresh vomit. His bloodshot eyes widened a bit, and all he could say, in a tone that dripped in disgust, was, "Oh,

Jesus Christ."

"Yeah," I said in response. He didn't say anything else, just turned back to the roulette wheel with a grunt, though he'd occasionally cast a distrustful eye my way. I put the phone up to my ear and said, "This is my fucking vacation, man."

"I know," Todd's voice said with a note of weariness.

"It took me ten seconds to sketch a shitty logo out on a cocktail napkin," I said. "You telling me that a bunch of hotshot designers can't get us a single mock-up? Not one?"

"They don't get it," Todd said.

"How is that possible?" I asked, raising my voice.

"I dunno," Todd said. "Let's ask them. They're dialing in right now."

There were a series of clicks, some labored breathing of unknown origin, and then Dwight's voice on the line, saying, "Hey, guys. Why are we putting a *Q* in the logo?"

I closed my eyes, took off my glasses, and rubbed the bridge of my nose. There was a killer headache lying in wait somewhere at the end of this conversation, I suspected, and the only medicines I had available were wholly unsatisfactory: Tylenol, alcohol, and gambling money I didn't really have. "Hi, Dwight." I ignored what he'd asked. "Is your team on with you?"

"Yeah, this is Daniel," a voice said, and I swear to God I could hear Third Eye Blind playing in the background. Another voice piped up and said his name was Mark. Neither sounded old enough to shave, drive automobiles, or walk down stairs without holding an adult's hand. "These are my best guys," Dwight said. "Absolute best. You should see the stuff they can come up with."

"Well, you know, I really would love to," I said, trying but failing in keeping the sarcasm from my voice. "I'm stoked. I'm ready to be dazzled."

"I told Heath that there was some confusion on the logo concept," Todd added helpfully.

"Oh . . . yeah," Dwight said. "Yeah, my guys are struggling with it."

"Well, can your guys give me a little to go on?" I asked. "I'd be happy to point them in the right direction."

"We're just not sure what you want," Mark said (or maybe it was Daniel).

"Yeah," the other one chimed in. "We don't get what you're going for."

Suddenly, I realized my margarita glass was empty. *Didn't I just get a refill?* I wondered. *Where the hell did it go?* I looked around for my waitress, all set to accuse some casino ninja of snatching my margarita. I considered asking Captain Gump if he'd seen where the margarita had gone, but he was inching as far away from me as he could get.

The night was looking up.

"Okay, guys," I said, reaching deep for whatever patience I possessed. "What we're looking for is to use a dialogue bubble as the key piece of the design. We want to tell people that Todd Allen is different because he's willing to engage in an actual dialogue."

"Oh," Dwight said. "I get it now. It's not a *Q*."

"It's not a *Q*?" Mark (Daniel?) asked, clearly confused.

Todd stepped in smoothly, probably sensing that I was split seconds away from an outburst of fairly epic proportions. "It's a speech bubble," he said in his best teacher voice. "And we want to use it as a symbol because politics has become all about screaming and people are sick of that. I'm sick of it. You're sick of it. Heath's sick of it. Voters are sick of it. We just want people to know that we can be better, and that it's okay to expect more of our candidates. Got it?"

Silence on the other end of the line. I had the sneaking suspicion that Mark, Daniel, and Dwight had never paid attention to politics, politicians, political campaigns, or your average high school government course. Finally, Mark (Daniel?) said, "Does a speech bubble say all that?"

"Maybe," I said. "Maybe not. Maybe we need to get a fluttering flag in there somewhere."

I was being sarcastic, but Daniel (Mark?) immediately sounded enthusiastic. "Yes! That's what I was thinking—"

I cut him off. "But we're not going to do that, because everyone has a fucking flag on their logo. I want us to be different. Maybe a dialogue bubble won't work, but we won't know until we've got a mock-up. Something on paper more substantial than a cocktail napkin. I sent y'all something to get your creative juices flowing. Took me ten minutes. I'd love to see what you can deliver in twenty-four hours."

More silence. I could tell what they were thinking, which was probably along the lines of, This design really needs more flags, maybe an eagle or two.

"Alright." Dwight had reluctance in his voice. "I think we can get something ready."

"Awesomesauce," I said. "Thanks for your time, gentlemen. Now, if you'll excuse me, a roulette wheel is calling my name."

Then I hung up.

An hour later, after I'd slowly won back most of the hundred I'd lost betting it all on black, Captain Gump leaned over. "What is your friend running on?"

I sighed a bit as the marble landed on a number that I had no interest in. "Mostly coffee and milkshakes."

Seeing his look, I said, "If you're talking about what his platform is, we haven't really figured out how to get it in a ten-word soundbite. I'm playing with saying he wants to work twenty-four seven for the nine-to-five American."

"I don't know what that means," Captain Gump said dismissively.

"Well, *you* tell me what we should say," I snapped, deciding that if we were gonna have this conversation, we were gonna fucking *have* this conversation. "My buddy and I are teachers. We work hard. We got student debt, which is our fault for going to an expensive school and then deciding to work in education. We got mortgages. He's got kids that need glasses and braces and doctor visits. Every year I have a little bet with myself about what unexpected bullshit expense is gonna come up to wipe out my savings. We're just normal guys, is what I'm saying, okay?"

"Normal guys don't run for Congress," Captain Gump pointed out grumpily. He'd just lost twenty bucks, system or no.

"No shit," I said. "That's what I'm saying. It feels like there's nothing for us in politics. No one is standing up for us. No one gives a shit about us. I'm not talking about causes or culture-war bullshit, I'm talking about someone out there giving a damn about making *my* life just a little bit easier. A larger tax return, maybe a system where if I come into a little bit of money the government doesn't immediately decide it belongs to them. How about schools that respect parents, students, *and* teachers so I don't feel like the world sees me as a babysitter? Or maybe a visit to the doctor's office not breaking the bank, how's that for progressive? Student debt relief would be nice, you know, so I could pay off school loans before I retire at the ripe old age of ninety. Shit that matters."

I shut up. I'd been ranting, I realized, and at a virtual stranger in a casino. I'd become *that* guy.

I shrugged and turned back to the roulette wheel, in the mood to put a lot of money on black thirteen and let it ride until I was broke or I won. I was embarrassed that I'd let all my frustrations boil out on a guy who was probably just trying to pass the time of day before pocketing his winnings and heading back out to his boat and shrimp nets.

Captain Gump let the silence hang over us for a moment before he took a nice long pull from whatever he was drinking and said, "Just looking out for us normal folks, huh?"

I was drunk. "We can't say normal folks," I pointed out. "Or ordinary people. Or average citizens. Or regular Americans. Not unless we want to get dragged into a dark alley by activists and have the shit kicked out of us. Half the trouble I have is figuring out how to say ordinary without using any of the synonyms for ordinary."

The old man shook his head, said, "Politically correct horseshit is gonna ruin this country, swear to God."

I didn't necessarily agree, but beggars can't be choosers when it comes to drunken casino companions and their political proclivities.

So I told him about something Todd once told me when trying to describe what he thought America had come to and what it was going to take to fix it. He'd said, "It's like . . . we've got these islands. These islands formed in this political gulf years ago. And liberals and conservatives jumped onto these islands, built McMansions, and didn't give much of a shit about the people on the other island. They just honed their talking points and loosed their arrows across the water. But that's not most of us. I think most Americans aren't on either island. They are in the gulf, drowning. And those people need something to save them. Or, at a minimum, a guy with a raft handing out floats and blankets."

I took a big drink from my latest, and last, margarita. Captain Gump was staring at me, puzzled. He said, "I'm not sure what the hell your friend is trying to say."

I shrugged. "Well, that makes two of us."

Then it was his turn to sigh. His grizzled visage looked sad as he looked off, either into the dim recesses of a time long lost or at a cocktail waitress sashaying by in a short skirt. Maybe both. "Feels like no one really cares about folks like me," he said. "Not anymore. Used to feel different, anyway. My dad was a lifelong Democrat. Lot of folks in the South were. Loyalty going back to the days when the party was looking out for the small farmers and fishermen and such during the Depression. Way he told it, they were trying to make lives a little easier for us normal folks. Sounds like your buddy is a bit of a throwback, isn't he?"

"No," I said thoughtfully. Something clicked. "Not a throwback. Not something old. Something *new*. Not the same old blue causes *ad nauseam*, the culture wars, the red meat for the base, but a blue that gives a shit about people. A *new* blue." I paused. "A new blue. Hashtag New-fucking-blue."

I reached for my phone and dialed Todd's number. He picked up on the third ring. "Hey," I said. "Give Dwight and the Wonder Twins the news that we've got a slogan they can start to plaster on everything in the campaign. Todd Allen for Congress, a #NewBlue for Texas." I paused again. "Yeah, I know it's good."

Captain Gump looked up from the wheel. "What the fuck is a hashtag?"

Cue the music, John Williams.

Introducing a #NewBlue
for the Texas 24th

Todd's First Email to Potential Voters

FROM: Todd Allen for Congress
SUBJ: Introducing a #NewBlue for the Texas 24th

My name is Todd Allen, and I wanted to take the time to reach out to you to introduce myself and what I stand for. Several months ago, I decided that I was going to run for election as a representative of the Texas 24th Congressional district. You probably don't recognize my name and want to know a little bit about who I am, what I represent, and why I'm suddenly sending you an email. The bottom line is simple: I want to start a conversation with you. I want to listen to what you think is important about the Democratic Party, the 24th Congressional District, and what you expect and hope a congressman to be.

My life has been spent as a teacher, working in our communities with the next generation, teaching my students the foundations and fundamentals of American government. I've spent my years in the classroom and on the playing fields, trying to lead by example and educate where I could. For the last couple of those years, happy as my wife and I have been raising our two children and being educators, I've been aware of a nagging sensation that there was a responsibility that I was not fully living up to. I'm writing to you today because I can see the writing on the wall. Day after day, I would paint over that wall, but whenever I'd look up, I'd see the same words just bleeding through. I would see the same phrase, over and over: it doesn't have to be like this; do something about it. I'm writing because I believe we can be better, and I am ready to take responsibility, personal responsibility, to do all that I can.

I am not a career politician. I am a teacher. I am proud to be a teacher. There are a thousand different reasons for me to ignore the writing on the wall, to keep painting over it. But the words keep bleeding through: it doesn't have to be like this; do something about it. So I'm stepping up to take a stand for what should be and what can be.

What kind of candidate do I intend to be? An active one: starting in August, I'd love to meet with any groups of local voters, Democrats or not, and introduce myself. More importantly, though, I want to listen to what they have to say. I want to have a conversation. There is a reason I've chosen the "message" icon as my campaign logo: it symbolizes what my candidacy is all about. We used to be able to talk to one another, as Americans. I believe we can again.

I also am running under the idea of a #NewBlue, a new branding for the Democratic Party that refocuses on putting more money in American pockets, providing more peace for American minds and more opportunities for American children.

Please feel free to look at my campaign site, and then please let me know any questions, comments, or concerns you have. Start a conversation; I'll listen and I'll reply.

I hope to hear from you soon.

Todd Allen

RE: Introducing a #NewBlue for the Texas 24th

The First Response From Todd's First Email

FROM: {Redacted Precinct Chair Name}
SUBJ: RE: Introducing a #NewBlue for the Texas 24th

I've never fucking heard of you.

The Launch

I came home from the wilds of a Louisiana casino feeling like a million bucks, even if I was a couple of hundred dollars poorer for it. For a moment, it seemed like the campaign had it all, and I was basking in it. A media team. A message. A slogan. A logo (assuming Dwight's team figured out what the hell I was talking about). A candidate who stood for everything that could redeem politics for Main Street America. Now all the campaign had to do was take those things and tell the world that Todd Allen was running for Congress and wait for the good word to spread.

It was easier said than done.

There was a date circled in red on my calendar: July 4, 2017, Independence Day, the launch party, and the glorious moment when Todd Allen would appear on the political scene as if by magic. Or, at least, that was my plan, which, looking back, was either genius in its simplicity or the worst form of naïvete. To tell you the truth, I was looking forward to that day. It was supposed to be our day of jubilee, the day when we could stand up in front of our friends and say, *Yeah, we did something about*

Is it an album cover or is it Lauren Allen, setting up for Todd's launch party?

it. Lauren Allen had gone all out in planning a campaign launch party at their house for Todd's friends and families, apparently buying up all the red, white, and blue tinsel in the Mid-Cities. Even the flowers in the vases on the kitchen table were patriotically hued. Todd said his house looked like a 1980s Springsteen album cover. He wasn't wrong.

Unfortunately, by the time I pulled up that day, I was in no mood for parties.

The source of my anger was our secret weapon, Dwight the Keychain Guy.

Frustratingly but predictably, contact with Dwight and his team had been sporadic since our casino-set conversation about the symbolism of dialogue bubbles, and the tension had been growing with each unanswered email. I liked the logo Dwight's team finally delivered, which turned the *O* in Todd's name into a stylized speech bubble (even if they had also managed to put the design of a Texas flag into that same bubble). It was a slick logo. It was professional. It made me feel as if Dwight and Co. really could deliver, even if it was going to take moving mountains to get each graphic or video. Unfortunately, moving mountains turned out to be an understatement: ever since receiving the logo, we hadn't seen the deluge of media materials that I had envisioned for our McDonald's strategy to work. We hadn't even seen a mock-up of the website that was supposed to go up on the same day as the launch.

Sitting in my car out in front of Todd's house, I checked the campaign website on my phone to see if it was *finally* live.

It was.

I lost my shit.

I charged up the drive, which Lauren had lined in tiny American flags, building up a head of steam as I went. I damn near took the front door off the hinges as I blew into that party riding a cloud of wrath that would make John Doe proud. Spotting Todd talking to a friend in the kitchen, I waved my phone at him and managed to sputter out, "Have you *seen* this shit?"

Todd grimaced, so I assumed he either had seen the website or he was embarrassed by my outburst or both. Toss-up, either way.

"Yeah, I saw it was up," he said as his friend escaped into the living room, out of the line of fire (but only just).

"That's one way to say it," I responded, showing him my phone and raising my voice. "Another way would be to say that my four-year-old nephew designs better shit on his fucking LeapFrog!"

Yeah, I was *pissed*, and at the one thing guaranteed to anger me in any situation: the failure of someone to produce what they had promised to produce. After a month of design, what Dwight's team had allowed to go live in front of the masses was something that made my eyeballs bleed. Underlying all my anger was a sense of the ingratitude of it all: I hadn't pushed to see draft designs of the site or dictated hard-and-fast deadlines because I had trusted in Dwight's professionalism. Scratch that: I hoped he had professionalism and had given him the benefit of the doubt. That faith had not been rewarded. That faith had been hit from behind with a billy club, shanghaied onto a tramp steamer, and drowned when that rust bucket finally sank with all hands.

What I saw when I pulled up ToddAllenForCongress.com on my phone was that the site was a single page that wasn't even formatted for phones. Todd's logo was cut off in the banner image, as was the top of his head and most of his last name. His policy positions were listed under the banner image in block text that looked like the jumble of coding rain from the beginning of the *Matrix* movies. I was mortified that Todd's first exposure to voters was going to be this absolute *monstrosity* of a website.

The Allen clan at the launch party, minus Sam, who I assume is eating a hot dog offscreen

And I was mad at myself, 'cause I had known, deep down, that this is where things were going to wind up. Because I hate people, conversation, and conflict (in no particular order), I had ignored it. Now my friend was going to pay the price of that cowardice. People were going to equate Todd Allen, not with quality and professionalism bursting onto a quiet political scene, but with amateur hour at the graphic design improv. My only consolation was that maybe people wouldn't know it was Todd Allen being introduced to the world in such a half-assed way since, after all, the graphic was cut off and advertised the campaign launch of someone named "Odd Al."[1]

Anyway, Todd looked at the phone for a long couple of seconds. "Yeah," he said softly, and his eyes narrowed. He was keeping cool, which is one thing I've always admired about Todd Allen. Decorum in public is something that matters to him, and above all else, when in the company of people, he is going to be in control. I might have admired it, but I didn't always *agree* with it, and right then what mattered to me wasn't decorum, it was finding Dwight at that party so I could impale his head on a fucking pike.

I was fuming and making a scene, and at that moment, I think Todd was more upset that I was obviously throwing a hissy in the middle of his day of jubilee than the fact that Dwight had basically crapped out on us. It was maybe the only heated argument we ever had.

"Look," Todd said, "this obviously isn't good. We'll fix it. Dwight's got some family problems."

This was news to me.

"That's news to me," I said. "What *kind* of family problems?"

"I dunno, something to do with his baby mama moving to another state or something. He was vague."

"Okay," I said, trying to remember to breathe. "Okay. So what the hell does that have to do with this Jackson Pollock of a fucking website?"

Todd got angry. "What do you want me to do, fire him?"

"Yes!" I almost screamed.

"Calm down," he said in a low voice. "You're scaring the normal people."

Then he walked by and out into the yard to mingle, and I helped

---

[1] Come to think of it, I might vote for Odd Al.

myself to some Doritos lying out on the counter while trying to figure out what to do next. By the time the bag was empty (I stress eat, as if you hadn't already figured that out), I was calmer and more collected. I no longer wanted to pull a Tristan Ludlow and go out into the night looking for Germans to scalp. It was time to be a grown-up, face failure, and figure out what came next.

I found Todd out by the grill, looking grim. I followed his eyes, guessed his thoughts, and said, "Not a very auspicious start, is it?"

His mouth tightened a bit as he admitted, "Somehow in my head this was bigger. More people. More . . . well, *more*. This is basically my folks, Bobby, and a few neighbors." He looked down at the grill. "I'm gonna have some leftover hotdogs."

"I may be able to help you with that," I said, leaning up against a porch railing. "And with that other thing. The website."

The basic gist of my plan at that moment was to quietly take over from Dwight and start from scratch on the website. We'd delay a few days on the campaign announcement until it was done, but until then I'd take the site down and hopefully no one would ever see what was essentially the Todd Allen for Congress campaign's beta test. I had never built a website before and had no idea how to get started, but neither Todd nor I were much worried about that. Todd was worried about hurting Dwight's feelings in his hour of domestic upheaval, and I was worried about being able to teach classes the next few days operating on nothing but coffee, Doritos, and leftover hotdogs.

I did it, of course, because that's what I do.

We were off to a rough start.

Your Sons Are Dead
Because They Were Stupid

As soon as the woman in the green dress stood up to ask a question, I knew that we were in deep shit, and not just because I was out of chili cheese fries and the waiter had taken a powder. For a local burger joint made up to resemble a fifties-era diner, the chili cheese fries were actually pretty damn good. I had decided they were either a fluke or the best-kept culinary secret in the Mid-Cities, because the place was nearly empty, except for the fifteen or so local activists crammed into a small event room off to one side.[1] A hand-lettered sign propped up outside the door boasted "Democrats Welcome!"

Even naïve as I was, I had my doubts about that sign.

It was Todd's first appearance at a public event since announcing his candidacy, his first chance to meet and greet local Democrats. Up until the woman in the green dress stood up, things had gone all right, which is a technical term reserved for endeavors that succeed in not totally

---

[1]Sadly, the place didn't survive the pandemic, like a lot of mom-and-pop establishments. The fries were damn good, though.

fucking things up. Lauren and the kids were there to support Todd (and eat a fairly decent hamburger). I had caught the local activists casting glances their way all night, and I knew what they were thinking: Holy shit, someone wants to run as a Democrat who is good looking, fairly charismatic, has a beautiful wife and two cute-as-fuck toddlers? Sign me up, this is who we need to save democracy!

Turns out that was *not* what any of them were thinking, but I didn't know that then.

I was busy congratulating myself on how well things were going. There had been bumps in the road to get there, but by mid-July we had a functioning website and social media, and Dwight had moved on to tackle his domestic issues full-time. By then, I felt we had overcome most of our hiccups and growing pains, and I was ready for us to be off to the races—or to the local burger joint, as the case turned out to be.

Todd showed up to the Burger Barn that night cocky, nervous, and overdressed. He wasn't the only one: I was sporting a suit and tie, which usually only made an appearance for job interviews or funerals. I sat down at a table in the front of the room, set out some freshly printed Todd Allen for Congress business cards, and settled in for an introvert's nightmare. We showed up in suits 'cause we imagined that is how the characters in the movie version of the campaign would dress. We had business cards because we wanted people to know that we were serious; later, it would occur to us to wonder why a little bit of card stock equated to the capability of holding public office.

I don't know what Todd had expected or how nervous he really was, but he waded into that room with a grin and a handshake for everyone. They didn't know him from a hole in the wall, but Todd walked in as if that didn't and shouldn't matter, and man, for a bright, shining moment I thought that maybe, just maybe, he was gonna pull this off. I trailed along behind him as he made his way through the room, watching and listening and doing no small amount of judging. What the hell am I supposed to do at these things, I wondered, other than follow him around and nod occasionally?

I settled, unsurprisingly, for following him around and nodding occasionally. I didn't try to contribute, figuring that people were wanting to talk to Todd, who was a nobody running for office, and not me, who was just a nobody. It felt a little like following Liz around a department store,

How most Allen for Congress campaign events started: me in my Challenger, waiting for Todd to waltz out the front door

bored out of my mind but unable to really come up with anything else to do.

Call it awkwardness or irritation, but it must have shown on my face, because Todd turned to me and suggested, "Hey, man, why don't you go sit down, have a Coke or something?"

Subtext: Heath, go sit down before you scare someone.

"Sure thing," I said, relieved.

I sat down, waved for the waitress, ordered some more chili cheese fries, and wondered what terribly important thing a campaign manager was supposed to be doing that I wasn't.

Oh, well, I thought, I guess ignorance is bliss. I tucked into the fries and watched Todd's first half hour as a politician unfold. It was entertaining and not a little inspiring, because Todd had a gift of being able to mingle without embarrassment. Maybe to some people that isn't uplifting, but to me, that's damn near "Ask Not What Your Country Can Do For You"–level inspiration.

Todd has a technique that I've long admired, which is this kind of faux-laugh that everyone seems to appreciate. He was using it on full power that night, and it was quite the show. He'd wait for someone to say something that could, in some universe if not in ours, be found humorous, then he'd smile, throw his head back and to the side, and laugh. It was great, 'cause he got to use it to break eye contact and end the conversation, but in a nicer way than saying, "Hey, I'd rather take a swift kick to the groin than converse with you for another split-fucking-second." That faux-laugh made people think he was invested in what they were saying. It was disarming. I'm sure he had and has no idea that he does it.

The leader of the little activist group, Ronnie, was basically the stereotype of the people we'd meet during the primary: older, fairly well-off, and white. Before long he got up at the front of the room and introduced Todd formally and thanked him for coming out to visit. Then he gave Todd five minutes to talk about himself, which was a pointless exercise considering Todd had just spent the last half hour doing that very thing. Todd stepped up, cleared his throat, set his feet, and barked out, "Hello, I'm Todd Allen!"

Turns out that, amidst congratulating myself on running a congressional campaign, I had forgotten to remind the candidate to practice his speech.

It's not as dumb a stunt to pull as it sounds. I mean, sure, you're thinking, "How the fuck do you not practice your speech at your first engagement in a run for the United States Congress?" While you're thinking that, think about this: Has *your* name ever been on a ballot?

Okay, then.

Truth be told, neither Todd nor I had given much thought to how he'd succinctly introduce himself to a crowd. He opened his mouth and what came out was too loud, too strident, and too much. The Todd at the front of the room giving a speech wasn't the same Todd who had been mingling with a laugh and charming smile a moment before. Nope. Suddenly, with something like a stump speech to give, he was going full-on Coach Allen, addressing a locker room full of football players at half-time. It didn't get any better over the next few minutes as he struggled to tell them what they all already knew: his name, a little bit about himself, and what he was running for. There was never a moment where he hit a stride or nailed a line that made the audience perk up and do anything but wonder, Hey, where the hell is that guy with my fries?

I gave him a look that he'd come to know well, the kind that mingled irritation with deeply felt disappointment.

I'll be the first to admit that I hadn't prepared him well for this little gathering. I'd basically sent him in there without much more than a firm handshake and a whispered, "Good luck, man." Later, he'd have a full stump speech to memorize. Later still, after we realized that he was a hell of a lot better speaking off-the-cuff than trying to perform my Kennedy-esque phrasing, he'd work off a "punch card" of issues and lines that he could mix and match at random. That night, he was all on his own; he was nervous; he was out of his element, and it showed.

To crown it all off, Todd couldn't find a way to *stop* talking. Sounds easy, doesn't it? Well, it turns out that not all speeches end with applause lines and rising music, and when they don't, it's hard to know exactly how to quit them. This was Todd's first political speech, and both of us realized, after five minutes of grueling, meandering twaddle, that neither of us had any clue how he should gracefully end a speech. So much of Todd's run for Congress was so based in Hollywood-inspired idealism that I had never considered that we'd need to work on a dynamite exit line to use when the crowd was stone-cold silent and unimpressed with our very existence.

My eyes swiveled to Todd, hoping he'd pull a homerun out of his ass.

"Anyway," Todd said weakly, "I'm Todd Allen. Thanks."

People clapped. They shouldn't have, but they did, which was nice of them.

Then, in the awkward silence that followed, Ronnie stepped forward and asked for questions.

And, ever so slowly, Todd began to redeem himself. For the next twenty minutes, I got to be proud of both Todd Allen and, God bless 'em, that little activist group at the Burger Barn. As the primary contest went on and on, the questions we'd receive at forums, gatherings, and meet and greets started to roll together into the same boring, pointless quagmire where candidates stop being individuals and start being an extension of the political base. You'd get so many versions of the same purity test questions that you could answer them in your sleep, just like your primary opponents. Abortion. Guns. LGBTQ Rights. Important issues, sure, but issues where most primary candidates have not a sliver of daylight between them, and everyone, including the voters asking the questions, knows it. What we didn't know back then was that what mattered in a primary is not the substance of what you say, but how you say it.

Man, but for twenty minutes that day in July, I gained a new respect for the American voter, or at least these American voters. Unlike most of the attendees in the forums we'd speak at in the months to come, these fifteen activists were ready to take a damned AP Government exam and pass with flying colors. The first question, from an elderly gentleman in the back, was, "How do you think we can escape the Thucydides Trap?"

And in my front-row seat, I tried to keep my face from showing what I was thinking, which was more or less, What the fuck?

I honestly don't remember if Todd knew what the Thucydides Trap was or if he even attempted to pronounce it correctly. I do remember that I was suddenly reminded why I thought my friend would be a good congressman. Whether he was bullshitting or not, Todd answered the gentleman's question in a deep, thoughtful way while I was still wondering who the fuck Themistocles was. Then he proceeded to answer the next five questions, all of which I couldn't have begun to answer without taking a break to look something up on my phone. The situation revolving around work visas for computer technology workers? The issues facing airline industry personnel at DFW Airport? Trade concerns with China and Southeast Asia? Todd took a legitimate swing at all of them, and unlike his quasi-stump speech, his answers seemed to be connecting. Distantly, maybe playing over the Burger Barn's loudspeaker out in the main room or on the radio of a parked car, I'm sure I heard the stirring notes of *The West Wing*'s theme song playing triumphantly. There was a milkshake in Todd's future.

Then the woman in the green dress stood up.

I took one look and knew that somehow we'd fucked up. We had walked right into an ambush. Charlie was in the fucking trees, and we didn't have time to bleed. Everyone looked at the woman in the green dress expectantly, and I knew that what she was about to say was going to matter to this group more than any questions Todd answered, now or in the future. It felt like witnessing a religious experience for people who worship differently than you, in a church that wild horses couldn't drag you to. This woman was about to deliver *the Word*, and we were the interlopers. We were the heathens.

"Did you know," she said, "that your Facebook page shared an article recently that referred to illegal immigration?"

Todd took the bait.

"Yes, ma'am," he said, nodding. "And on the possibility of bipartisan solutions as long as everyone is willing to sit down and talk to each other."

"Well," she shot back, "I want you to know there is no such thing as an *illegal* human being and your use of that term is offensive."

The room erupted into applause.

I looked at Todd. He looked at me. I scrawled one word into my notebook.

Fuck.

Then I reached over to Todd's nearly untouched plate and took a chili cheese fry.

Minutes later, we walked out into the parking lot and into the warm July air as two moderately wiser political animals. Well, no, scratch that: what we were wasn't *wiser*, it was *politically shell-shocked*. Todd bid Lauren and the kids goodnight and saw them off, then walked over to my car, probably to find out how many times I could use the word *fuck* in a single sentence.

I was up to the challenge. I was pissed off at the activists, the world, myself, and congressional candidates who stumbled over well-honed lines—in no particular order. Todd's smile had dropped off his face the minute we hit the pavement, and now he was wearing a blank expression that suggested he wasn't drinking heavily yet, but he sure as hell was thinking about it. He shook his head slowly, stared off about a thousand yards into the murky night of Bedford, Texas, and finally exhaled a plaintive, "What the fuck?"

"I'll tell you what," I said, wishing I was a smoker so I could light up a cigarette and wave it around indignantly. "These sons of bitches are the reason Democrats lose so fucking always. They heard you talk about civility and conversation, and they decided they just can't have that shit. These people don't want politics to be civil. They don't want to talk to the other side. They want to fucking murder Republicans in their fucking sleep! They don't care who wins as long as they can be self-righteously pissed off all the fucking time. That's what matters. Not policy. Not getting something done. Just being mad."

I paused. "You know, the great thing about being mad as a lifestyle is that you never have to worry about what comes next. They can strut around with the mental attitude of a three-year-old on a long car ride.

They've got a great attitude that is gonna do really fucking well in a plus fifteen Republican district. It's gonna win over converts. It's gonna heal the sick. The blind are gonna fucking see."

I mentally flicked away that imaginary cigarette and added, "Or, you know, they are gonna keep losing by double digit margins."

I could tell Todd wasn't listening to most of what I was saying. He was already making the shift into his primary mode of reflection, which was, essentially, to blame himself.

Softly, he said, "I had a bad feeling about tonight."

"Yeah." I wished I was a real smoker. I need the prop.

"I was at AP training today out at SMU," he said. "Renewing my certificate. Guy leading the training, Dr. Kleinshmidt, I caught him during a break and let him know I would be gone for the afternoon session because I had a political event I needed to attend."

Todd sighed, continued, "He asked if I was part of an activist group or something. I said, 'No, sir. I'm announcing my candidacy for Congress.' He looked up at me and asked, 'The United States Congress?' I nodded and he just looked at me for a long time, then finally just said, 'Good luck with that.'"

Talk about a gut punch.

"Good luck with that," I repeated, shaking my head. "Guy should be a motivational speaker."

This wasn't an out-of-the-ordinary reaction, we'd come to find out. Reactions like this are probably why I just stopped telling people close to me what we were doing. For example, I had close family friends who were big-time activists and liberal flag-wavers, good people that I enjoyed being around. It was almost a guarantee that any conversation with them would swerve into a political discussion within a hot minute. During Todd's entire candidacy, they seemed curiously disinterested in the fact that I was running a congressional campaign. They didn't want to talk about it. It didn't interest them. I never figured it out, but it was a reaction we got from family, friends, and acquaintances all the time.

I looked over at Todd's face and I knew I'd missed my window to complain about Democratic activists and their demands about campaign language. He was already mentally reviewing his performance that night, and by his expression I knew exactly what he thought of that performance. I'll tell you this: I've never met anyone as prone to negative self-reflection as Todd Allen. *Cynical* doesn't begin to describe his view of his own efforts on damn near anything. I've heard Todd referred to as "arrogant" before, which always makes me laugh since absolutely no one is as hard on himself as Todd is.

Plus, he didn't need to get mad or rant and rave. He had me for that.

I took a deep breath, calmed myself, and said, "Well . . . what do you think?"

His answer was pure Todd Allen.

He shrugged and said matter-of-factly, "I think we need to do better."

PART II

Our Guts Have Shit for Brains

A Real Campaign Has Envelopes

Even though politics had invaded my life and colonized some significant territory in my mind, most of my fellow Americans weren't exactly wrapping their day-to-day existence around the machinations of elephants and donkeys. No, the waning months of the summer of 2017 were all about animals of a different sort—dragons. *Game of Thrones*, the poster child for epic fantasy (not to mention ultimate disappointment) was steaming towards a conclusion, winter was coming, beloved characters were dropping like flies, spoilers were being shared with abandon, and in stolen moments between campaign-centered conversations Todd and I speculated on the lessons learned from too many hours spent throwing money at HBO.

"The answer to our failing public education system is *Game of Thrones*," I said one morning on the phone. "Who needs teachers when you have dragons and nudity? There's literally nothing you need to know about life that you can't learn by subscribing to HBO."

"Hang on, I'm putting that in an email to our superintendent. Cancel curriculum. Just show *Game of Thrones*. Got it." Todd responded. Somehow I doubted he was actually sending an email, but maybe I'm just cynical.

"Since you're doing an email," I said, "I've got the bullet points for you: Never get to know a sibling in a biblical sense. Never trust a brothel owner. Never hunt boar while drunk—"

"Couldn't we add 'while drunk' to the entire list?" Todd interjected, laughing.

I was on a roll, so I ignored him.

"And never, under any circumstances, attend a wedding," I concluded, sure that George R. R. Martin would be proud that I'd successfully encapsulated his multithousand-page epic in such a succinct phone conversation.

"No weddings under any circumstances, huh?" I could almost see the smile on the other end of the line as Todd pointed out, "You know, that last one's gonna be kind of hard for you to avoid, isn't it?"

I waved away his concern and reminded him that the rules of Westeros didn't apply to my own forthcoming nuptials (to be certain, however, there wouldn't be a violinist or crossbowman in sight). No, my wedding was exempt from the rules of fantasy epics.

"The wedding I'm not invited to," Todd reminded me.

"The wedding you're not invited to," I confirmed.

Liz and I had marched into a judge's chambers in May to tie the knot officially, celebrating with a bowl of authentic Texas chili at Tolbert's in Grapevine, which is basically how all life events should be marked. We quickly decided that we wanted something more personal and celebratory than a bowl of chili, as odd as that may be, so as July 2017 came to a close we planned to head to a cabin in Broken Bow, Oklahoma, to have a more traditional wedding. We would spend a few days with our most immediate family before having a small, personal ceremony out on the cabin's back porch under green leaves and blue skies. It was the kind of wedding that appealed to us both (though she hides it better, Liz is as averse to extroversion as I am). Parents, siblings, and a handful of young nieces and nephews, gathered under a bright summer sky with no pretensions, no overly elaborate pagan rituals, and no lurking assassins.

And no politics or political candidates.

Liz had been worried that Todd would take his non-invitation to the big day as a mortal slight. I knew better, so Todd's apparent giddiness at

An early campaign event, when I was still wearing a tie; I'm afraid neither Todd nor I seem to be masking our feelings very well

not having to wear fancy clothes, sit through a ceremony, or chat with people he didn't know was both palpable and entirely predictable. I can't say for sure that he did cartwheels, but there might have been a small smile of satisfaction, perhaps a sigh of pure relief. The joys of life are few, but I was happy to be able to hand my friend this one tiny moment.

It was the least I could do for being at least partially responsible for making him a political candidate.

This seems like an excellent and auspicious point to pause this political narrative to focus with laser-like precision on an aspect of this story that I might not have been totally clear about: my wife Liz is, without a shred of a doubt, the most perfect woman, companion, wife, and mother that anyone could ask for. Seriously, she's smart as a whip, sexy in a way that would embarrass our kids to read about, and so kind and loving that little birds burst into song whenever she appears outdoors and flutter around her head like a halo. Lucky does not even begin to describe my life condition as it relates to this wonderful woman and what she's brought into my day-to-day existence.

Now, if this paean of praise seems a tad unusual and out of place in what has been, up to this point, a fairly irreverent accounting of two teachers blundering through politics, I'd like to point out two things that might shed some light on the situation. First, absolutely none of my praise of Liz is exaggerated; she's a goddess, final answer.

Second, I might have gotten up and left the table at our wedding rehearsal dinner to take a political campaign call.

If you're shaking your head and saying to yourself, No, surely he didn't actually do that, I would like to reassure you that life has matured me to the point where I would obviously not commit such a serious faux pas on such an important occasion.

Except, yes, I did, in fact, do exactly that.

As mistakes go, it was on par with bringing a diary inscribed with a map to the Holy Grail to a castle full of Nazis while attempting to rescue my father and/or James Bond. Similar risks, similar stupidity, similar potential for world-shaking consequences. I caught a curious look from Liz as I excused myself from the table. An entirely understandable look, even an understated one from a bride watching the groom take a call at the rehearsal dinner. In my head, Sean Connery was narrating the moment in his Scottish brogue, commenting with increasing desperation, "You didn't do that, did you? You didn't, did you?"

I did.

I held the phone up to my ear, pushed open the restaurant doors, and said, "Okay, what do you want?"

"Well, we don't have envelopes," I heard Todd say as I stepped out into the parking lot of the restaurant where my future bride and the rest of my family and soon-to-be family were feasting on some of the best pizza a person can get anywhere.[1] "Did you know we needed envelopes? Because apparently we need envelopes."

I paused, brows furrowed. "I'm sorry, what?"

"We don't have envelopes," Todd said again, then, with a hint of frustration and sarcasm. "So, you know, I'm gonna need you to get right on that because apparently real campaigns have envelopes."

Deep breath. In, out. Smells faintly of pizza on the breeze, so that's a positive to focus on. Certainly don't think about the fact that you just

---

[1] Shout out to Grateful Head in Broken Bow, Oklahoma.

left your rehearsal dinner to talk about envelopes. Don't even begin to ponder how to explain it. Focus on the now.

"Focus on the now," I muttered aloud. I wondered if Liz would throw pizza at me when I went back inside. Then I wondered if I would pick the slice up off the floor and eat it. Then I wondered if the slice would be pepperoni and sausage or one of those joke pizzas that comes covered in nothing but rabbit food and an unsettling sense of a misspent life. Then I wondered if Liz would be merciful or something more like God in Old Testament mode. Then I wondered if Shirley Jackson had ever written a short story about a wedding party tying up the groom and slowly torturing him while mumbling arcane prophecies about envelopes.

Then I wondered what the hell Todd was talking about, because I obviously hadn't been paying sufficient attention.

I wrenched my mind back onto the conversation at hand and managed to pick up the gist of what Todd was complaining about because, unlike others I could name, I was paying attention in third grade when Ms. Kirkpatrick taught about context clues. Long story short, Todd had been to a political event at a neighbor's house and felt most of it had come off well. He showed up, did his little spiel, smiled a lot, did the fake laugh thing, nodded quite a bit, and was all prepared to make a successful exit.

"That's when this old dude waddles up wanting to make a donation," he said, with bitterness that surprised me. Still a little confused, and with at least three-quarters of my mind on that looming Shirley Jackson scenario, I said, "I don't understand. Usually someone wanting to give us money is a good thing."

"I'll let you know when it happens more often," Todd commented dryly. "Anyway, I gave him my card and told him how to use the online portal to make a donation. He shook his head, put his arm around my shoulder and pulled out a twenty-dollar bill. He said, 'That's why I can't take your campaign seriously, son. Real campaigns have envelopes at these kinds of things. I could fill in my donation information, put the money inside, and you'd be twenty dollars richer.' He kinda chuckled and shuffled away and it took all I had not to tell him exactly what he could do with those fucking envelopes."

"Which we don't have," I noted.

"Which we don't have," Todd confirmed. He sighed, and I knew the rant was over. "So, yeah, we need envelopes."

"Do we?" I asked. It was rhetorical, but just in case Todd was under the mistaken idea that I wanted to spend any more of my rehearsal dinner talking about envelopes, I switched topics. "Look, I don't want to give the impression I don't care, even though I mostly don't, but I'm having a bit of a life moment this weekend."

"I know that," Todd said, exasperated. "I assumed you wouldn't take the call if you were doing anything other than sitting on a porch drinking a margarita." He paused, then asked, "What are you doing?"

"Well, the rest of the family is sitting at a table enjoying the rehearsal dinner," I answered.

There was a stunned moment of silence, then laughter. It might have gone on for an inappropriately long time, but what do I know? I had left my rehearsal dinner to stand in a parking lot to talk about envelopes. Maybe it was the exact right amount of laughter; it might even have been far less than I deserved.

"Jesus, dude," Todd finally said. "Who the hell does that? Let it go to voicemail."

Somewhat testily, I said through gritted teeth, "So, other than the envelopes, you said the event went pretty well?"

Todd, being a functioning human being, had continued right on with his campaign schedule while I absconded to Oklahoma to tie the knot. At this point in the campaign, most politicos and activists in the district still didn't know who he was, what he stood for, or where he'd come from. We were just starting to find our way on social media, and Todd was just starting to get into a kind of swing when it came to shaking hands and kissing babies.[2] To say that we were outsiders would be to put it mildly, and as we were discovering, primary voters and activists rarely felt like putting anything mildly.

"It was okay. My elevator speech was a lot cleaner this time. I felt like I was answering questions pretty well, which made me hate myself a little less," Todd said. "But I gotta tell you, dude, we were wrong."

---

[2]Actually, I'm not sure I ever saw a baby, or even a child, that wasn't related to either of us at any event or meet-and-greet. Do politicians kiss babies? Do people take infants to events so politicians can kiss them? Why would anyone *do* that?

"Wouldn't be the first time," I said. "In fact, you might have to be a little more specific. And make it quick, huh? I think my pizza is still warm."

Todd continued without missing a beat, "Just for starters, the whole idea of conversation and how we need to be able to talk to each other again just isn't resonating. I might as well have said that Trump seems like a swell guy who we can work with."

"Jesus, you didn't say that, did you?"

"Yes," he said sarcastically, "because I typically express my appreciation of the unsung virtues of our forty-fifth president." He paused to let that one sink in a bit. "The idea of compromise plays even worse than talking about having conversations. When I said 'compromise,' they looked at me like they just smelled a dog fart. I hate to say it, but they want red meat, dude. Trump bad. Democrat good. It's everyone I meet operating within these activist groups. Everyone. I talk about dialogue, and they want to talk about how I'm gonna dissect Mitch McConnell on live television."

Here's the thing about Todd: when he starts in with the hyperbole and exaggeration, you know he's pretty far gone down the road of frustration. I could say something to console him but fuck it. He'd called during my wedding rehearsal dinner. It wasn't his fault I'd taken the call, but whose side are you on, anyway?

After a second or two, a calmer Todd delivered the Too Long, Didn't Read summary of the event by saying, "I've been called Republican-lite about a dozen times this weekend. I don't even fucking know what that means other than, I guess, I foolishly believe government works best when we work more and hate less."

I sighed and rubbed the bridge of my nose, feeling a headache coming on that didn't have enough to do with the fact that I'd walked out of my rehearsal dinner. Ever since the Green Dress Lady had stood up to scold Todd at that first event at the Burger Barn, he'd been called Republican-lite at every campaign activity. It was a label thrown around with the kind of hostility elves on Middle-earth reserved for talking about Sauron (incidentally, in quieter moments I'd wonder if that meant I was Christopher Lee or just an orc, and usually wound up deciding I'd probably rather not know). What did Republican-lite mean, exactly? Was it a policy label? Was it a form of beer that tastes like water?

"I think I've had a can of Republican-Lite once," Todd said reflectively.

"Well, yeah, when you couldn't afford Lone Star," I noted somewhat sarcastically.

I struggled with understanding why Todd was drawing fire from people like the Green Dress Lady (in much the same way as I struggle with basic algebra). Todd's policy positions were quite liberal, so I could never see where the invective was coming from. I suspected it had less to do with actual ideas or ideals and everything to do with the picture Todd presented to the world. He walked into one of those meeting rooms and he was instantly cataloged as a good-looking, ever so possibly smug, middle-aged white male. Anything short of full-throated calls for revolution and absolute dominance of the political sphere brought on accusations that he was not, in fact, a liberal at all, but a dirty, no-good, baby-devouring Republican wolf in sheep's clothing.

No wonder no one brought babies to be kissed.

The truth had been slowly dawning on me over the last few weeks, and now was as good a time as any to confront it. "I know what the problem is," I said finally. "The problem is I'm stupid."

"Go on," Todd said, ever willing to listen to a good self-flagellating confession when one was around to be had.

"The problem," I continued, "other than my stupidity, is that we've confused why you wanted to do this and why people might want to vote for you. What do you tell your government classes about the average makeup of people voting in a political primary?"

"That they are, in bulk, the ideological extremes" Todd said immediately.

"Yeah," I said, then, after a second, "shit."

Todd gave a long, slow sigh. "We're idiots," he said. Then, after another long pause, "Shit."

Excrement indeed. We had jumped into this with an overarching feeling that everyone around us was tired of the political circus playing out on the nightly news and on our Twitter feeds. The whole crux of our campaign was that a large mass of Americans wanted a return to civility, conversation, and some form of actual fucking statesmanship. We should have known better, because nothing about what we saw playing out on the political stage encouraged us to think otherwise. Moderate voices weren't being rewarded. Statesmen weren't being honored; hell, who was the last person we'd heard even being described as one?

"We might hate what's going on in politics," I said bitterly, "but, dammit, what the fuck makes us think anyone else does? Especially primary voters?"

The reality of politics, which both of us should have damn well known, was that the political primary process was not set up to reward the voices of moderation, but the extreme idealists. Of course Todd's message of civility and conversation wasn't appealing to the people he met with; these were activists who were heavily invested in policy positions and brooked no dissent.

"I have to believe they are out there," Todd said after a while. "I have to believe that most of us don't like turning on the television to watch adults behave like toddlers. Surely there are folks out there who just want that all to stop."

"I don't know, man," I said, shaking my head. "I don't know how we're going to reach those people if we have to get the approval of the extremes first. How the hell does that work?"

"Maybe it doesn't," Todd said. "Maybe that is how someone like Donald Trump gets to sit in the White House."

Cheerful thoughts on my wedding weekend.

"I'm beginning to think we might need some help, dude," Todd said finally.

"A real campaign has envelopes," I muttered tonelessly. Our own inexperience with politics was hurting us in ways we couldn't imagine. Todd was right: what we desperately needed was help—someone who knew the political groups and their language, who would be able to suggest a course through the dangerous shoals ahead, who would know that a real campaign had envelopes. It was a move more successful campaigns took on first, before ever announcing their candidacy. It was a move we should have made weeks ago. Now, we didn't have help, we didn't have envelopes, and damn it, we could have used twenty bucks. Unfortunately, no one we'd met so far was interested in helping us. After all, Todd was Republican-lite.

"But, hey, good news," Todd said, interrupting my pity party. "That big group in the Mid-Cities has agreed to let me come speak finally. Monday night. Maybe that'll be a turning point."

"Maybe more than ten people will be there," I said hopefully. I'd been leaving messages for the organizers of this particular group for weeks, asking when it would be appropriate for Todd to attend and introduce himself, maybe speak to the group as a whole and answer questions. For a month there had been radio silence, but it appeared Todd had finally proven that maybe he wasn't going to disappear into the political night. He was going to get some time in front of the group at their next meeting, glory hallelujah—

Then I fully realized what that meant.

"Ummm . . . Monday night? *This* Monday night?"

"As in the day after Sunday, yes," Todd confirmed.

I sighed.

Liz and I had planned to stick around at the cabins until Tuesday morning in lieu of an official honeymoon. Both our day jobs expected us on Wednesday, and neither one of us was a half-hearted or half-assed worker. Starting mid-week, we knew everything was going to get harder, so a day or two of relaxation at the cabins seemed like a small but necessary respite. Now, of course, here comes the congressional campaign of Todd Allen, knocking on the door with an important event.

Todd was a grown man who didn't need me sitting in the audience frowning in order to make a speech. There was nothing preventing me from telling Todd to have a good event and I'd see him on Tuesday when I returned. Certainly I didn't need to compound leaving my rehearsal dinner to talk about envelopes (or a lack of them) with cutting short my already short honeymoon. Surely, life had taught me enough to realize that a campaign event, no matter how potentially consequential, was nowhere near as important as a precious day of relaxation with a wonderful woman in an amazing environment on a once-in-a-lifetime occasion.

I sighed again.

"I'll be there," I said, then walked back in to face the music and the cold pizza. It could have been worse; at least the pizza place wasn't filled with Nazis.

Tony's Clown Car Candidacy

You know, it's amazing what margaritas and marriage to a soulmate can do for self-confidence. Luckily, my dad was both the officiant at my wedding and the weekend's designated bartender, and, equally fortuitously, he shared my preference for sentimental but short speeches and a quality mixed beverage.[1] At the ceremony, Liz walked out looking like some kind of woodland elf princess and I forgot to breathe for a bit—and then everyone was offering congratulations and the time had come for dancing and drinks and laughter. A good deal of those laughs, both with me and at me, came from talking about my adventures in the strange realm of politics. We drank margaritas, we laughed, and, somehow, even though I was sharing the litany of my screwups and missteps, by the time Monday morning rolled around, I was feeling great and ready to conquer the world, one Chinese buffet at a time.

It also had a lot to do with the woman driving back to Texas with me. Liz was going to attend the event with me that night, a first for her, and she seemed to be honestly looking forward to it. We didn't know it

---

[1] My mother rarely makes the margaritas, but when she does it is something special. Essentially, she shows a lime a shot glass of tequila and threatens it with immersion before granting a reprieve and serving the result. It certainly is not for the faint of heart.

then, but by the time the election rolled around, Liz would have handed out more campaign literature and attended more events than anyone but Todd and myself, something that makes me grin with pride every time I think about it. I'm not sure if Liz shares that feeling, given that a political campaign involves attending way too many meet and greets at way too many Chinese restaurants and extroverting until your face feels ready to slide off your skull if you force a smile just one more time.

On that Monday, however, all those interchangeable buffets of General Tso's chicken and bad conversations were in the unanticipated future, and Liz seemed happy that we were about to jump into something so monumental together. She seemed excited.

"I'm excited," she said, which is how I knew she was excited. I'm perceptive.

I said, "Well, at least that makes one of us."

She shot me a look from the passenger seat. After a moment, she asked, "This isn't working out quite like you imagined, is it?"

Well, of course she had been paying attention over the weekend during those laughter-filled story sessions on the porch. She had realized that there was some deep-seated anxiety under the laughs and the margaritas. She did, after all, teach middle school.

"No," I said quietly. "No, this isn't what I thought it would be at all."

"What did you think it would be?" Liz asked.

"1952," I finally said.

Liz, to her eternal credit, waited patiently for me to expand on that nonsensical response rather than asking me exactly what the fuck I was talking about. That was for the best, really, since it gave me the time I needed to figure out for myself what in the actual fuck I was talking about. It sometimes occurs to me that life would be a lot simpler if people would just accept what I occasionally blurt out as an article of faith—to be puzzled over and interpreted, certainly, but with the underlying assumption that I know what I'm talking about. You know, like the Bible, or like how Republicans believe in the infallibility of trickle-down economics.

"In my head, it's 1952 America," I finally said. "Todd campaigns in a fedora because everyone wears a fedora. He holds it in his hands and gestures with it when he makes a speech, which he always does from a flag-bedecked bandstand or gazebo because it's 1952."

Todd greeting voters at Grapefest

"Gazebo is a fun word to say," Liz said.

"You see 'em a lot in Norman Rockwell paintings," I told her. "Gazebos and bandstands."

"And fedoras," she helpfully added.

"And fedoras," I confirmed. "Anyway, that's the America where I pictured Todd running: Norman Rockwell–inspired Main Street America. Where people would be drawn to him because he was a normal guy and he was running and that would be enough. He talks to Rotary Clubs and at Legion Halls. He walks down the street and shakes hands and kisses babies and the women pushing the baby carriages smile at him and offer him a slice of apple pie. He has real discussions with people who don't agree with him, serious discussions where everyone involved looks somber but still talk quietly and nod occasionally. I picture Todd sitting up in the stands at a football game, a hotdog in one hand, his tie loosened, talking foreign policy and the intricacies of the single wing offense with everyone sitting around him—"

"And all of them are smoking," Liz said with a smile, and I smiled back because I knew she got it, she was right there in the 1952 that never was. God, I love her.

Todd's go-to campaign photo. Is he gazing into your soul? Is he?

"That's the campaign I thought I'd run," I said wistfully. "*Naïve* doesn't even begin to describe it, but that's what I wanted. I wanted Todd to give a speech in front of a small-town crowd with the sun setting behind him and snow beginning to fall because why the fuck not? He'd look up and at the edge of the crowd he'd see me giving him a thumbs-up and then, just over my shoulder, Robert Kennedy would give him a slow nod and then turn to walk back into the corn with the ghosts of John, Jimmy Stewart, and Shoeless Joe Jackson."

I fell silent, running out of imaginative gas. It happens more often than you'd think.

Liz finally said, "I don't know what the single wing is, and I don't think I've seen most of the movies you're referencing. But I do know that you're going to figure it all out. I know that for sure."

"Maybe so," I said, smiling over at her. Liz has a lot going for her on any given day, but always, rain or shine, she brings this to the table: she can make me a believer. Teacher or politician, I don't know of any quality that should be celebrated more.

"So, other than the fact that men don't wear snappy hats anymore," Liz asked, "what is the biggest problem with the campaign?"

"The problem is that we're not talking to any of those people," I said without a moment's hesitation. "We're not holding court at ball games or walking down Main Street. We're not talking to all those voices I was pretty damn sure I've been hearing for the last couple of years—the voices that keep saying they are just normal Americans, and man, they are sick of all this politics shit."

Liz was quiet for a minute, then asked, "So who *have* you been talking to?"

"The groups," I said, and I tried, I really tried, to keep my voice from betraying exactly how I felt about that answer.

"The groups?" Liz repeated, puzzled.

She didn't say it right, and I bet you didn't either. First, even if there was no capital letter at the beginning of that phrase, you'd be wrong not to include it. Rookie mistake: *the groups* is a proper noun, capitalization or not, and rightfully so, because as anyone involved with them will constantly tell you, they are important. A staff of life, even. You've got to acknowledge that importance when you speak of them, but to get the tone right you also need to have the faintest note of bewilderment and no small amount of disdain; try saying Senator Herschel Walker aloud and you'll hear what I'm talking about. Then knock on wood, toss some salt over your left shoulder, spit three times, and think seriously about sacrificing a chicken to whichever deity seems most appropriate, because no one needs to vocalize that shit and tempt fate. Whenever I hear some-one talk about the groups today, my eyebrows twitch like Captain Hook catching wind of a cuckoo clock, and I swear some hidden orchestra strikes up a rendition of "The Imperial March."

"Why are you humming that?" Liz asked.

I cut my John Williams–inspired rendition short and said, "The activist groups are all we seem to talk to. Funny thing is, I used to think that they'd be a good thing for us. Before we started, I knew there would be activist groups and political clubs, and I thought, Great, here are organizations that will be friendly places for Todd to start and get his feet under him before he tackles those Main Street conversations and gazebo speeches. But I was wrong, 'cause we never seem to find those gazebos, and the group leaders don't like us. I thought they would, but . . . I was wrong."

Was I ever.

By the time we pulled into the parking lot at a Mexican restaurant in Hurst, Texas, I had filled Liz in on everything I thought I knew about the local groups, which was quite a deal less than I should but a whole lot more than I had known before I walked into the Burger Barn a few short weeks before. Back then, I had been pleasantly surprised when I discovered that CD-24, because it sprawled across so many communities over three different counties, hosted quite a few political clubs and activist groups. I had assumed that the people walking into Chinese and Mexican buffets to attend these meetings were not only hungry, but also a lot like Todd or myself—Americans shaken out of apathy into doing something more. As a point of fact, many of them were exactly that: recent converts to the religion of civic involvement, and as such, I thought they'd understand exactly who Todd was and why he was running. The online chatter from these true believers was encouraging as well, because it was filled to the brim with frustration towards the perennially poor quality of the candidates running for office in the area. This is awesome, I remember thinking while scrolling through Facebook feeds; these are our people.

There was a lot I didn't know about politics at that point. Hell, the total tonnage of what I didn't know about politics could float a battleship, stun an ox in its tracks, or shatter mountains. One of the few things I did know by the time I walked through the doors of that restaurant in Hurst, however, was this: most of the members of the political clubs did not, in fact, consider themselves to be our people.

"Why don't they consider themselves to be our kind of people?" Liz asked as we opened the doors.

I took a moment to savor the smell of melting cheese, cheap beef, and freshly made tortillas before I shrugged by way of an answer. The truth was that I didn't know what to tell her. I didn't quite understand why we were hitting a wall, repeatedly and violently, with each interaction Todd had with the local political leaders. It was a lot like those old eighties commercials showing a crash test dummy slamming into a dashboard over and over. I was a little surprised Todd wasn't showing up in a padded helmet instead of a suit and tie.

"We're gonna need a bigger boat," I muttered, almost to myself, surveying the people in the small room every restaurant reserves for political groups, local PTA meetings, and Girl Scout troops. Liz wasn't as much a fan of cinema history as I was, but she'd been a part of my life long enough to translate my bizarre mix of celluloid quotations and know what I really meant. What I really meant was, We need help.

I spotted Todd, who was already inside doing his thing, namely mingling and trying to keep a smile on his face. He saw me and gestured me over to where he was conversing with a short, elderly lady with closely cropped silver hair. She seemed vaguely familiar, but that wasn't much of a surprise by this point: nearly everyone who attended group meetings, no matter the group, was short, elderly, and sported hair that resembled an Oakland Raiders helmet.[2] They were also, almost without exception, kind, infinitely willing to listen, and seemed to deeply appreciate the time Todd spent talking to them. It was exactly the kind of audience and reception I'd pictured in Technicolor-shaded, 1952-themed campaign daydreams. And yet, I thought, somehow these individual conversations aren't translating when it comes to the groups as a whole. It was a puzzle I had yet to crack, the source of no small amount of frustration and queso consumption.

"What should I be doing?" asked Liz as we walked over to Todd. She seemed eager, but I knew better: she was an introvert's introvert, emerging to extrovert as the best damn teacher in the world, but preferring if most people, you know, left her alone. A room full of strangers that she was expected to engage with, long after school was out of session, was basically her idea of a nightmare.

But you wouldn't know it to see her that night.

"Okay," I said, "I need you to go around to each table with this clipboard and tell people about Todd and encourage them to sign this petition to put his name on the primary ballot." I paused, aware of the anxiety that must have been flashing through her mind. "I really appreciate you being here tonight."

She took a deep breath, flashed me a thumbs-up, and then she was off, clipboard in hand and warming up her best teacher voice to unleash on a room full of strangers.

Meanwhile, I was close enough to Todd to see his smile faltering just a bit as the woman he was talking to (she of the patient smile and Raider-

_____

[2] Yes, I know they have been in Las Vegas for a while now. No, it doesn't matter.

shaded hair) was frowning and saying, "Ryan said you could speak tonight?"

Uh-oh.

"Yes, ma'am," I heard Todd say.

Then Ryan appeared.

Look, I am not what you would call the most observant of individuals. Heck, I recently gifted Liz with a pair of earrings for Christmas, which might have been better received if, after years of marriage and two kids, I had noticed that Liz does not, in fact, have pierced ears. However, my failings as both a husband and an observer of my surroundings aside, I can tell you the one thing that activist groups, sewing circles, book clubs, PTAs, and just about any organization with a supposedly elected leadership have in common: they are democratic in the same way that Russia is democratic. Does that mean that dissenters are pushed off balconies or die of radiation poisoning after a spat about Jane Austen at the neighborhood reading circle? Probably not, but what it does mean is that there is someone who rules, elected or not, and they govern with an absolute iron fist.

Ryan was the Vladimir Putin of this particular group. In a lot of ways, he looked a lot like Todd: a middle-aged white guy in a suit, no tie, and at least twenty years younger than most of the folks eating chips and queso and talking politics in that room. I had a feeling that a big day for him was cutting loose by wearing jeans with a blazer.

By the time I got over to Todd, Ryan had swooped over, frowned along with Ms. Raider-Hair, shook his head, laid down the law, and gently but firmly escorted her away, both looking as if the night had just been permanently stained by the conversation. Todd might have had an amiable expression on his face, but I could tell he was struggling mightily to keep it there. Call it the experience of a long friendship or, if you'd rather, call it the result of clues to his true feelings, such as his first words when I sidled up beside him and asked what was going on.

Those words, incidentally, were, "Mother. Fucker."

"You gonna kiss babies with that mouth?" I asked. "So . . . that looked like it was productive. You gonna fill me in?"

He let out something between a sigh and a growl of frustration. "Okay. Okay. It isn't what we hoped for, but we're here and it's something."

"Mmm-hmm." I pushed my glasses back up on my nose. "What, exactly, is 'something'? I'd love to be part of this conversation. After all, I should be relaxing on a cabin porch with a margarita right about now."

"Long story short," Todd said, "is that we can have thirty seconds."

"Wow," I said. "That's generous. Thirty whole seconds for a congressional candidate to address this group, which is ostensibly gathered here to talk about politics. I can feel the love."

Todd looked over at me. "You know, I don't often hear the word 'ostensibly' spoken out loud."

I shot him a look that told him exactly what he could do with his opinions. Ostensibly.

He sighed again. "So, I can have thirty seconds. So can every candidate in this room. Glad you didn't stay up all night writing a speech I'd just have to throw out."

"Well," I said, "at least it is thirty seconds you wouldn't otherwise have had. A lot can happen in thirty seconds." I reached back into our shared past as football coaches and added, "How many games have you coached where everything changed because of one play?"

"For my team or for the other guys?" Todd asked, then, as something caught his eye, "Hey, is that Liz?"

"Yup," I confirmed. "She decided the Todd Allen for Congress campaign should ruin both our nights. For better or worse and all that."

He looked absurdly pleased. "That's awesome. I'm gonna go thank her."

That's my friend, ladies and gentlemen. Todd Allen, who might be Republican-lite (whatever that means) and only worth thirty seconds of time, but dammit, he was worth a vote. If I knew how to bottle up that moment, film it, and edit it into a nice thirty-second TV spot, I'd do it, just to show people why I thought this guy, this teacher, needed to be sent to Congress. He might not know shit about the nitty-gritty of primary politics, and he might not be the cultural warrior the left yearned for, and he might not have custom envelopes, but he was worth twenty bucks and a vote. Somehow, I had to convince people of it. That was my job, after all. That was what I had volunteered for.

And, so far, I wasn't doing a great job of it.

Like Scarlett said, though, tomorrow is another day, and I was nothing if not an optimist. For what it was worth, I'd seen my share of football contests that had come down to one pass, one play, one yard on the goal line, one second on the clock. Thirty seconds could change things, and Todd was about to get thirty seconds. That was more than a lot of people ever got. Thirty seconds on the stage, with a captive audience.

Of course, Todd had to be invited up onto that stage, which was something that Ryan seemed increasingly reluctant to do. My first hint that something was up came when I caught Ryan eying Todd apprehensively as he was making a hushed phone call. Something about that moment sent up red rocket flares of warning in my head (sue me—I'm a little Machiavellian). Then the parade of politicians began as Ryan invited each candidate for office in the room to speak his or her piece. He took his time introducing each and every one, too, awkwardly so, and those red rocket flares in my head were soon joined by blaring klaxons, flashing lights, and a voice a lot like William Shatner's calling out, "Red Alert! Shields Up! Mr. Sulu, get us out of here!"

Mr. Sulu has no power against the might of local activist groups, I discovered.

After working his way through every county judge, clerk, and dog-catcher running for office (in unopposed primaries, I might add), I saw Ryan's glance fixate on the door. His expression became one of relief. He actually smiled. Trying to be nonchalant, I turned ever so slightly to see what Ryan was so relieved about. Faintly, a Scottish brogue cried out, "Captain, she can't take much more of this!"

Todd said, "Huh."

Liz whispered, "Is that . . . ?"

Jan McDowell was standing in the doorway. It was the first time I had seen her in person: a woman of sixty or so, wearing glasses and a purple blouse and an expression that seemed permanently affixed into a frown. Her hair was a little askew, and she looked flustered, harried, and not a little bit annoyed, and I suspected why: she had been roused from a perfectly relaxing Monday evening to hurry out to this meeting. It wouldn't stand up in court, but I knew just the same that good ole Ryan had made a quick phone call to Jan, then stalled until she could arrive. I imagined overhearing his end of the conversation:

"Jan, it's Ryan. No, the other one. Can you get out here for the meeting? . . . No, nothing important, it's just that this guy is here claiming he's running for Congress. . . . No, I have no idea who the hell he is, some guy with an entourage going table to table getting signatures. . . . Yeah, an entourage. Can you get out here? . . . I mean, if you have an entourage, that would be great, bring 'em too. Okay. Okay. . . . Yeah, the *cerveza* is half off till seven. Bye."

It would have been absurd if it wasn't also exactly what had happened. I almost laughed, it was so ridiculous. Surely, I remember thinking, this is not what politics is. Surely. I was still half chuckling to myself when Ryan sighed audibly and announced, "Ladies and gentlemen, I'd like to take this opportunity to introduce a candidate that has always been a good friend of this group, and to all voters in District Twenty Four. The hardest working candidate I've ever seen in this district, and come November, it'll be our pleasure to vote her into the United States Congress. Here is our friend, Jan McDowell!"

Polite applause, followed by a halting, rote speech from an annoyed candidate. I glanced over at Todd, who was trying not to stand up and cuss out Ryan on the spot. He was succeeding, but I could read between the lines: what the actual fuck?

Liz whispered to me, "That seemed pretty biased, right?"

I nodded and braced for what came next.

It was every bit as awful as I anticipated.

After Jan left the front of the room, Ryan frowned and looked puzzled. "So, uh," he began, looking down at the floor as if a script was written there. "There is someone new here tonight who is, uh . . . running for . . . what was it?"

As if you didn't know, I thought, gritting my teeth.

"Congress," Todd said cheerfully, standing up. "District Twenty Four."

"Right," Ryan said. "Right. Anyway, here is, uh . . . Tony Allen, who wants to talk to us about our district."

No applause. How could there be, after such a ringing endorsement? It was done so bald-faced, so ham-handed, you could tell most people in the room were embarrassed. As Todd made his way up to the front of the room, putting on his customary swagger like you'd put on a favorite sweatshirt, I whispered sarcastically, "Good luck, *Tony*." Beside me, Liz patted my hand, either to console me or to warn me (or both). I don't wear masks very well, or hide my thoughts, so I'm sure that any eyes turned my way would have seen exactly what I was thinking at that moment (which was, incidentally, picturing how Torquemada would have reacted in a similar situation).[3] Todd, somehow, was smiling as he reached the front of the room. You're a better man than me, Gunga Din.

"So, my name's actually Todd," he said with a laugh, launching into his thirty seconds. "Todd Allen. I'm a teacher, a husband, and a father, and I'm running for Congress."

It wasn't an interception for a score or an onside kick recovery as the clock ran down, but Todd made that thirty seconds count. Through the haze of my own irritation, I saw people smiling at him, nodding, listening respectfully, and when he was done, the audience in that room clapped and some followed him with their eyes as he came back to our table. "Well done," I said as he sat down. I pushed the basket of chips over his way. "Now get some fuel and get your ass to mingling. Go win some more votes."

I didn't want to mingle. I'm sure he didn't. What I really wanted to do was spend a solid ten minutes bitching about what had just gone down. What I really wanted to do was corner Ryan and ask him exactly what he thought he had accomplished and, for the love of God, why he had thought it was necessary. Judging by the annoyed look on Jan McDowell's face, she might have been thinking along the same lines.

Almost as soon as the program wrapped up, Todd pushed back his chair and walked over to Jan, sticking out his hand to introduce himself. It gave me a chance to lean back and ponder how the campaign was going (and also to eat the rest of the basket of chips while also calling for a second). Running through my mind was a litany of the failures I had overseen so far as the campaign manager of what should be one of the most important endeavors in my friend's life. The website. The announcement party. The failure to curry favor with the activist groups. The lack of envelopes. It seemed like I was stumbling from one fumbled attempt at competence to another. It felt like I was running a clown-car candidacy, and my friend deserved better.

---

[3]Look it up.

It was time to face the truth: I couldn't do this on my own.

We needed help.

That's when Liz walked up to the table with a young woman beside her and said, "Hey, honey, this is Kelsie, and she wants to help."

Life is funny that way.

Loserville

A nd then there were four.

Before Todd got done shaking hands and assuring everyone in attendance that his name wasn't, in fact, Tony, his campaign had a brand-new communications director. To be fair (and perfectly accurate), the campaign hadn't had an old communications director. The campaign had been operating as a cause and a candidate in search of a staff.

"Which you probably already guessed," I told Kelsie that night after she expressed interest in coming on board to help Todd's candidacy out. "Out of curiosity, what was your first clue that maybe we could use a little help? Was it when I decided to introduce Todd to local precinct chairs with a well-written, heart-felt bid for support that would have been more effective if I had actually emailed it to Democrats instead of, wait for it, every Republican precinct chair in three counties?"

Kelsie laughed. "Oh, wow. I didn't know about that."

Beside her at the table, Liz looked chagrined and said, "That was actually my fault. He asked me for the precinct chair emails and . . . well, I gave him the wrong list."

"It was a good email, though," I insisted. "I think we changed some minds." I paused, munched on a chip, and reflected. "Well, we didn't change any minds, but it was a damn good email."

What does the answer to a political prayer look like? In the case of the Todd Allen for Congress campaign, it looked like Kelsie—a young woman who was politically engaged, smart as a whip, articulate in ways I could only dream of, experienced in campaigning, and, most importantly, someone who didn't sneer, spit, roll her eyes, compulsively vomit, or spontaneously combust when Todd's name was mentioned in conversation. Rolled into one package, Kelsie was exactly the kind of help we needed, which is probably why, when Todd finally worked his way through the crowd and back to the table, I introduced her as both a recent acquaintance and as the campaign's savior.

"Great, we need one of those," Todd said, introducing himself and shaking her hand. "You tell her about the precinct chair screw up?"

"Yeah," I said.

"And our appalling lack of knowledge?"

I nodded and said, "I thought that went without saying, but, yeah, I might have mentioned it."

"And our rejection by the Aggies?"

Kelsie shot me a puzzled look. I had not told her about the Aggies. Liz, it turned out, was a fairly militant graduate of Texas A&M,[1] along with her siblings, her friends, and, according to most Aggies, just possibly anyone worth knowing or speaking to at all. With that background in mind, I had reached out to the Aggie Alumni Association's local chapter, hoping to book Todd a chance to speak, introduce himself, maybe mention his overt fondness for border collies, starched shirts, and making weird exclamative noises in lieu of conversation. Luckily, we never had to find out if Todd could have hidden his distaste for all things Aggie, because the response we received from the leader of the Aggie alums was pretty unequivocal: No thanks, the email read, we are all pretty big supporters of Kenny Marchant around here. Liz still grinds her teeth when we talk about it. Aggies, it seems, just don't vote Democrat.

As Todd and Kelsie chatted, the Aggie I married squeezed my hand and whispered, "I like her."

I did, too.

I was feeling pretty good about the night in general. Aside from the

---

[1] Do they come any other way?

"Tony" debacle and the many ugly looks Jan McDowell shot my way, the whole event was turning out to be a net positive. Todd had met some new folks, shaken a few hands, expressed a willingness to kiss babies that weren't in attendance. Voters had gotten a chance to see Jan and Todd together in the same room, and I could only hope the differences between their levels of energy, charisma, and ability to speak extemporaneously had been noticeable. Not only that, but Liz, in her first campaign appearance, had not only gamely dived headfirst into the excruciating exercise of gathering petition signatures for Todd's ballot access but had also found us a communications director. In the time it had taken me to decide if I wanted to order nachos or stuffed jalapeños, the campaign staff had basically doubled in size, and absolutely none of it was due to any effort or talent on my part other than being lucky enough to marry well. We might not have had envelopes, but the Todd Allen for Congress campaign had momentum, *damn it*, and that was something.

And, for the curious, I did wind up ordering the stuffed jalapeños.

"Okay," Todd said, shifting the conversation ever so subtly into shop talk. "Tell me what we're doing wrong, Kelsie. How do we get better?"

Kelsie had a ready answer, which she probably would have had even if I hadn't already grilled her for ten minutes on the exact same subject. "Look," she said, "what you need is to inoculate yourself from the party infrastructure anointing a different candidate—particularly a woman— if your image is caricatured as white, benevolently sexist, Republican-Lite."

"And it is," I muttered under my breath.

"Well, at least I'm benevolent," Todd mused. "So how do I keep people like Ryan from handing the nomination to our good friend Jan?"

Kelsie answered, "You're vulnerable because you're running as a pragmatist that these people don't know against a woman that they know and are comfortable with. You can't give voters any ammunition to discount you, and you've got to focus on getting support from credible leaders in the party who can vouch that you are who you say you are. You're viscerally progressive, but no one knows it or believes it."

This time it was Todd who glanced my way, and I knew why: we had unintentionally given primary voters enough ammunition to stock a survivalist's bomb shelter and see him through the coming apocalypse. I also found myself thinking that what I really wanted, just once in my life, was for someone to describe me using the word *visceral*. How often does that ever happen?

"Alright, Kelsie," Todd told her later as we were all walking to our cars. "Here is what I'd like your first task to be: go through everything we've done, every post on social media, and grade us. Dig deep and figure out what we've done wrong. We need help, we need someone to hold our hand and tell us what to do next, and what we need more than anything is an ambassador to groups like this one. Does that sound like a good place to start?"

Good or not, that is where Kelsie started.

It would have been a pretty big ask from a miracle worker, much less a politico: to help us connect with those "credible" leaders in the local party who could give Todd Allen the nod and a swat on the ass to urge him to get after it. Luckily for us, Kelsie jumped right in, which is why, a few days later, I found myself sitting at a table overlooking Lake Lewisville at a Mexican restaurant a few blocks from my house.[2] I was waiting on someone that Kelsie had hooked me up with, a staffer with some influence who worked for a local Democratic official. I don't know who reached out to whom or what was said, but to my eyes, Kelsie was proving her worth and the campaign was starting to move into the Aaron Sorkin territory that I'd pictured all those months before at Todd's kitchen table. I had high hopes that maybe, just maybe, this meeting was the start—maybe, just maybe, I was about to become the campaign manager of a real campaign.

I didn't know it at the time, but I was in the wrong movie. Aaron Sorkin wasn't writing the script for this scene; Oliver Stone was. Peak Oliver Stone, though, not the Oliver Stone who decided slapping a blond wig on an Irishman was enough to pass him off as a Macedonian conqueror.

All ribbing aside,[3] I usually enjoy the heck out of Stone's films, and his *JFK* is one of my all-time favorite movies. Every time I watch the film, I'm right there with Kevin Costner's character, wholeheartedly believing that the leader of the free world was assassinated by the nefarious forces of the military industrial complex and Kevin Bacon.

---

[2]Didn't I tell you in one of the first chapters that everything essentially happens at a Mexican restaurant? If Italian joints offered queso, I'd consider eating somewhere else, but they don't, so . . .

[3]And coming from someone who has seen all of the various cuts of *Alexander*, I figure have a right to kid Mr. Stone a little.

My favorite scene in *JFK* occurs about three-quarters of the way through the film. Costner's beleaguered district attorney character is visiting the Lincoln Memorial in Washington, DC, to meet clandestinely with a mysterious intelligence official played by Donald Sutherland. The scene is absolutely an example of a *deus-ex-machina* character showing up to give the hero all the answers in an exposition dump of astounding proportions. Sutherland's silky-voiced Mr. X admits that Kennedy was killed in a conspiracy involving the CIA, the Mafia, LBJ, Fidel Castro, and apparently everyone else short of green-skinned Martians. As a scene, it shouldn't work, but it does, and it has me on the edge of my seat every single time.

Now you have context when I tell you that the Mexican restaurant on the lakeshore was my Lincoln Memorial, and Donald Sutherland was about to walk in . . . if Donald Sutherland was in his late twenties and Hispanic, that is. Not that I don't think Donald's got the acting chops to pull that kind of transformation off, but let's just say instead that I was meeting with someone played, in this movie, by Lou Diamond Phillips the year *Young Guns II* came out.[4]

Are we all on the same page of the script now? The one written by Stone, not Sorkin?

So Lou walks in, sits down, and I'm thinking as we awkwardly chit-chat that this is *it*: this is the moment it all comes together. Like Kelsie, Lou was at least a decade younger than me, which was something I was getting used to. In the political world, I had discovered, there are two distinct population sets, two demographics, and I didn't really fit in either one. The first were the members of the activist groups and political clubs, who were usually retired folks with time to kill but not just a ton of years left on their warranty. The second were political operatives on the area campaigns, kids who were inevitably college-aged or a little older. They were the mercenaries of the political wars, marching into battle under a different flag each week. The takeaway was that my existence as a middle-aged man was as obvious a sign as anyone needed (along with my clothes, haircut, and obvious lack of social graces) that I shouldn't

---

[4]Fun fact: as young teachers, my parents taught LDP at Flour Bluff in Texas. They took me to see *Young Guns* when it came out, not because it was at all appropriate for, I dunno, an eight-year-old but because he was in it. They fondly remember him as a brilliant, creative, and, most important to new educators, a very polite young man.

really be taken seriously, politically speaking; anyone my age should be chief of staff to someone important somewhere, or making a living consulting.

Not, in other words, having lunch with a young staffer like Lou.

He knew it, too. He mercifully cut short the introductory *how-do-you-do*-type icebreakers before the waiter had time to fetch his diet soda. He leaned forward over the tortilla chips arrayed between us and asked pointedly, "What are you guys hoping to get out of this, anyway?"

I tried not to let my confusion show. "I'm not sure what you mean . . . ?"

He shrugged. "What are you hoping to get out of this? What do you want? Positioning for a run for municipal office in '20? Getting your name out there? Building up a donor base for something down the line? Maybe looking to jump on a real staff somewhere? What are you hoping for?"

The warning lights were going off in my head. I had caught that offhand use of the word *real*, and it didn't bode well for the rest of the conversation.

"Well . . . I guess what we're really hoping for is a seat in Congress," I said, half laughing.

Wrong answer.

Something changed in Lou's demeanor. He seemed to deflate a bit, to relax. If he had been wearing a tie (and he wasn't), he would have reached up to loosen it. He even smiled a little, though more discerning and observant individuals might have said it was a smirk. Smiling or smirking, Lou reached for a chip without showing any inclination to respond to my comment. I took a sip of my drink to hide the disappointment and dismay—I knew, without a shadow of a doubt, that somehow I'd failed a test. This meeting wasn't going to change anything about Todd's campaign, except maybe to cement an impression party leaders had that he was a nobody. This had gone from being a meeting to being an opportunity for Lou to get a free meal on my dime. He could relax because nothing that was going to be said was going to matter.

I had no idea what I'd done wrong.

Lou leaned back, crunching on a chip. "You know you're not going to win the election."

"No, I don't *know* that," I said, fishing absently through the chip basket to hide my embarrassment. "I mean . . . I think we've got a chance. Sure, a long shot, but a chance. Marchant's complacent. The district's trending our way. Everyone says 2020, but I think 2018 is gonna be the year we can surprise 'em."

Lou shook his head. "You're not going to beat Marchant 'cause you're not going to run against Marchant. You're going to lose the primary." He bit into a chip. "I walked in here wondering if you knew that or not. You just answered that question."

I was too disappointed to be angry. Because I had to say something, I said, "I don't understand. No one thinks Jan McDowell can beat Marchant. All over the internet, people are asking for anyone but Jan. Well, we're not Jan."

"You're not," Lou confirmed.

"So . . . why can't we win?"

"Because you're running in Loserville," Lou said, reaching for another chip, "and no one wins in Loserville."

I tried to process that. "I don't get it," I finally said.

Lou wiped his hands on a napkin. "I can see that. Okay, because you're buying lunch and because the queso is pretty decent, I'll stick around and answer some of your questions, okay? Sounds fair?"

"Depends on the answers," I muttered.

He looked at me speculatively, probably wondering how much to tell me and how truthful to be. He must have decided I wasn't going to understand half of what was said, because he clearly thought, Fuck it. The queso is pretty good, and there's half a bowl left. He leaned forward. "You think your guy is the *better* candidate, right? You think he's a *good* candidate. But you show up to these activist groups and none of them seem to like him or want to support him. Looks like they'd rather run a boring lady that lost the last election by double digits. And you have no idea why it is happening. Why no one is donating or volunteering. Why no one gives a shit. Am I close?"

I nodded.

"Okay," Lou said, warming to his subject (or the queso). "You know what gerrymandering is, right?"

I said, "Yeah, I teach high school government."

Lou's expression didn't change. It was as if I had confirmed that I breathed oxygen or that I was, in fact, still sitting at the table. I guess, in his world, respect for teachers was in short supply outside of a campaign event.

"Alright," he said, finally. "Well, most districts in this country are gerrymandered. They are sure things for someone. Cake walks. You don't even have to campaign, except to raise money. There are a handful of competitive races out there, and those are the races everyone pays attention to. The others . . . " He shrugged and gestured my way. "Loservilles."

I absently stirred the ice in my soda, waiting for more, waiting for it to make sense.

"You know what Loservilles are filled with?" Lou asked. "Losers. Losers and people who are so used to losing, race after race, decade after decade, that some part of their brain accepts an ass kicking as a natural occurrence. It's the way things are, like the sun coming up. They always fucking lose so the race doesn't even matter."

"So what does?" I asked bitterly.

"Take your pick," Lou said. "Could be the ideological purity of the candidate. They are gonna lose, so they might as well lose while spouting the correct bullshit, right? Could be they vote for whoever has been in line the longest, you know, whoever has paid their dues. Or, take Jan Mc-Dowell: it's the year of the woman, and she's a woman and you're not, so maybe that's why she'll get their vote. Or maybe just because she's there, man. She's *there*. Week in and week out, she's gonna be at those diners and buffets, chatting at your table and talking about your kids, about the weather, about the fucking Cowboys. You wanna talk about awkward, try telling her you're voting for someone else, then spending the rest of your retirement sitting at a table with her, pretending you didn't."

The chips were gone. I was stress eating.

Lou leaned forward, almost whispered. "But have you figured out the scary part yet?"

"People voting for a bad candidate 'cause it's her turn isn't scary?"
He shook his head.

"No, that's human nature. That's politics, man." He smirked again. "The scary part is that the losers in Loserville know they are gonna lose, they know they are making decisions based on the fact they are gonna lose . . . but they'll pretend otherwise. They'll pretend they are gonna win. They'll pretend so fucking hard that they forget they are pretending. How many posts have you seen on Twitter from someone in Loserville talking about a blue wave election? When they should know they don't have a hope in hell? Like someone swearing up and down gravity doesn't exist and then marching calmly off a roof, even though they've watched literally every jumper in front of them pancake against the fucking sidewalk. They'll know gravity is an absolute law of physics, but they'll climb right back up on that ladder, time after time."

After a long pause, Lou finally said, "Then they'll lose. Again. Always. And the cycle will start again."

"Is there anything we can do? To break through?"

Lou shrugged. "Sure: money, friends, influence. But if you had those things, we wouldn't be sitting here, would we?"

He stood up. "Thanks for the queso."

I held up a hand. "You're telling me nothing we do matters," I said. "You're telling me we won't get the nomination because everyone knows Democrats won't win the general election. And you're telling me we won't get the nomination because everyone is pretending Democrats absolutely will win the general election. What the hell am I supposed to do with that?"

"Get off the roof," Lou suggested. "Hell, the only reason I told you any of that is because you don't matter. Your guy isn't gonna win and we're never gonna see each other again. And, if some miracle happens and he does and we do, I won't remember ever having this conversation."

So long, Lou. Fuck you very much.

I sat at that table for a long, long time. I got another basket of chips, ordered a margarita, and I thought about what I had just heard. The closer I got to the bottom of the basket (not to mention the bottom of that glass), the clearer it got: if Lou was right, we were fighting a losing battle against forces we couldn't control. The voters we were trying to convince were lemmings lining up to jump off a cliff, over and over again. The more I thought about it, the more it made a twisted kind of sense—and the less sense it made. Paradox. Contradiction. We can't win because everyone knows the battle is lost, but everyone acts, and maybe even believes, the war is won. In the end, could even a politically astute fighter like Kelsie make a difference against the Loserville mentality Lou took for granted as the natural order of things? Could having a candidate like Todd, who genuinely cared about doing good in the world, make a difference?

What do you do with someone who refuses to believe gravity exists?

When Todd called, I picked up the phone with a heavy heart.

"Well, how'd it go?" he asked.

"It went."

"That's on brand for us," Todd said after a moment. "Did you get a list of contacts or anything, something we can use?"

"No," I said.

"No numbers? No advice? *Nothing*?"

"Nope."

I could hear the disappointment in Todd's voice as he asked, "Did we get *anything*?"

"Yeah," I said as I drained the last of the margarita. "A reality check."

Less Nuance, Please

L iz took one look as she walked in the door, wrinkled her nose, and said, "I just don't get the appeal of bad pizza."

"It helps if you don't think of it as pizza," Todd said, handing her a clipboard with the dreaded ballot access petition sheets just waiting for signatures. "Just think of it as . . . I dunno, not pizza. Manage expectations." The expression on his face suggested he wasn't entirely following his own advice. To be fair, it's hard to maintain a positive culinary outlook in the face of the constant disappointment of fast food and buffets where local political groups tend to thrive. Someone should do a study on the correlation between the cumulative grease output of a kitchen and the number of political activities hosted.

Manage expectations, I thought dryly. Not something I'm especially good at. It was true: despite my gruff exterior and grumbling, I was the optimist on the campaign. Todd was the knee-jerk pessimist while I was the idealistic optimist, the one who believed that not only would everything work out, but it would work out spectacularly, with fireworks, a winning lottery ticket, and a three-picture development deal in Hollywood. That optimism wasn't always grounded in what you might call reality, though, a fact which Todd often brought up when my Pollyanna routine wore on his nerves. Maybe I shouldn't have been optimistic about my friend's political chances, especially after the recent revelations about politics in Loserville . . . but I was. After all, we had an honest-to-god politico now to keep us from falling too far into amateur hour, and it seemed as if the local activists were starting to accept that Todd Allen was a real person, maybe even a Democrat. It was just a short step from acknowledging the fact of a person's existence to checking the box beside their name in a primary, or so I hoped.

I smiled and tried to spread a little of that unreasonable optimism around by telling Liz, "Hey, this is gonna be a good day, I can feel it." Liz didn't look convinced, but she took the clipboard anyway and started making the rounds like a good soldier. If you ever get it into your head that working on a political campaign is fun, I'd like to talk to you about this bridge I have to sell outside of Iraan, Texas. It's a good investment, I promise.

The entire Todd Allen campaign staff was appearing en masse that day at a local Hurst pizza buffet (though I doubt the French ever envisioned the term applying to only four people, and I very much doubt the Italians would recognize, appreciate, or, you know, ingest the food being served). You'd think the place would be packed during lunch hour on a Saturday, but you'd be wrong—there were a handful of diners, mostly families, and, in a back room, a half dozen retirees I recognized from our previous adventures in Activist Land. Judging by the plates in front of them, none of them were really there for the pizza, either. Todd was already moving their way, his campaign-issued smile on his face, Kelsie a step or two behind him, ready to run interference if an activist suddenly decided Todd was a Republican in disguise and needed to be put down, *Old Yeller*–style.

As far as I could tell, the only one that desperately needed to be put down was whoever was back in that kitchen whipping out the pizza. You'd think your typical cheap pizza buffet franchise would be right up my alley; after all, what's *not* to like about all-you-can-eat carbs slathered in melted cheese? The answer was—well, most of it, 'cause it tastes like wet cardboard run through a microwave and served behind an oft-ignored sneeze guard. You know the kind of place I'm talking about, the

Todd at a coffee shop during any number of meet-the-candidate opportunities the campaign offered; my wife Liz sits next to him.

ones with a menu seemingly constructed by a hungry four-year-old constantly asking questions like, "Well, what would a pizza taste like covered in macaroni and cheese?" We're talking about shit no one above grade school age really wants to eat, but, hey, it's all-you-can-eat, so, sure, I'll try a slice of glazed apple and gouda.

I still wasn't a fan of the pizza when the Todd Allen campaign staff walked into that restaurant in Hurst ready to meet with a local political club to discuss subjects of utmost importance. At least, Kelsie assured me it was important, and she was the expert. As Todd shook hands and did the meaningless chitchat he was so good at, I sidled over to Kelsie and whispered, "So, remind me what we did wrong this time?"

"Todd used the word *entitlements* on the website," she said.

"Referring to Social Security and Medicare?" I asked.

"Yes," Kelsie confirmed.

"So . . . they are mad we used the word *entitlements* to refer to entitlements?"

Kelsie pulled me a little further away from the table, probably so my ignorance wouldn't accidentally inspire one of the activists to commit a hate crime. "They're mad because Todd just showed up out of the blue a few months ago," she whispered. "They're mad because they don't know him. They're mad because he doesn't speak their language. They're mad because he doesn't attend every meeting. And yes, they are mad because they don't like the word *entitlements*."

Smirking a little (and I'm known for my smirk), I said, "Are we sure they aren't mad because they like being mad?"

Kelsie glanced over her shoulder, confirmed that Todd was still doing fine glad-handing and that no one had overheard my sarcasm, then said, "I don't like the term *entitlements*, either, which you'd have known if you had asked. So I get it. I get where you guys are coming from, too, but that isn't enough, because I need *them* to get it, and the easiest way to do that is to get *you* to get it."

It was the single most complicated sentence I'd ever heard in my life, so naturally I encountered it at a cheap pizza buffet. I had next to no chance of actually understanding it. I shook my head, finally said, "But Obama used the term *entitlements*. In a State of the Union address, even. Clinton did. Hell, the textbook I teach from does! When did Republicans convince us it was a bad word? The way I see it, I paid for it, so I'm fucking entitled to it. Shouldn't we be focused on how to make sure people actually get Social Security when the time comes rather than arguing about what to call it?"

Kelsie laughed a little. "Ah, but see . . . this is not about you. They want their Social Security, and they don't want to call it an entitlement, and that's what they care about. They want both. If you don't care that they care, that might explain why the campaign has been struggling."

Well, that was a little punch to the emotional solar plexus.

"I care," I muttered. "I just think it's a stupid thing to care about."

She shot me a look.

"Which I'll happily keep to myself," I added. "Also, I think you'll find that there are actually a lot of reasons we're struggling. That's why I'm glad you're here to fix things."

Switching gears, Kelsie said, "You know, a lot of activists think Todd is a plant."

I blinked. "You mean, like a *Little Shop of Horrors* situation?"

"No," she said. "I mean they think he's a Republican in a Democrat's clothing."

My moment of introspection was over. I rolled my eyes. "What, exactly, screams Republican about our guy? I get that he uses words they don't like, but other than that . . . ? He's pro-choice, pro-LGBTQ, pro-migrant, pro-not being shot while he's teaching one day, pro-not being fucking crazy. I really do get what you're saying about language, but substance has to count, too, right?"

"No," Kelsie finally said. "Not until the way he says things connects to people, and right now it isn't. They can't get past the terms to see the ideas. Ronnie feels pretty strongly that we've got to change the language on the website *now*. He's got some suggestions."

Look, the good angel on my shoulder said firmly, this is why you brought Kelsie onboard, right? She knows a hell of a lot more about politics than you do, so maybe just shut up and let the communications director communicate. All of that was true enough, and good advice to boot: if Kelsie thought we needed to sit down and let an activist group draft the campaign language, then maybe I should just swallow my pride and my misgivings and see what happens. Besides, this wasn't just any political club we were meeting with, it was Ronnie's group, the very first activist group we'd ever met with. If anyone could be called Todd Allen supporters, it was these people.

Sure, that first meeting at the Burger Barn had been rough, but it hadn't been the last word. Over the first few months of the campaign, we'd gone back to Ronnie's group repeatedly and they had kinda become, in our minds at least, our political "home." I liked them, all in all. They were a newer group on the local stage, and they seemed filled with people who were a lot like Todd and myself—newly energized, frustrated with politics, taking time out from working-class jobs to meet and figure out their place in this weird political world and maybe find a voice. That voice, incidentally, didn't belong to the infamous Green Dress Lady, who you may remember had rained on Todd's inaugural political parade by chiding him for using the phrase "illegal immigration" aloud. From what Ronnie and Kelsie told us, she had stormed out of the group shortly after that first meeting with Todd, intent on forming a splinter cell of fellow activist commandos, so we felt as if those who remained were a safe space. If any group was going to have a hand in revising what we said and how we said it, it might as well be Ronnie's group.

And they were smiling at him. They might not have liked some terms on his website, but they were smiling and laughing and seemed genuinely pleased to see him. This is how it starts, the good angel on my shoulder assured me. This is how you go from a campaign staff of two to having volunteers fetch you coffee before you give an interview to Walter Cronkite.

The bad bloke on my other shoulder (because it certainly couldn't have been me) pointed out sarcastically that Cronkite's dead, this pizza stinks, and there is a difference between supporters and fucking hostage-taking emotional terrorists.

I sat down at the table with some misgivings, cracked open my notebook, and let Kelsie run the show. Not that she was able to say much, because almost immediately Ronnie held up his phone and said, "Can I read you something from your website?"

Todd gestured as if to say the floor was open. "Go ahead, that's why we're here."

Ronnie cleared his throat.

"So, you don't have a policy section on your site—" he began.

"Well, I do, I just call them—"

"Conversation Starters," Ronnie finished for him. "So, I wanted to read what you say at the top of the Conversation Starters page: 'Very few things in this life can be rendered down to black-and-white terms, with absolute rights and absolute wrongs. Life is more nuanced than that. I intend to be a representative for everyone in the Texas Twenty-Fourth District, not just the citizens who happen to agree with my beliefs and identify with my party. Part of that is being willing to listen, to discuss, and keep nuance in mind.'"

Ronnie paused, looked up from his phone and stared pointedly at Todd, as if he'd just read out incriminating evidence at a murder trial. The other members of the group muttered and grumbled a bit around bites of bad pizza. Kelsie looked stone-faced, clutching her notebook to her chest. I kept my eyes locked on the pages of my own notes, scrawling out my true feelings in blue ink: Are you fucking kidding me?

With what I thought was infinite patience, Todd asked, "Is there something problematic about that?"

"Why don't you just say what you think?" Ronnie responded. "You make it sound as if you've got no beliefs. How are we supposed to know if you—"

"And what's with this word, *nuance*?"

I looked up from my notebook. The question had come from a gentleman in a worn Metallica T-shirt and faded jeans, wearing a ball cap and a handlebar mustache I could only ever aspire to.

"Nuance?" Todd repeated.

"Yeah, you expect most people to know what that actually means?" Handlebar said with a grunt, leaning back in the booth. "All your positions are too long for people to read. No one's got time for shit like nuance. Simplify it, alright?"

The table was filled with people nodding slowly. Ronnie picked up on what Handlebar was putting down and added, "Bullet points is what you need, I think. Keep it simple and just say what you believe in so we can feel comfortable voting for you."

My eyes sought out Kelsie. She was nodding right along with everyone else. And there was a smell coming from the buffet table that surprisingly seemed appealing, so I decided that maybe I could best serve the campaign by keeping my mouth closed when it wasn't filled with pizza. "Gonna grab a plate real quick," I said, pushing back from the table with what I hoped was a passable smile. As I headed off towards the heat lamps and slices of disappointment, I heard Handlebar say, "And stop saying you're not a politician. Trump says stuff like that."

I took my time once I got up from the table. I used the restroom. I checked on Liz and her noble quest to get the line workers behind the counter to sign a ballot petition. I tried to decide if the lettuce offered at the salad bar was better described as wrinkled or wilted. I stood in front of the heat lamps and pretended to weigh the individual merits of selecting a slice of pizza covered in taco spice or one with sad little cubes of chicken swimming in a sea of what smelled like barbecue sauce. You know things with me aren't quite right when I can't get my head in the food game, even if the food in question was bad pizza.

Suddenly Todd was standing beside me, a plate in his hand, facing the same sad choices (referring to the pizza, not my mental struggle with the reality of politics). He reached for a slice of pizza covered in a neon-orange sauce, then seemed to hesitate.

"I wouldn't," I cautioned him.

He withdrew his hand. "I'm just pretending to be hungry, anyway."

"Just forget about the pizza and load up on cinnamon rolls."

"Or maybe we should just escape out the back without anyone noticing," Todd said.

I didn't have high hopes on that score: Liz was still collecting signatures, Kelsie was deep in conversation with Ronnie, and there were at least five pairs of activist eyes on Todd and me, eyes that were clearly attached to brains that were wondering when we'd sit down so they could go over our lack of communication skills. Suddenly, I felt like Butch and Sundance, desperately needing an escape, which seemed increasingly unlikely. LaFors and the posse and that fucking straw boater were waiting on us outside of every door.

Todd reached for a slice of barbecue pizza, which everyone knows is a horrible choice under any circumstance, glanced over his shoulder to make sure no one of the activist persuasion was within earshot. "So they finally decided I should say that I haven't *been* a politician."

Just to be contrary, I picked up a slice of the taco pizza. "Well, that'll certainly be a game changer."

"Kelsie also says we should look at the language that makes me seem benevolently sexist."

"Hmmm," I said, instantly regretting my choice.

"I'm not benevolent, am I?" Todd asked.

I looked at him, straight-faced. "I'm afraid you are."

For a moment we just stood there, unwilling to head back to battle and certainly unwilling to take even tentative bites of the pizza. Finally, Todd said, "Does it seem like we're seeing the same fifteen people no matter which group we talk to?"

"Yeah," I said.

"Does it seem like maybe this isn't any fun anymore?"

"Yeah."

"Does it seem like they want us to be politicians when the whole reason we got into this was because politicians are all horrible fucking people, and we thought it'd be nice for a normal person to run for office for a change?"

"Yeah, it does," I confirmed. "What do *you* think?"

He grinned. "I think we should go to Bolivia."

Conversation works a lot better when our minds are running through the same movie references at the same time, which happens more often than you might think. The bad bloke on my shoulder knew what Todd was talking about (aside from *Butch Cassidy and the Sundance Kid*). He meant it was time to get away from those same two dozen people who formed the super-posse of activists dominating every club and every group, chasing us from forum to forum and grumbling about language before deciding what they really wanted to do was yell some more. He meant maybe we shouldn't spend time fighting a battle we couldn't win. And, just maybe, he meant that when they took us down, we should go down in a blaze of glory as who we were and not who they wanted us to be.

Bolivia.

"We're not folksy," he said suddenly, a faraway look in his eye. It was the kind of look he got when he had come to a decision about something big and was struggling to explain why he had made it. "I don't mind bullet points. I don't mind rephrasing things. But I'm not a simple guy. I don't talk that way. I don't write that way. You sure as hell don't; you've never met a semicolon you didn't like."

That was absolutely true, but Todd didn't wait for me to confirm it. "I am not spending my time and money and effort to find the simplest way to say what they want me to say," he said. "You know what my biggest problem is?"

I was noncommittal. "I have some theories."

He leaned toward me, said, "My problem is that I want to be successful. I don't want to lose. I don't want people to see me struggle. Here I am, and people are telling me I need to do this, this, and that to be a successful politician, a respectable progressive, and I'm just following along, doing what they suggest because I want to be a success . . . but then I remember why I'm here staring at bad pizza on a Saturday when I should be playing with my kids."

"You know," Todd continued, "if we do win, it won't be because we sold progressive ideas better than Jan or convinced moderates to go blue because the people wearing red are acting crazy. It will be because we made people believe we can be better. That all of this isn't completely fucking broken. That I honestly believe there is hope that this isn't all a shit show."

"Is it?" I asked.

He looked up at me and softly said, "I don't think it has to be."

Then he jerked his head over toward the table where Ronnie and his compatriots were hammering Kelsie on the changes Todd needed to make if he wanted to get their vote. He said, "You think that will be enough for them to understand me? To like me? To vote for me?"

"Let's find out," I suggested.

Moneyball

I'll admit it: I've been known to make a mistake or two. Anyone who has ever known me, lived with me, or worked with me knows that I'm not immune to my own bad ideas. Fortunately, those ideas usually never make it much further than the speculative stage, killed in the cradle by raised eyebrows, startled expressions, and an assurance that the thought just uttered was, perhaps, historically awful. In my defense, I'd like to think that most great ideas have a little bit of a bad idea in them (which is why people hadn't tried that particular idea before), and that my occasional forays into the ridiculous were justified by the once-in-a-blue-moon, honest-to-God amazing thought emerging from my melon. Still, there was no shortage of bad ideas to choose from when it came to the file labeled Heath's Contributions to the Todd Allen Campaign.

For instance, at that very first kitchen-table meeting, I'd floated the suggestion that Todd needed to wear jeans and a button-down red shirt to every event to create an iconic look that could be called a uniform. Todd called it stupid, and I was forced to agree. Never mind the fact that Todd was always more comfortable wearing pastels; I could only imagine how the activist base would have viewed a candidate sporting the enemy colors. At the very least they would have wondered if Todd was a college kid with only one dress shirt in the dorm closet.

Nix Bad Idea #1 of Many.

There was also the time that I suggested that Todd's campaign logo be designed in black and school-bus yellow. Look, I remember saying, this will remind everyone that you are, at heart and in reality, just a teacher trying to make good. It might have been Todd's wife, Lauren, who gently reminded me that most people don't like teachers so maybe we needed to cool it with the education references. It turned out to be true: you'd think in a congressional district where the top employer was the public education sector you'd find plenty of supporters of a candidate with a teaching background, but you'd be wrong. I know I was. Join the club, we'll have T-shirts made.

Scratch Bad Idea #2.

Mired in a vision for the campaign seen squarely through rose-colored glasses fixed on Kennedy-era nostalgia, I'd also come up with a whopper of a bad idea that involved taking a page from the Mama Rose playbook. Wouldn't it be great, I thought, if we could send Lauren out on her own on weekends to have tea with area voters and give her perspective on the candidacy of her husband? It worked for JFK's mom, why not for the Allen campaign? Well, it was a bad idea, and not just because I have serious doubts about whether the modern American woman actually sits down to something like tea and cookies. No, Bad Idea #3 was bad because it forgot that Todd's wife wasn't just a political prop; she was a mother of two kids and a respected professional with a career, and her time was too valuable to be squandered on a bad idea.

Adios, Teas with Lauren and Bad Idea #3.

You get the picture. I wasn't infallible, and the campaign I was ostensibly running (which felt sometimes like holding onto the horns of a bucking bull for dear life) wasn't error-free. We were learning, though, or trying to, one event and one email blast at a time. Where language was getting in the way of ideas, Kelsie stepped in to try and massage that language so the people she knew best, the activists and politicos, could engage us in discussions about policy instead of throwing rotten fruit at our skulls. Todd was trying to balance the reality of being a successful candidate with the truth of why he was running in the first place, and where he felt he had to disagree with someone, he learned how to do it

The Allen clan at one of the few "fancy" political meet-and-greets during the campaign. There was silverware and everything.

with a smile, a shrug, and a comment that made them feel as if he would listen even if he didn't agree. For my part, I tried to stay out of their way, sticking with our media strategy and focusing on getting Todd and his message to the right place at the right time.

Turns out that there were a lot of right places to be at, and it was taking up a lot of time. Or, more to the point, it was too much time, and how right the places were was up for debate. I wasn't exactly thrilled at a campaign schedule that saw us committed to visiting the same activist groups, never getting outside a small bubble of maybe a hundred people, and certainly never having those gazebo-based conversations with Main Street Americans that I envisioned back when the campaign started and I was still worried about how Todd should dress. It was annoying and frustrating, but it was also becoming routine, so I wasn't really questioning the necessity of it. I was moving from day to day and event to event.

Mistakes were made.

One Saturday, sitting in the back of a restaurant as Todd finished up a speech and Liz and Kelsie were making the rounds with campaign literature, I found out just how big of a mistake I had made by getting complacent and accepting a campaign schedule and style I knew wasn't right. It began as Todd shuffled over, the veneer of the candidate beginning to slip as he started to mentally shift into off-the-clock mode. Sure, there would be a few more hands to shake on the way out, a few more smiles to force, and a few more pleasantries to exchange, but for all intents and purposes, the night was officially over and in the books.

He sat down and tried not to sigh in relief.

"Good job up there," I said. I meant it, too. Doing what Todd managed to do at these things was nothing more or less than a job, hard work, and he did it well.

"Thanks," Todd said in his usual post-event tone of voice, the one that indicated that he was deeply disappointed in himself, the political process, and life in general. "What are you working on?"

I held up my phone, where I was just finishing drafting an email with the campaign's schedule for the next seven days.

Todd looked and made a noise a little like a whimper. "That's brutal."

I sighed as I pushed send. I agreed that the schedule wasn't anyone's idea of a good time (at least not in households with the name Hamrick or Allen on the mailbox). We had meetings to attend at local groups on Monday, Tuesday, Thursday, and Saturday, a Facebook Live event on Friday, and a meet and greet scheduled on Wednesday. Probably an easy schedule for your average candidate with nothing but time and a staff to somehow fabricate more, but for a regular Joe working a nine-to-five job and only *then* getting out on the campaign trail, it was a beating. These kinds of weeks were becoming the norm, and neither one of us was happy about it. A typical day for Todd involved getting up before dawn, getting kids to school, teaching for eight hours, getting in the car and driving in rush-hour traffic to meet me at some random Chinese buffet or Mexican restaurant, extroverting and performing for another two hours, and finally getting home just in time to grab a solid five hours or so of sack time before getting up to do it all over again.

Like the man said: brutal.

That's when my phone binged to let me know a text message had come through. I shivered a bit at the sound; call it intuition, but I knew it was nothing good. I'm not the most sociable of people, and I can count on one hand the number of folks who text me on a regular basis. And I could see both of them from where I was standing. Maybe it's Barack

Obama, I thought, texting to tell me he loves our media and wants to endorse Todd on national television.

I looked at the name on the message.

It wasn't Barack Obama.

"Oh, sweet Jesus," I muttered, aware that I was, technically, now in deep shit.

It was from Todd's wife, Lauren, and it was short if not necessarily sweet. I'm paraphrasing here, but the message said something like the following: You ever schedule Todd for more than two nights a week, I will personally wreak havoc on your life and rain hell on your day-to-day existence. I'm sure she said it in a polite way, but, you know, I'm cutting to the chase here.

Wordlessly, I handed my phone over to Todd so he could read the message. He took one look, then took a deep breath and handed the phone back to me. Standing up, he said, "Let's step outside." I followed him without protest. There are some conversations that need to be had in the comforting environs of a dirty parking lot next to a busy interstate.

After a long minute spent shuffling our feet and inhaling gas fumes I asked Todd, "How long has this been coming?"

Todd looked down, kicked the gravel around a little before he met my eyes and said, "For a while."

"Okay," I said. "How bad is it?"

He didn't answer.

"Does she want you to quit?"

He shrugged. I have a vivid imagination, and I'd had at least two margaritas at the event, so it was easy for me to read a lot in that single shrug. I imagined what must have been hours of tense, terse conversations between Todd, struggling to find meaning in an increasingly meaningless process, and Lauren, who was trying to keep the family ship afloat without much help. Nothing about that kitchen-table meeting we'd had a couple of months ago had suggested that her husband was going to virtually disappear for an extended period. No one had mentioned that she would have to set aside her own hopes and dreams for the future so that Todd could chase his. If the campaign had been embraced by the locals from the get-go, things might have been different. I tried to place myself in Lauren's shoes: working to the point of exhaustion every day as a teacher, then as a mother, and finally as a doctoral student, before watching Todd come in late at night to gripe about how all of it was essentially in vain anyway.

I don't know if any of that happened, for sure. There are some pages in the book of friendship that I don't ask Todd to turn to. But, as I said, I have a vivid imagination.

"Do *you* want to quit?" I asked.

I needed to know the answer. Part of me, maybe even most of me, wanted him to say *yes*. All I needed was a nod, and I'd cheerfully walk back into that Chinese buffet, grab Liz, rip up the petitions, tell Ronnie and Handlebar and Jan and Ryan where they could stuff the rest of the campaign literature, give a lecture on the joys of nuance, and then waltz out with a margarita to-go and a final suggestion that they could all go fuck themselves. Who knows, it might have been a campaign highlight; we might have even won a few votes out of it.

But Todd didn't nod. He shook his head and said, "We've come too far for that. I put my name on a ballot. I'm gonna finish."

"Well, technically, we still have a couple hundred more signatures or a few thousand dollars to go before your name is on the ballot," I said. "So, you know, if there was ever a time . . . "

"I'm not quitting," he said. "I'm going to finish this. I don't know if my kids will ever really care that their dad ran for Congress. I'd like to think they will. I'd like to think that at some point down the line, when life gets a little rough for them and they've got to make some tough decisions, they'll remember that I did this, that I took a chance, that I kept going. So, no, I'm not quitting."

His head bowed, he repeated, almost to himself, "I'm not quitting."

Then he looked up at me. "But we may have to run a different campaign."

"A different campaign," I muttered. I took out the phone, looked at the message again to be sure I'd read it right the first time. "Before we do anything drastic and I flip out and start throwing shit, let's just take a step back. Lauren's saying I shouldn't schedule anything without asking her first, which, okay, I can live with, but she's also saying that I should never schedule more than two events a week. I get where she's coming from but—"

"Yeah, I'm not sure you do, dude," Todd said flatly.

I rose to the occasion (or took the bait, whichever seems more accurate to you). I said, "Then help me out, man. We were all at that same kitchen table, right? You know, the night I had big ole binders ready that basically said that we shouldn't do this if everyone wasn't on board?"

"I know," Todd said. "I was there. The binders were nice."

"They were nice," I confirmed. "Anyway, Kelsie says we are already taking fire from the activists 'cause you can't be at all the little coffee get-togethers they have during the school day. We get by because everyone knows you have a real job, and while they don't like it, they don't feel too hot bitching about it. But now, we start missing these evening events, they'll break out the fucking pitchforks." I ran out of energy. "I just . . . I don't know how we do this if we can't do this."

"I just told you," Todd said quietly. "We have to run a different campaign."

I was already trying to figure out what that would look like. One thing I've always been good at is the art of the pivot—changing targets, behavior, or plans because there absolutely were no other good options. It was maybe one of my few advantages in any given gathering: while everyone else was still bemoaning fate, I'd be in a corner somewhere, two chess moves farther into the game. They weren't always great moves (and sometimes they were those aforementioned bad ideas), but at least I was moving.

A different campaign. Alright, then.

Todd being Todd, he was deep into damage control, trying to get me to understand where Lauren was coming from. Truth was, I was barely paying attention. I was gaming out a new campaign scenario, and, besides, I knew where Lauren was coming from. Todd has often said that his wife and I had very similar personalities, which usually leads to one of two situations: a passionate, star-crossed love affair or a bloody feud that would put the Hatfields and McCoys to shame.

Well, I've never been to Kentucky, but I imagine Lauren and I would get on well there.

Anyway, Todd held out his hands, almost pleading. "Look, just put yourself in her shoes, okay? Your husband says he wants to do this great, big, noble thing, and all it's gonna take is money and time and all your patience and understanding. And all you have to do is support his bullshit dream, raise the kids, drive an hour or so twice a week to campus because you are getting a doctorate, a doctorate in fucking statistics by the way, which is basically goddamn rocket science. Oh, and work a full-time job. And while you're doing all that, your husband is out at Chinese buffets arguing about stupid bullshit that doesn't seem to matter, which he complains about in those few minutes he gets to see you at night and in the mornings. So . . . yeah, maybe she's got a right to be a bit upset."

He took a deep breath, stared hard at me. "Were you even fucking listening?"

"No," I admitted. "Not really. Shut up for a second."

Cars were roaring by in the evening Metroplex traffic, which made the long, drawn-out silence between us a little less awkward. Todd had his phone out, but he wasn't doing anything other than staring at it blankly, probably trying to decide exactly what to say to his wife, who was bearing a lion's share of the burden of a campaign that wasn't showing the promise any of us had hoped for. For my part, I was glad of the silence, if only because I was deep in thought. Something Todd had said was nagging at the corners of mind, something that was important, if only I could grasp it (and avoid getting even further on Lauren's shit list along the way). Then it hit me.

"We're wasting our time," I said suddenly.

Todd looked up from his phone sharply, probably wondering if I was about to toss my notebook into traffic and tell him in no uncertain terms where the campaign could shove that weekly schedule. I held up a hand. "A different campaign. You're absolutely right. We've been needing to do a different kind of campaign all along. You've known it, I've known it, Lauren knows it, and as long as she isn't on the way here to cut off my balls, starting right now, this minute, I think we can turn this campaign into something new."

Todd was looking around the parking lot. Maybe he was looking to see if Lauren's SUV was about to come screaming around a curve. "Well, okay," he said. "Why don't you cut the suspense and tell me what you're thinking?"

I smiled. "*Moneyball.*"

"*Moneyball?* You mean . . . like the movie?" His eyebrows furrowed in confusion. "You're doing that thing where you skip entire exchanges of conversation, you know that, right? Start over from the beginning."

I glanced back at the restaurant, where Kelsie and Liz were still fighting the good fight and activists were slowly beginning to trickle out into the night. I hoped none of them would come over to say hello and ask Todd about his views on foreign policy. We had important shit to straighten out—namely, making sure the Todd Allen campaign got down to Lauren-approved levels of constituent interaction while still remaining a viable candidacy. And, not to put too fine a point on it, making sure my balls remained firmly attached in the process. I've read about the Hatfields and McCoys.[1] It ain't pretty.

"Okay," I said. "You remember last week at that pizza place, where Ronnie told us that *nuance* was a bad word? You told me that you felt as if we see the same twenty people, over and over. We're spending all this time, all this energy, all this effort, on a couple of people who might, one day, decide they don't hate us as much as they used to. Time is money, man, and we're being really stupid about where we spend it."

Todd was starting to nod. "Rightly so. Okay . . . so how does a base-ball movie fit in?"

The answer is *barely*, but just go along with me for a second. For those unfamiliar with professional baseball, or at least the Aaron Sorkin–writ-ten drama about professional baseball, *Moneyball* stars Brad Pitt as a general manager for a ball club with little talent or money to import it. The solution to his dilemma turned out to be thinking about a baseball team in a different way: seeing players as tools for getting on base instead of as total-package all-stars. Rendered down to that simplistic metric, the team had recruited relatively unknown, cheaply signed athletes who no one recognized but who could get on base reliably. The result was inspirational: money was spent where it could most effectively achieve the desired result—in other words, victories. And I liked victories, even if I didn't necessarily like baseball.

"Your time is our money," I explained, warming to the subject. "We have to spend it wisely and where it'll do the most good. This, what we're doing tonight and every other fucking night on the campaign trail . . . this . . . isn't it. Shit, maybe Lauren's text is a good thing."

"Is it?" Todd asked.

"For *me*, no, absolutely not, it scares me shitless," I admitted, "but for the campaign, yes, because it makes us confront what we're doing and

---

[1] I lay claim to the Kevin Costner portrayal of Devil Anse Hatfield as my spirit character, by the way: epic facial hair, badass dialogue, and, spoiler alert, getting through the entire miniseries without marrying a crazy woman or drunkenly setting his house afire.

how stupid it is. We need a metric, a scorecard, that is all about *your* time and *my* time and how many points each activity is worth—and then we decide how to spend that time based on the metric. Ask yourself: What would have the biggest impact, Heath sitting at that table in there pretending to argue about nuance with a dozen activists or Heath editing a campaign video that might reach a thousand people on a slow day?"

Todd smiled and, for the first time, stopped looking around the parking lot for the imminent arrival of a pissed-off significant other. "Moneyball. We let Kelsie do what she does best, run interference with the groups and keep them from roasting me alive if I can't attend every event. Meanwhile you can do what *you* do best, pump out media and graphics and policy . . . "

He was starting to get it.

Nodding, he said, "This can work. I hit the events that are worth it according to the metric, and Lauren hates us less." He paused and corrected himself. "Well, hates me and the idea of a congressional campaign less. You're fucked."

"Yes," I acknowledged. "I absolutely am."

"Moneyball," Todd said. I could tell he liked the sound of it.

"Moneyball," I echoed, deciding that what I really needed to do when I got home was find my copy of the film and see what wisdom I could learn from the acting chops of Brad Pitt and Philip Seymour Hoffman. "I'm telling you, that's the answer. We don't do things the old-fashioned way just because everyone says we have to. And, as an added bonus, you don't get served with divorce papers, and I don't wind up dismembered in a ditch in Alabama."

"No, it wouldn't be Alabama. Lake Lewisville maybe. But you're right. That would be ideal," Todd said. "Alright, well, problem solved. Why don't you head home and figure out how to make this work so that tomorrow we can start moneyballing the shit out of this thing?"

Was *moneyballing* an actual word? Did it matter? Not a bit. We headed back into the restaurant, feeling a hell of a lot better than we had when we walked out. We had a plan, at least, that wasn't dependent on seeing either of us broke, exhausted, or divorced, always a net positive.

Moneyball.

Every great idea starts with a bad idea, right?

Article I, Section II

Everything Todd and I know about the US Constitution we learned from the King of the Wild Frontier himself. History buffs and children of the 1950s will get the reference; everyone else will probably need some context, assuming they aren't up to speed on cultural phenomena of the Eisenhower era. Here's the context. Back in the early aughts, Todd and I were political science students at Trinity University, doing our damnedest to focus our efforts and attention on anything but political science. Our college advisor tried to steer us onto a more practical and useful course for our lives, but, alas, here we are, conspicuously *not* successful millionaires, writing memoirs without the usual justification of impressive achievements.

But, to be fair, we are rather funny once you get to know us.

Anyway, our college advisor had the misfortune of walking around a campus located in San Antonio, Texas, while being named David Crockett. The fact that he was ex-military, and that he left the armed forces as a colonel, probably didn't do anything to limit the giggles from undergrads and the occasional colleague breaking out into a stirring rendition of a theme song meant to remind everyone of the sheer awesomeness of a certain legend born on a mountaintop in Tennessee. The poor guy had enough to deal with as the only conservative on a political science staff packed with kooky eccentrics and liberals. He was the guy showing up to class in a crisp suit, while others made a habit of wheeling into the lecture hall on a bicycle in crumpled clothes and helmet hair that might have been last combed sometime during the Reagan administration.

Luckily, Dr. Crockett was one of the most calm and unassuming men I've ever met, not to mention an absolute expert on American politics (particularly the presidency). Todd and I once cajoled him into appearing in one of our amateur comedy films, an endeavor we were sure would end in our acclimation in Hollywood as the next Kevin Smith. It did not and we weren't, which I'm sure Dr. Crockett knew even before we asked him to run lines that involved his character having a conversation with our film's hero between the walls of a bathroom stall. He did it because he had a sense of humor, or maybe just a sense of the ridiculous, or, and this just now occurs to me, maybe because he was pretty confident no one would ever see that particular magnum opus.[1]

Todd and I learned a lot from good ole Dr. Crockett, including the ins and outs of a little document our textbooks call the Constitution. You might be familiar with it, but probably not in a way that would be acknowledged as adequate by Dr. Crockett. Every week, he'd throw us a five-minute timed quiz on the details and eccentricities of the text, expecting us to know each and every paragraph inside and out, backwards and forwards, before we either passed the class or went to the registrar's office to drop it in defeat. The result, at least in our case, was the production of two newly minted Constitutional snobs.

Our profession didn't exactly help matters in the snobbery department. Teaching government only allowed us to wallow in our snobbery, like pigs in a pen. Most of my experience was in charter schools, teaching underserved youth, and spending weeks on engaging lessons about checks and balances. Todd, meanwhile, was teaching Advanced Placement Government to kids who routinely wound up at Harvard or Stanford, grilling them on constitutional law until their eyes glazed over in parchment-toned hues and they mumbled about the Federalist Papers in their sleep. Dr. Crocket would be proud.

So what happened on the soon-to-be infamous phone call with Myra

---

[1]Jokes on you, Doc. It took twenty years, but the secret is out!

was inevitable, maybe even destined—hell, *fated*, really. Written in the stars.

But that's right—you haven't met Myra yet. We're gonna need to take care of that.

The political moneyball metric that was inspired by Todd's desire to run a different kind of campaign (not to mention my own deeply rooted inclination to avoid castration) wasn't, by any stretch of the imagination, what you would call an exact science. It ranked campaign activities by how much time they required, how much they cost, and how likely they were to produce a concrete outcome for the campaign (donations, volunteers, petition signatures, and other campaign currency). It was all pretty subjective. In fact, Kelsie probably summed it up best after I explained it to her on the phone the next day.

"This doesn't make any sense," she said.

"Well, doesn't the fact that it makes no sense actually make sense for this campaign?" I asked jokingly.

"Todd can't go around telling people they aren't worth his time," she said with no small amount of worry.

"He won't," I assured her. "That'll be your job."

Pause for laugh.

Longer pause. Maybe . . . wait, there it—nope, it wasn't happening. Time to switch gears.

"Kelsie, this is one of those times where necessity is forcing us to get outside the box," I said. "We're not doing this to be obstinate, and we're not doing it because we just enjoy how it feels to have everyone be mad at us. I might be used to it, but I don't necessarily enjoy it. The truth is that Todd isn't just a political candidate. He's a dad. He's a husband. He's a full-time teacher. He can't just put those things on pause because he's running for office."

"But he *is* running for office," Kelsie said, and if anything, the amount of hesitation in her voice had only grown.

I sighed. "Look, our job is to take the reality of his life and do the best we can with it. And I think . . . you know, I think that's what makes him appealing as a candidate. He's just a normal guy. He doesn't have a ton of oil money in the bank, he didn't jump out of a Black Hawk helicopter to single-handedly win the war in Iraq, he doesn't spend his days as a district attorney and his nights as a crime-fighting masked avenger, and

God knows he's not a celebrity. He doesn't have the talent. He's just a guy who gives a shit."

Kelsie finally exhaled, so I had either convinced her or she was doing anger-management exercises and working on her breathing techniques. Either way, she was vocal again, even if she wasn't ready to agree (and she wasn't). "Well," she said, switching gears, "there's a line in Todd's stump language I think we need to stop using."

"Okay," I said. "Tell me."

"It's that line about how he wouldn't want his son to grow up to be like Donald Trump," Kelsie said, "or his daughter to date him."

"Uh-huh?"

"It's sexist," Kelsie said.

I furrowed my brows as I pondered that. Seriously, my brows furrowed, I felt them furrowing, and even in the moment, I was thinking: Huh, my brows are furrowed. In fact, that's what I actually said aloud. Not anything about sexist language or Donald Trump or even Todd's children and his hopes for them; nope, what I said aloud was, "Furrowed."

Kelsie paused, puzzled, and said, "Huh?"

I shook it off and said, "How is it sexist? I'm not seeing it."

"I assumed that," Kelsie said dryly. "That's why I'm here. There are things you guys just don't think about because you're men and most men just don't ever think about some things."

"Closing the toilet lid?" I asked.

"Sexist subtext," Kelsie shot back. "For instance, that line in Todd's speech, and y'all use it over and over, by the way, assigns the daughter a position that is purely related to her relationship appeal, and it is even more apparent because you put it in direct contrast to his son." She paused. "Let me simplify this. The line might as well be that you don't want Todd's son to be a billionaire who acts like Trump, and you don't want Todd's daughter to have *sex* with Trump. See the difference?"

"Well, when you put it like that—" I said haltingly.

"Oh, and I just got off the phone with Ronnie, and he's pissed at y'all."

"Shit. Is this about that event the other night?"

"Yeah," she said.

"The event he berated us for not attending that we did, in fact, attend?"

"Yes," Kelsie said.

"The one where we have photos of us attending? The one where we actually have a picture of Todd having a solo conversation with the keynote speaker, the Democrat candidate for lieutenant governor? The one where Todd actually waved at Ronnie when he saw him?"

"He's mad," Kelsie said. "He says he can't keep supporting Todd if he won't bother to show up to important events—"

"We were there! There's evidence!"

"Important events," Kelsie repeated, "that Ronnie and other activists expect to see a congressional candidate at. They didn't see Todd. He might have been there, but they didn't see him, because he went home before the speeches started."

Irritated, I said, "He went home because Lauren had a paper due, and I suspect writing doctoral research summaries is best done sometime *other* than 3 a.m. Todd went home to watch the kids for once, and I went home to congratulate myself on not having to listen to the same speeches for the hundredth time, which is exactly what Todd tried to explain to Ronnie after getting his irate email."

This time it was certain. Kelsie sighed. "Okay, I get it," she said. "But you have got to get it through your head that activists don't care if Todd is just a normal guy. They just want him to show up."

She paused, as if mentally clearing the conversation. "I told Myra that Todd would be calling shortly. That still the plan?"

It was. One of the first things I had asked Kelsie to do when she had come aboard the campaign was to serve as a liaison between Todd and the leaders in the activist community. "Court the Kingmakers," I had told her, and Myra was definitely among that number. She was a bigwig with liberal groups in Dallas County, which is where the money came from in our congressional district. Unfortunately, the district was also made up of voters living in Tarrant County, the reddest metropolitan county in the entire United States, and also a good chunk of Denton County, whose elected officials, not to be outdone, had fought tooth and claw to save a statue dedicated to the memory of Confederate veterans. None of that mattered in a primary, of course, which meant that Myra, and the votes and money she represented, were a big deal. Kelsie had been trying to get a one-on-one with her and Todd for weeks.

Now all we had to do was not screw it up. At least, that was all Todd had to do.

I was just going to listen in.

"We'll do our best, Kelsie," I promised. "We really will."

"Okay," she said. "Good luck. Let me know how it goes."

I laughed and said, "I was about to tell you the same thing!"

She chuckled a little as she hung up, so maybe the campaign was still on the rails after all.

About that time Todd walked in the front door, a notebook in one hand and a milkshake in the other. I breathed a quick sigh of relief: the milkshake was a good sign. If he hadn't had one coming in, I'd have run out to Whataburger to fetch one; after all, I had promised Kelsie my best effort.

"Doctor," Todd said as he sat down at the kitchen table. "How are we doing?"

"Ask me after this call," I said.

Maybe my nervousness was apparent, because Todd looked up from his notebook with a grin and said, "Hey . . . it's me. Don't worry."

I might have appreciated the *Star Wars* reference more with a bowl of queso on hand. I sat down at the opposite end of the table with a cup of coffee and my own scratch pad, hoping the Todd Allen for Congress campaign was going to have better luck with Myra than our track record with activist leaders would suggest.

Then I didn't have time to worry anymore because Myra was picking up the phone.

I've never quite figured out where Todd gets the energy to start a political conversation with a stranger, but somehow he does. He smiles as if the person on the other end of the phone could see him and chatters away as if he hadn't just driven across Metroplex traffic after putting in a full day in an urban classroom. It's awe-inspiring and exhausting to witness.

"Afternoon, Myra," Todd said. "How we doin' today?"

The voice on the other end was cultured, smooth, and guarded. It reminded me of school administrators I had known who made entire careers out of saying absolutely nothing and making as few decisions as possible. Hush, I told myself (or the bad bloke on my shoulder), being careful isn't a crime. What Myra said was a perfectly reasonable, perfectly cordial, "I'm doing well, Todd. How are you?"

Civil. Polite.

I could tell Todd's grin was growing even though I was looking down into my coffee cup. He's got an audible smile, if there is such a thing. Sometimes I wonder if the conversation would have gone down a different path if Myra had been sitting right there in the kitchen with her own cup of coffee, seeing that smile and maybe also seeing the humble furnishings of a home belonging to a lifelong educator.

"You know," Todd said. "I'm good, but between work, two little kids, my wife getting her doctorate, and campaigning, it, uh . . . it's a thousand miles an hour around here. It's like three full-time jobs."

"I can imagine," Myra said, noticeably noncommittal.

Hmmmm. That's what I wrote at the top of a blank page: Hmmmmm.

"But hey," Todd said, still chipper, still smiling, "that's why I earn the big bucks, right?" He laughed, just in case she was unclear that he was joking. "We're all here to make things better for folks, whatever it takes."

But Myra had other things on her mind, and it was starting to seem as if maybe she was in a hurry to get to them. "That's right," she said, confirming that she agreed that trying to make a better world was a worthwhile ideal. Then she said, "Todd, I wanted to let you know why I can't allow your campaign to post materials on my group's Facebook page. That page isn't really for candidates. It's for activists to discuss how we're going to organize ourselves to get things done, like letting Kenny Marchant know we're not satisfied with the job he's doing. If we let candidates post on that page, I am afraid it will be flooded with solicitations and ads, and that's not what I want it to be."

Which is a place to bitch, I thought.

Kelsie had warned us that Myra was unhappy with the social media saturation our campaign was engaged in, though I still wasn't quite sure why letting candidates reach like-minded activists was a bad thing. Our posts and shares were being routinely deleted. Myra's explanation wasn't clearing things up for me any, but then, I sensed she really didn't care much if it did or not. What her tone really reminded me of was that email you get from a potential employer that starts out applauding your myriad skills and talents before dropping the truth hammer of rejection.

Did Todd sense that hammer? He didn't show it. He just nodded his head and plowed forward and said, "So, I'm glad we're getting a chance to talk. I know you've spoken with Kelsie about the campaign——"

A flicker of warmth. "Of course, I love Kelsie. She's a strong progressive voice."

Hmmmmm, I wrote again.

"Absolutely," Todd said. "I couldn't be more excited to have her on staff. She basically keeps us on the straight and narrow around here. She's great, so I know she's filled you in on the campaign, what we're trying to achieve . . . but what I'd love to do today is talk one-on-one about who I am and why I'm running."

After a moment, Myra said, "Todd, that's not necessary."

It is a life truth, I've found, that when someone uses your first name mid-conversation you should brace yourself for a scolding. It was true when I was five and it is true now, and I have no doubt it'll be true when I'm in a nursing home, stealing Jell-O and bribing the nurses to bring me some queso. I looked up from my pad as Todd hesitantly said, "Really?"

Myra's voice picked up a bit of speed, as if gathering momentum. "Yes, I've read your website," she said. "I've seen your social media. Your campaign certainly posts quite a bit."

She paused and added, "I know who you are."

I would have given any amount of money if Todd had taken advantage of that opening to growl out, "I'm Batman!"

Instead, he looked up at me, eyes a little wider, and I knew what was actually going on in his head. Never in the history of dramatic literature has the phrase "I know who you are" been followed by anything cheerful, heartwarming, inspirational, or even remotely warm and fuzzy. Usually, it's followed up by someone offering to read Miranda rights while a *Law & Order*–style sound effect rings out an ominous *dun, dun!*

"I have some concerns about you as a candidate," Myra said.

"Let's hear them," Todd invited cheerfully. "That's why I'm here."

She refused to be softened by his attitude. She was on a mission. All I could do was sit at that table and wait for it to be revealed, ass clenched and unfortunately running low on coffee.

"Todd," Myra said again, "some information was shared with me a few days ago that I found really concerning."

Holy shit, I thought, this woman could teach Alfred Hitchcock a thing or two about suspense. What was she concerned about? Todd's policies?

His failures both personal and professional? His lack of campaign staff? The fact that he wasn't actually named Tony and didn't have custom envelopes? Jesus Christ, Todd, what have you done? Were you the gunman on the Grassy Knoll? Did you invent New Coke?

What the fuck, I wrote in letters big enough to be seen from space. Or, at least, from the other side of the table.

Todd saw them and frowned.

"I'm listening," he prompted.

"It's about your voting record."

"My voting record?"

"You just don't have much of one."

"Oh," Todd said involuntarily. He didn't say, Is that all? He didn't say that. I did, though, and probably loud enough for Myra to hear me on the other end of the line.

He waved at me to shut up, then said, "That's certainly true, ma'am. I haven't always been as involved as I should have been."

"You didn't vote for Obama," Myra said.

"You didn't vote for Obama?" I asked before I could stop myself.

Todd shot me another look that suggested, in no uncertain terms, that I was more than welcome to step outside to find a way to fornicate myself.

"I didn't vote for Obama," Todd confirmed. "But, in my defense, I didn't vote for anyone that year."

Myra said, "That's my problem with you, Todd. You want me to support you and your vanity run for Congress—"

Todd interjected. "I certainly don't think I'd still be doing this if it were about vanity. I'm not stepping out there each night and taking body shots for vanity."

I was a little surprised that Todd was keeping his voice so calm; I was fighting mad, and I *had* voted for Obama. Maybe it was all the practice he'd been getting lately taking one on the chin from all sides, but he wasn't picking up the gauntlet that Myra had thrown down. He was keeping it cool.

Myra, on the other hand . . .

"Todd," she said, persisting in her use of his name as a launch pad for an insult. "Here is what I know: there was a transformational candidate in 2008, and as far as I can tell you didn't care. You weren't involved.

You couldn't be bothered. I knocked on thousands of doors for Obama. I made thousands of calls. And you did nothing. And now you think someone like *you* can run for Congress?"

And still, Todd kept it together. God bless him, he was giving it the good old-fashioned college try.[2] "Well, I understand how you'd think that," he said calmly. "But the whole idea of my campaign is that there are a whole lot of us out there who should have done more and didn't but are now waking up . . . and we're ready. I'd like to think that there are a lot of people like me who need to hear that they have a place in this process, that they *can* make an impact, that they *can* make a difference. Those people, they're the difference makers in this election. And those people, Myra, well, they're people like me. They're people who want the government and their leaders to be better. I just . . . well, I'm just like them. I just want us to be better."

Ding. A lightbulb switched on, Looney Tunes–style, in my head. I jotted down We Can Be Better on my notepad and kept listening.

"What is *that* supposed to mean?" Myra asked. Maybe she didn't like being on the defensive, or maybe she was annoyed at the idea that politics wasn't always about who spent the most time in the right group complaining the loudest.

Todd started talking more quickly, which was a sign that whatever hold he had on his patience was beginning to slip. He was making a last effort, and he wanted to get it out there before it was swallowed up by something else. He said, "What I'm trying to say is . . . I can't control the past, okay? I can't step back to 2008 and tell my younger self to get to the polls so we wouldn't have to have this conversation. All I can do is fight for today. I feel like I have to. It's not vanity. I'm not masochistic. It's just what is right. And you know what? Come November, healthcare will be on the ballot, reasonable gun regulations will be on the ballot, taxes will be on the ballot, but I'm damn sure my voting record won't be."

Myra snorted. She actually snorted. I've read about someone snorting in disgust but I've never run across it actually happening in the wild.

Anyway, she snorted and said, "That's a fine speech, but your voting record disqualifies you from running for Congress."

––––––––––––––––––––––

[2] I've never understood this reference, by the way.

And that's when it ran out.

Todd's patience was done taking an ass kicking and so was he.

"Well," he snapped, "luckily, Article I, Section II of the Constitution says differently."

"Don't talk to me about the Constitution," Myra shot back.

I looked up at Todd, shaking my head in disbelief. She was actually upset that he'd dared to fight back. She'd been sniping and swiping and Todd had been taking that shit with a smile and a pleasant tone that apparently signaled, Yes, please keep feeding me shit, I love shit, it's my daily diet. She had flat out told him that all his work, all his effort, all his time, *all of it* was fucking pointless because he hadn't passed her personal test of worthiness, and she'd expected him to just take it until she was tired of dishing it out. It reminded me of parents in the stands of any given public school sporting event, loudly complaining about the coach as if it were their right, and then being shocked, no, outraged when that coach addressed those concerns directly by turning to them and telling them to fuck off.

Anyway, it was like that.

And Todd was embracing the dark side.

"You sure you don't want to talk about the Constitution?" he asked pointedly. "Because you're throwing out terms like *disqualify* when what I think you mean to say is that you just don't like me."

"This conversation is over," Myra said flatly. "Good luck."

Then she hung up.

Todd held the phone up for a bit, gingerly, as if it were a bomb that still might explode at any moment. There were angry spots of color on his cheeks. He probably needed nothing more at that moment than a margarita and some good queso; being a good friend and proper campaign manager, I was already reaching for my car keys. He took a deep, shuddering breath and muttered, "I don't think she really wishes us good luck, do you?"

I just shook my head.

He set the phone down and stood up slowly. "Well . . . I think that went well. What do you think?"

I looked down at my notebook and the list of potential kingmakers Todd needed to court to gain favor with the activists. I took my pen and drew a thick line through Myra's name.

We Can Be Better

It was late September. I was parked outside of Todd's house in Hurst, waiting to ferry him to the next in a long series of campaign events. I sat stiffly in the driver's seat of that Challenger, waiting for a candidate who was worth the time and effort, even if I had my doubts about his campaign. Self-doubt is a cruel thing, and I had enough doubts that weekend to go around and then some. I wondered if all I was really managing was a remarkably effective campaign of self-sabotage and political suicide. After all, the most consistent message Todd and I were hearing from activist leaders and experienced operatives like Kelsie was that we needed to focus a hell of a lot less on doing what we thought was right and a hell of a lot more on doing what we were told would be successful.

The only problem, I thought, is that doing what we think is right actually feels good. And I think it's working.

Donations were trickling in at a steady pace, even if the total dollar amount wasn't enough to pay a fancy Washington consultant for a week's work. They represented the support of teachers, mechanics, nurses, retirees, firemen, mothers, fathers, grandparents, and others who never got out to an activist event but had found us through social media and liked what they saw. They were also from people who did show up to all those activist meetings, willing to listen and talk and keep an open mind about something new. The people at the front of those rooms might not have been superhot on an Allen candidacy, but once you got to the cheap seats, it seemed as if Todd's message was resonating. They smiled as he approached their tables, they laughed at his jokes, they signed his petitions, took his literature, and seemed to think that it was a great idea for a normal person to take a shot at Congress for once.

And they weren't alone.

Where the campaign was really picking up steam was in the digital world of social media, where local Democratic candidates consistently faltered and fumbled—and based on their infrequent posts, terrible aesthetic sense, and complete lack of humor, seemed to agree that media wasn't worth a campaign's quality time. Of course, whenever I heard one of the veteran politicos try to explain this near-total disregard for media to me, I couldn't resist pointing out that Nixon probably said something similar right before heading into that televised debate with Kennedy. In the world of social media, a voter in the Twenty-Fourth District had a clear choice: a candidate with a growing digital presence or a candidate who had once, maybe by accident, fired up a browser using AOL Online (and that venerable bit of programming had gone the way of the dodo while Todd and I were still assuring Dr. Crockett that we intended to be lawyers).

But likes weren't translating into love with the powers that be in the Democratic Party, where the activist leadership was sending a pretty clear message our way: You're not one of us.

Have you ever seen *Citizen Kane*? If not, you should, and not just because it's often acknowledged as the finest film ever made, or because you feel like watching Orson Welles, at fucking twenty-four years old, give a master class in acting that honestly makes me feel jealous at how effortless it all seems for him. Watch it for the performances, watch it for the direction, the editing, the story, the cinematography, the cinematic innovations, yes, watch it for all those reasons, but be damn sure you watch it for the life lessons the script tosses out like instructional candy. Did *Citizen Kane* have anything to offer a thirty-eight-year-old newbie campaign manager with confidence issues?

Absolutely.

There is a scene that occurs shortly after newspaper magnate Kane's second wife, a trophy blonde with a sweet disposition, attempts to kill herself with an overdose of sleeping pills. Kane had been aggressively pushing poor Susan to be an opera singer, despite her all-too-meager talents. "Charlie," she whimpers upon regaining consciousness, "I couldn't go through with the singing again. You don't know what it means to know that people are—that a whole audience just doesn't *want* you."

Preach, Susan Alexander Kane. Preach.

Todd's call with Myra had left no doubt in my mind that there was a large slice of the primary electorate who just didn't want Todd, and probably never would. In a way, that call marked a huge turning point in the campaign. Before that call, we had been doing our best to adjust our ideas to what we were being told the voters wanted and trying to do the things a successful campaign does to get elected. But that wasn't why we decided to run for Congress, and we had started pushing back, little by little, just for our own sanity.

A dozen times since that call, I turned back to my notes and saw a phrase Todd had uttered that struck a chord with me. I had jotted it down, then underlined it, then circled it, and that was just while the conversation with Myra was ongoing. In fact, every time I turned back to that page since, I had added an underline or sketched the letters in a bit darker, a bit bolder.

Those words *mattered*. I was convinced of it.

And we had said them before. They showed up in Todd's earliest stump speeches, in the copy of social media posts, and even tucked away in the text of those nifty binders I'd prepared for that kitchen table meeting way back in the spring. Before we'd run with a triptych like *Civility, Conversation, & Change* and before we settled on a campaign slogan of *#NewBlue*, we'd been dancing around the language that actually seemed to matter most: *We Can Be Better*. Were we talking about Americans, Democrats, activists, or ourselves?

Or all the above?

I was still staring at that line in my notebook when Todd opened the door with his customary greeting and flopped down with all the grace of a six-year-old forced to sit through a two-hour church sermon. "Alright, let's roll," he said, all his attention focused on mentally rehearsing a two-minute spiel he was expected to give at the event, introducing himself and his candidacy using a phrase I'd come up with months earlier at a roulette wheel while shooting the political shit with a shrimp boat captain. Then he'd try to tell them why he was running for Congress.

For all the changes we had made, for all the good I felt we had done, I still had too many days where I wasn't sure we were telling our story in a way people would give a shit about. I felt like we were still lost in the process, lost in campaign semantics, wandering, searching for our real voice. We'd been using a slogan I'd stolen from a character right out of Winston Groom, and I wasn't sure it was working anymore.[1]

So I asked.

"Why are you running for Congress?" I asked.

Todd frowned, probably a bit annoyed at what seemed like a rhetorical question interrupting the sanctity of a five-minute car ride that was usually reserved for talking about movies or bitching about work. He looked at me with a raised eyebrow, which I took as a subtle suggestion that maybe I should answer my own rhetorical exercises or switch the topic to something more exciting, like the new *Star Wars* movie coming out.[2]

"Is this a quiz?" he asked

"We keep telling people to vote for Todd Allen," I said. "If they went and cast votes for you today, I'm not sure I know what they just voted for."

Todd wasn't slow on the uptake. No one could accuse him of that (well, they could and often did, especially in the underworld of local Democratic politics, but that didn't make it true). Nodding to himself, he settled back into his seat. "You know . . . Lauren asked me why I wanted to keep running the other day." He paused. "I gave her an answer, but it wasn't a good one. I don't even remember what I said."

"Maybe we don't have a good answer anymore," I pointed out.

He looked at me for a long moment. "I would agree with that."

I forged ahead. "Right now we've got a mix of Todd Allen, the guy I want to see in Congress, and Todd Allen, the candidate that activist groups would maybe support if they felt like it that day. I know we're

---

[1] Remember *#NewBlue*? No one knew what it meant. I wasn't sure we knew what it meant.

[2] It was *The Last Jedi*. I loved it; Todd wasn't a fan. Different strokes, folks. We both agreed that anything was better than the live-action cartoons that George Lucas pumped out during our college years. At least these were real films.

trying to stay true to who we are *without* pissing off the activists. I know we want to be successful, even if it means using bullet points on the site and clearing our language with Ronnie just in case his buddy Handlebar doesn't understand the words. I know Kelsie thinks we're not doing enough to do things right, that we're already giving good advice the middle finger. But the Todd Allen who's running now doesn't feel worth fighting for."

"We pushed back on simplifying the language," Todd argued. "We pushed back on wasting our time at events."

"We need to push harder."

"Look, I don't want all of this to be pointless," Todd said sharply. "I don't want to be the guy that everyone laughs at because he thought he could run for Congress without help. We've never done this before. These people have done it—"

"And *lost*," I interrupted. "They've done it and lost. Over and over."

I gave him a minute to chew on that one. I understood what was going through his head. Neither of us were afraid to take risks, to jump into situations swinging, to tell people that didn't think something could be done to hold our beer while we proved them otherwise. But he also didn't want to be ridiculed while he was busy finding out that he was wrong, and it was all impossible after all. There was always that glimmer of hope, glimpsed just outside the corners of our eyes, that all we had to do was take the right advice, tweak what we said just a little, show up at the right event, shake the right hand, and suddenly everything would work out.

Maybe that was all overthinking it. To Todd, losing wasn't an activity with inherent nobility.

Come to think of it, I wasn't fond of it either.

"Dude," I said after a moment, "all I know for sure is that we're not going to make it to March, much less next November. Not like this. As far as I can tell, we're running for the privilege of being told how we're upsetting people. I can deal with people hating my guts as long as I'm proud of why they hate me. But right now, this campaign is all about how we're saying the wrong words to the wrong people at the wrong events."

I took a deep breath, because either what I said next changed everything or we were going to have to find a way to enjoy the gooey middle of a compliment sandwich—hold the compliments.

I held out my notebook to him. "If we're going to be wrong, let's be wrong doing what we think is right. All the way. You said something the other day that was maybe the truest, most honest thing I've ever heard you say, and you said it to someone who hates your guts. I want you to take another look at it."

He took it and began to read. I could see his lips moving ever so slightly as he did, could tell he was picturing himself reading them in front of a camera, or at a meet-and-greet, or in a debate hall. But would he like what he was pretending to say?

Under my notes from the Myra conversation, I'd written:

> *It doesn't have to be like this. We can be better. I think Americans want civility. They want to be able to talk to each other. They want politics to change. I'm doing this for those Americans, those weary Americans who have just been waiting for something different. I'm doing this for them because I'm one of them. We can be better.*

When he looked up at me, he was smiling a little. He exhaled slowly, almost relieved.

"I don't think Kelsie is gonna be very happy about this," he said, gesturing to the book.

"What do *you* think?"

"I think this campaign has worn on us," he said. "I think all these little groups and bit players and constant revisions and suggestions that are actually demands have worn on us. I think some days I want to text you that I quit and then ignore your calls for two weeks." He paused, and for a moment I thought that maybe he was about to just skip the texting stage and go straight into the breakup.

"I also think you might be right," he finally said. "We can be better. We *need* to be better. If any of this is gonna be worth it, then we need to say what we actually believe and be who we actually are."

Todd looked out the windshield, maybe at something down the street, maybe at something a little farther away, a little more intangible. "I don't believe in absolutes," he said softly, more to himself than to me. "I don't believe the best thing we can do is yell louder and longer than the other guy."

"Only a Sith believes in absolutes," I reminded him.

Todd chuckled at that. "Alright, dude, let's go. If we're going to try to save this fucking campaign and our sanity, we might as well get started." Smiling to myself, I put the car into gear and heard Todd muse aloud, "Who knows, maybe the voters will go along with me on this one."

And just like that, it felt as if an elephant took his foot off my back and let me stand up to breathe for the first time in months. The Challenger shot forward when I put it in gear, seemingly eager to get us where we needed to go so we could finally be ourselves. That five-minute drive might have been the best moment of the campaign. Every song on the radio was a good one, every light was green, and the sun was shining in a blue sky that promised more than just a daily kick to the political dick. The candidate who stepped into that mom-and-pop restaurant in Bedford to speak to yet another political club was a man who had finally, *finally*, decided to trust his instincts.

Todd Allen had decided he was going to win or lose as Todd Allen.

Kelsie knew right off the bat that something had changed because we both walked into that restaurant smiling. I thought of Liz letting this campaign intrude upon what was supposed to be the happiest moments of her life, and I was amazed that she had put up with it for so long and determined that I was going to make it up to her. I thought of Kelsie, offering advice only to watch as these two amateurs took it kicking and screaming and acting as if she was pulling teeth. I even spared a thought for Myra, whose phone call with Todd was fast becoming legend, wondering if she would have been more forgiving of Todd's voting record (or lack thereof) if he had stuck to his political instincts from the get-go.

Probably not.

There was a different feel in the room when we walked in that night. By late fall, there was a discernible shift in the political world, as if some invisible border had been crossed. On the summer side of that line, everything was experimental, exploratory, and incredibly temporary; on the other side, the side we were approaching, the stakes were higher, the gauntlet of events more intense, and the scrutiny on campaigns moved from the spotlight of occasional interest to the harsh glare generated by a thousand activists narrowing their eyes. If for no other reason than that, I was glad the campaign had found its footing on a hill Todd and I were willing, if not happy, to die on.

Soon, each and every one of the local political clubs and activist groups would start hosting forums where every candidate would stand up on a stage to be judged, pigeon-holed, possibly ridiculed, and grilled by a moderator looking to see which of the primary candidates would crack under the pressure. As the round of forums ended, endorsement season would begin, and those same clubs and groups would vote on which candidate they'd officially support. Somewhere in there, we'd also confirm, either through turning in enough signatures or paying a fee, that, yes, Edward "Todd" Allen's name would be on the ballot. It was a roadmap for what remained of the campaign, and I'd be lying if I said I wasn't a little surprised we were still on the road.

But we were.

Kelsie kept shooting me curious looks, which was understandable considering that I was enjoying an event for the first time . . . well, ever. The guest speaker was Kim Olsen, a retired Air Force pilot who was the Democratic candidate for Texas Agriculture Commissioner. Hearing her speak was energizing—not because of what she said, which I honestly can't remember even though I have now heard her deliver that same speech a dozen times, but because of *how* she said it. She was a natural leader, but more than that, she was a natural public speaker, and she grabbed the attention of that little restaurant and wouldn't let go. Believe it or not, but most candidates running in Loserville are actually hopeless when it comes to public speaking, offering up awkward elevator pitches at best and stumbling and bumbling monologues at worst. Kim Olsen was something different. She was using language and charisma to open eyes and get hearts beating.

It was inspirational because I saw what Todd could be if given a chance. He was an ex-coach who had given his share of fiery halftime speeches. He was a teacher who could hold a classroom in the palm of his hand. He didn't need to be an ex-fighter pilot to give a good speech.

He just needed words worth saying.

That night, for the first time, maybe also inspired by Kim's example, he came close to finding those words. Given two minutes to introduce himself, he gave an off-the-cuff mix of his usual spiel and some of the phrases he'd just read in my little notebook. I could see some familiar faces in the room wearing an unfamiliar expression: they were listening. They were nodding. Some were smiling.

It wasn't a great speech. It wasn't even close. But he believed in it, and that made all the difference.

Afterwards, as Todd was making the rounds, Kelsie came over and for my ears alone said, "So, some of that was . . . new."

I nodded but played it close to the vest. I suspected Kelsie wouldn't like the new direction, and I didn't want to have an argument about it. Not that night. No, what I wanted was to take this feeling I had—could it be satisfaction?—and see if it would last until I could get home and examine it more closely. It wasn't as if we had spent the whole campaign being someone we weren't. We had pushed back and fought and resisted doing things we thought were wrong or ineffective. But for the first time, we had decided to make a leap of faith and to trust ourselves completely. Win or lose. Come what may. Just like those two college kids we had once been, hauling a trunk full of scripts on a hopeless quest down I-10 in the middle of a summer night.

We were on our way to California all over again.

"Hey, I want to talk about that RFK thing you want to run," Kelsie said.

I narrowed my eyes. I had a thing for Bobby Kennedy, a nostalgia for that last campaign of his before it ended in tragedy in '68 (if someone can *have* nostalgia for something they weren't even alive for). My favorite speech, and I mean ever, was one that Kennedy gave that year shortly after Martin Luther King Jr. was assassinated. It was titled "On the Mindless Menace of Violence," and it was something I could listen to for literally hours on end, it was that good. In it, Bobby cautioned Americans about the rising tide of violent intolerance in the land, using a voice that was sad and knowing, which I suppose makes sense when you consider who his brother had been and how he had died. Anyway, his conclusion summed up a lot of what Todd and I felt about modern times, and I'd worked it up into a graphic and post for social media:

> But we can perhaps remember, if only for a time, that those who live with us are our brothers, that they share with us the same short moment of life, that they seek, as do we, nothing but the chance to live out their lives in purpose and in happiness, winning what satisfaction and fulfillment they can. Surely this bond of common fate, this bond of common

goals, can begin to teach us something. Surely we can learn, at the least, to look at those around us, at our fellow men, and surely we can begin to work a little harder to bind up the wounds among us, and to become in our hearts brothers and countrymen once again.

"I think we should edit it a little," Kelsie suggested. "It leans a lot into that old-style sexist language: fellow men, brothers, countrymen. Maybe we can just rephrase that a bit."

"You want me to rephrase Bobby Kennedy?" I asked, and if she had wanted me to paraphrase Jesus I would not have been more aghast. I told you, I have a thing for RFK.

"Can you?" She asked. "I just want people to see Todd the way I see him."

"I can do that," I assured her, swallowing my objections and my nostalgic love for my political hero. After all, we were going to be shifting the campaign's message over her almost-certain objections; the least I could do was give her a *countrymen* or two.

"Speaking of . . . who's Todd talking to?" Kelsie asked, drawing my attention to where Todd was having what appeared to be an in-depth conversation with a young man I hadn't seen before. He was dressed casually, in a T-shirt and shorts, and for a minute I thought he might have been a student at one of the local high schools. Whatever they were talking about, they finished up by the time Kelsie and I drifted over.

"Kind of a weird conversation," Todd said as I walked up.

"What do you mean?" I asked.

"He asked me what my plan was for raising enough money to beat Marchant." "I told him we had some pretty robust digital fundraising plans in place—"

"Which is bullshit," I added.

"Absolute bullshit," Todd confirmed, "But, anyway, I told him that all the plans in the world didn't mean anything if people didn't buy into the message. I told him the campaign was focusing on reaching voters right now and spreading that message."

"Huh," I said, watching the young man walk out the restaurant doors with a determined expression on his face. Somehow, I didn't think he liked what he had heard.[3] Idly, I wondered if he was a spy from the

Marchant campaign. Kelsie told us they had a history of sending college students and young volunteers to rival campaign events to ask, poke, and pry and hopefully get a recording of a candidate giving an unpracticed, embarrassing answer to an awkward question. Kelsie's eyes were also on the retreating form of Todd's young interrogator, probably wondering the same thing. Tomorrow, I'd have to call her and explain the campaign's new guiding star, and I'd have to use all my cunning to sell it. Tomorrow was soon enough, I thought.

Except tomorrow would hold its own surprises.

Tomorrow, we'd find out that the young man with the question about fundraising wasn't a spy from Marchant's congressional office. He was actually a college professor, a self-professed "brain scientist," and he was getting all set to announce his own run for office as the Democrat candidate for US Congress in the Twenty-Fourth District.

His name was John Biggan.

---

[3]He hadn't. Much later, he divulged to me that Todd's lack of realism when it came to the role of money in politics was what inspired him to jump into the race.

PART III

That's How I Got to Memphis

Crooked

His logo was crooked.

"His fucking logo is crooked," I said when I dialed into the meeting. It was a campaign conference call, the kind of thing where the staff spent five minutes on important business and about a half hour on venting, bitching, and daydreaming. Usually, the Allen for Congress campaign provided no shortage of subjects for venting, bitching, or daydreaming; rarely, however, did something come up worth actually obsessing over. One week after John Biggan announced his candidacy for Congress, I had found something to obsess over.

Maybe not the right something, but something. Something crooked.

There was no shortage of important, dare I say dire, implications to the entrance of a third candidate in the primary for the Democratic nomination, all of which needed due consideration and complete attention from a crafty campaign manager. Unfortunately, the first thing I noticed about John Biggan's candidacy was the shitty logo, and that monopolized my attention completely.

"Let's focus on something other than the logo," Kelsie suggested over the line. "Guys, a third person in the race is a big deal."

"Is it?" Todd asked. He wasn't being serious, he just didn't want us to forget he was there.

"Yeah," Kelsie said. "It's serious. It's another name on the ballot."

"I get that," I said. "But don't you think a crooked logo says something about his campaign?"

"It says that they don't have someone on staff obsessing over aesthetics," Todd reminded me, trying (and failing) to redirect the conversation. "But I hear you, dude. Fucking thing is definitely slanted."

"Yeah," I said, "it bothers me. Seriously."

"The candidacy or the logo?"

I hesitated, then ventured, "Can't it be both?"

What had been a binary choice for the voters of the Twenty-Fourth District was now something infinitely more complex. Todd was no longer the shiny new candidate vying to snatch votes away from a proven congressional loser; he was just another name on a ballot getting too crowded for comfort. The spotlight for our campaign had always felt a lot more like the view through a sniper's scope, but that didn't mean I was all that excited about ceding our place in it to another candidate.

"I don't like what I'm hearing out there in the groups," Kelsie said. "This guy represents another chance for people to vote for someone that isn't you, and no matter how you look at it, it's not good. The people in the groups are actually excited about the race now. They haven't had a contested primary, I think, since redistricting, and now there are three candidates vying for their attention. I don't think Biggan is going to get the same reception you did. They're excited he's in it. They're excited about him."

I groaned. "We *just* got the campaign to a good place. We've got a message we believe in. We're being smart with our time and money. We're not spending all of our energy either apologizing for what we say or revising it by committee. We're getting donations. We're getting followers on social media. Hell, we're getting followers out in the real world, people who actually want to volunteer their time to help get Todd elected. Now a twelve-year-old waltzes into the race in jogging shorts and shakes that all up?"

I heard a chuckle, and Todd said, "I think he's our age, dude. Kelsie, is he dealing with that same Republican-lite bullshit people were throwing our way?"

"I suspect the groups will receive him differently than you," Kelsie confirmed. "I think you took a lot of fire because the first one through the door—"

"Like being one of the guys at the front of the boat when the ramp drops on D-Day," I muttered.

Kelsie had seen that part of *Saving Private Ryan*, too. I could picture her nodding as she said, "Almost exactly like that. Todd took the hits; Biggan won't."

"God, that's a great movie," Todd mused. "Okay, folks, let's just hope no one else is about to show up. Shit's getting crowded enough already."

Todd was right. The race was getting crowded, and that should have captured my complete attention. Unfortunately, there were questionable aesthetic choices being made, and I just couldn't focus on anything but Biggan's logo. It was nothing fancy, just Biggan's name and the state of Texas, but somehow the result was crooked. How is it that no one has popped onto Facebook to suggest that only secret Republicans have crooked logos? I wondered. Why hasn't Myra put in a call to warn Biggan that the inability to approve a symbolic brand for his ideals that wasn't off-kilter disqualified him from running for office? You could say I was losing sight of the bigger picture, which was that Todd Allen was no longer the default candidate of hope and change.

We had all been to a monthly meeting of a local activist group where John Biggan had made one of his first appearances, so we were all working from some distinct first impressions.

Kelsie offered hers first. "Look, the field is crowded," she said. "So we need to look at what we're doing and adjust. Tweak things a bit. From what I saw, Biggan doesn't seem to be well connected and he hasn't lived here long. He didn't go out of his way to talk to people." She paused, then added pointedly, "He *does* posture quite liberal. And when there are two male candidates and a female candidate, the woman usually has an advantage." I would have been happier to hear that Biggan could barely put two words together in a coherent sentence and practiced poor personal hygiene, but we can't have everything, can we?

After a moment, Kelsie added, "And Myra likes him."

Of course Myra liked him.

Liz had a disconcerting reaction to seeing Biggan speak, which I shared with the group.

"She said, 'Uh-oh.'" I told them.

There was a short silence as everyone tried to internalize that one.

"What does that mean?" Todd finally asked.

"Well," I said, "Liz was reluctant to admit it, but she finally told me that he was charismatic, he was a good speaker, he could make people laugh, he was as adorable as a lost puppy, and his smile was just as charming as Todd's."

"Oh," Todd said. "She thinks I have a charming smile?"

"Focus," Kelsie said. "Liz is right. Biggan comes across as—"

"Goofy?" I cut in.

"Authentic," Kelsie finished. "Non-threatening. A good guy. And you know Todd doesn't always have the best of luck with first impressions—"

"Which is bullshit," Todd interjected. "I work my ass off to be a pleasant, approachable guy."

Kelsie added, "I agree. But the way you look is threatening to some people."

This was a problem we could do without. I was incredibly aware that Todd didn't always come off as a cute and cuddly candidate for the common people. For whatever reason, at first glance people seemed to think Todd was stuck-up, arrogant, and ever-so-slightly smug (three words that all mean the same thing, but apparently sometimes having three of something is inevitable). On the other side of the coin, John Biggan, according to Liz, came off as the goofy kid who was every girl's best friend in a high school one-act play who suddenly became every woman's fantasy boyfriend after graduation.

Todd's reactions to our reactions weren't surprising. It bothered him that he wasn't the darling of the activist groups, but he had accepted it. It bothered him that he was stereotyped as an entitled middle-aged white male, but since he was, in fact, a middle-aged white male, he didn't think there was a whole lot he could do about it other than try to prove people wrong. It even bothered him that the Biggan campaign was running with a crooked logo (though he wasn't nearly as blinded by that aesthetic monstrosity as I was). No, what bothered Todd the most was that our campaign had clearly set a precedent that others were willing to follow.

"I've always been afraid that we'd prove that it could be done," he said thoughtfully. "And then we'd see others decide that if we could do it, they could, too." Before hanging up, he said, "Folks, we need to get serious about finding ways to stand out from the crowd."

A few days later, I was still working on ways to make sure that Todd was offering something to voters that the other candidates weren't. I was also still bitching about Biggan's crooked-ass logo as Todd, Liz, and I drove out to the town center area in Colleyville that weekend to find a spot to shoot a quick campaign video. "Maybe it isn't the logo that is crooked," I said as we pulled up next to a rock-walled church that I thought would make a good backdrop. "Maybe it's just Texas. Is Texas crooked? In a geographic sense, I mean?"

"I think you need to let it go. This looks good, by the way," Todd said, stepping out of the car and eying the broad, aged wooden doors of the church. The doors looked like something out of western Europe, something medieval, which was perfect for the tone of the video we wanted to shoot. Just to be sure, I turned to Liz and said, "Honey, you've got a good eye. Does that look like the kind of place where bloodthirsty warlords would congregate?"

She eyed the church doors. "Now, or generally?"

"Either." I killed the engine and grabbed my phone. "Let's see if we can hit a new record and get this video recorded in under five minutes!"

Liz was looking around, seeing nothing but a block of overpriced townhomes and cute little delicatessens which somehow managed to survive day-to-day on a noticeable dearth of customers. She looked back at me. "I don't see any bloodthirsty warlords. Is that going to be a problem?

"Nah," Todd said. "Heath will just fix it in post."

Despite the bombshell that was John Biggan, we were all in a good mood. Everyone in the car felt really good about what we were doing, and how we were doing it. The cherry on top was that we were seeing evidence that it was working: the message that *We Can Be Better* seemed to be resonating, people seemed to be responding, and even though a third candidate had jumped into the race (with his crooked-ass logo), it almost felt as if we were actually winning. For the curious, that essentially meant we weren't spending every waking moment worrying about who we were pissing off. Oh, we wondered about who was joining the ranks of the Angry at Allen Army, but we weren't getting any ulcers over it.

It felt as if we had hit a stride and found our niche, and that political sweet spot was located out in that mysterious land known as Social Media. The battlefields of Facebook and other sites weren't exactly slick with the blood of our foes, but that was only because our foes seemed to forget about social media for months at a time, leaving us to wonder where everyone had gone while we planted our victorious flag in the digital soil. We weren't doing anything new or different or revolutionary, so you might ask why we were finding so much confidence in our media game. The answer was simple: we were running a campaign in Loserville, which is, much like my knowledge of pop music, firmly entrenched on the sunny slopes of long ago. I'm talking about a time bubble of at least two decades, long enough for newfangled things like social media to still be considered an exotic tool (and more than long enough for Woodrow and Gus to be forgotten by surly bartenders, but that's neither here nor there).[1]

In big-time races with lots of national attention, social media was handled by interns who pumped out new content daily; it was an expected facet of any legitimate campaign and not exactly something that wowed voters. In Loserville, however, social media was something that a candidate did when they remembered that it existed. When the Todd Allen campaign started posting multiple times daily, and posting with quality original content, memes, and videos, that was something new. People started reacting, interacting, commenting, and generally just doing what they were supposed to do on social media. For my part, I made sure we kept in mind that content was king, and then kept that content flowing, on schedule and on theme. If we ran a meme on gun control on

---

[1] Seriously, go read *Lonesome Dove*. Or watch the miniseries. Time well-spent, either way.

Monday, there would be at least a few articles from national papers on that topic shared by Wednesday, along with a video on Thursday and a policy note on Friday. In short, my media strategy was to use the platforms available to us to serve as surrogates for all those activist meetings in bad buffets. And if the other candidates in the race saw all that content and felt pressured to match it by spending thousands of dollars a week that they didn't have, I was okay with that too.

"Okay," I told Todd. "You know the drill. Say the lines over and over until I say *stop*, and try to ignore the fact that I'm pushing the camera up your nostril."

"Yup," Todd said, nodding his head. "Got it. Let's do it."

We had a rule when it came to campaign videos: for the love of God, no fucking bookshelves. You already know what I'm talking about—the tendency of politicians to put out campaign videos where they stood in front of a handy bookshelf, stared earnestly at the camera, and then droned on for three or four minutes or terminal brain death, whichever came first. Only slightly less annoying to us were the campaigns that embraced a shaky-cam style totally out of sync with the subject matter; watching those kinds of videos was like trying to talk about the intricacies of health insurance while storming the beaches at Normandy. Our detractors (of which there were many) called the former "honest and substantive" and the latter "genuine and grassroots." I called them how I saw them: butt-ass boring and aesthetically painful, not to mention nauseating. Keep it short, keep it interesting, and keep it sharp—that was our philosophy when it came to videos.

The castle of some medieval baron, however? Fair game.

"So what's the idea for this video, again?" Liz asked.

"*Game of Thrones* is about to run the season finale," Todd said.

"And we're going to take advantage of that," I added. I turned to Todd, all business, and said, "Okay, dude, why don't you go ahead and try not to fuck this up."

Todd looked into the lens of my phone's camera, adopting what I called his "serious look," then did his best to spit out the lines I'd written in the car on the drive over:

American politics has become a game of thrones. An arena where an

Shooting the *Game of Thrones* ad, and probably mid-sentence on complaining about a certain crooked campaign logo.

entertainer reigns over complete dysfunction. It doesn't have to be like this. We can be better. I'm Todd Allen and I'm running for Congress. Let's keep the game of thrones on cable.

"Cut," I said, confident he'd gotten through the take without stumbling over a word and more than confident that I had enough to make the video I envisioned in my head. I made him do it five or six more times anyway, mostly to just be doubly sure I had sufficient footage, but also just to mess with his mind and inspire a better performance. Maybe it worked. By that last take, his tone was getting more and more frustrated, which just happened to be exactly what I needed.

"How is this all going to cut together?" Liz asked as I told Todd that we were done, and we piled back into the Challenger.

"Imagine what he just said," I explained, "but cut together with shots of crows against the snow, medieval battlefields, Vikings wielding big fuck-off axes, empty thrones, and, just for good measure, Donald Trump doing his best grumpy Queen Victoria impression, maybe a few shots of those idiots at Charlottesville waving tiki torches and Confederate flags. It'll be maybe a twenty-second ad, and we'll post it in every Democratic club social media page we can and hope a couple of thousand people see it."

"Not bad for five minutes of work," Todd said.

"Moneyball?" Liz asked.

"Moneyball," I confirmed.

Not that our moneyball strategy was always comprehensible. Our main destination for that evening was proof of that. After our little jaunt to the church castle in Colleyville, we were heading for Grapefest in downtown Grapevine. It was your typical town festival where Main Street was shut down for the weekend and lined with booths selling food that was unquestionably bad for you but did encourage you to enter any of the dozen wineries, bars, and restaurants nearby that were offering samples of homebrews and wines. It was the kind of event where you could chase a corndog with a thirty-dollar glass of wine and not feel out of place. It was also an event crawling with everyday Americans, many of them voters in the Twenty-Fourth District, and Todd and I wanted a shot at them. The three of us were clad in brand-new campaign shirts, a nice cornflower blue that fit Todd's fondness for pastels and my nostalgic love for the Houston Oilers. We were ready to shake hands and talk to voters . . . or, rather, Liz and I were ready to film Todd as he shook hands and talked to voters. We were a couple of introverts, after all.

"But this event doesn't fit the rubric," Kelsie had pointed out earlier that day. "You'll be there for a couple of hours and maybe meet a hundred people, who *might* be non-voters. They *might* be Republicans. They

After Grapefest, the brain trust of the Allen campaign meeting over what appears to be fried food and ice cream.

might live outside the district. How is this worth the effort?"

"Not at all, by the old metric," I acknowledged.

She said, "At least when you're at a group event, you know those people live in the district, are Democrats, and will vote in the primary. Every conversation is potentially worth it."

"You absolutely have a point," I told her. "But the thing is, I've added one more metric to the rubric, and it trumps all that."

"What is it?" she asked after a loaded pause.

"How does the event make us feel?" I answered. "Call it the new gold standard. Nothing is worth it if Todd gets to the end of February and is physically sick at the thought of being a public servant. His mood is our currency, and we have to worry about more than just how we spend it. We need to think about how we add to the bank."

"Hmmmm," Kelsie responded.

She didn't sound convinced. "Besides, we're covering our bases: You, Eric, and Mike will be out at the Metro event, so the campaign will be well represented. Best of both worlds!"

That's right, you haven't met Eric or Mike yet.

I'm not sure how it happened, but somehow, while our campaign was deciding that we could be better, it was also attracting people who believed in everything Todd and I were trying to say. It felt as if I blinked one day and boom, suddenly we had a campaign staff that, as far as I could tell, was bigger than anything our opponents could brag of. Yes, I know what Freud suggested about preoccupation with size as symbolic of quality (ahem), but in the grim political cage fight of a Democratic primary, size meant money and money meant a candidate was serious. I don't know about you, but I like being serious (ahem), so when I found myself one day having a conference call with Todd and Liz and Kelsie and Eric and Mike, I suddenly felt like the King of the World, hold the icebergs, please.

Eric and Mike. If anyone ever needed proof that sometimes politics is what it ought to be, then I'd direct them to these two gentlemen.

Todd and I had been at a Starbucks a few weeks before, wasting time waiting on volunteers for a blockwalk. We didn't wind up knocking on any doors that night, mostly because no one appeared with their tennies and an eager smile, ready and willing to knock on the doors of strangers and extol the virtues of one Edward Allen. After about twenty minutes of waiting, Todd and I were ready to chalk the event up in the bad idea column and head home. I was on my third white chocolate mocha.[2] Then Mike appeared, resplendent in a three-piece suit. I don't think I ever saw him in casual clothes during the entire campaign. He introduced himself (young, military, law school), and the three of us ordered some more caffeine and spent the next hour chatting about our ideas and what we thought we could do differently in politics. We didn't know

---

[2] Not sure this is pertinent.

it, but when Mike walked out the door that night, he was a committed Todd Allen campaign staffer. From then on, he was at every event, commented on every post, shared our media material, called local groups religiously to advocate for the campaign, bugged reporters, and hounded community leaders.

And he wasn't alone.

A week or so later, Liz and I met Eric at yet another campaign meet and greet at a Starbucks (if nothing else, running a congressional campaign made me intimately familiar with the locations and relative quality of every Starbucks in the Mid-Cities). A veteran and an airline pilot, Eric taught me about a world I didn't know a lot about and illuminated problems that I was only vaguely aware of regarding this nation's treatment of veterans. He was more than that, though: right as the campaign was deciding that our true message was that *We Can Be Better*, Eric showed up as a living example of the civility and good nature we were hoping to see in politics. This is a dude who would offer a ride to a volunteer for one of Todd's primary opponents, chatting her up amiably and knocking on doors together, he for his candidate and her for hers, never a cross word passing between them.

Eric and Mike. We got their vote.[3]

Man, I sometimes wonder if campaigns run outside of Loserville ever had moments like our meeting Eric and Mike. Did John McCain or Beto O'Rourke or Bill Clinton or Barack Obama ever have a moment when two people showed up willing to believe, and suddenly they weren't just names on a ballot, suddenly they were honest-to-God candidates? Do those big-time names *ever* start out with something as small and fragile as the faith and good will of just two people, or do they pop onto the scene with a small army of volunteers, never doubting their own worth? Did those campaigns have moments where their versions of Eric and Mike became dozens, then hundreds? And when and if that happened, do they remember where it all started? With just two guys and coffee?

I sometimes wonder.

As Todd and Liz and I made our way through the crowds at Grapefest,

---

[3]Worth bragging about.

My favorite campaign picture. No idea what the ladies in the background are doing, or what Todd is looking at; I'd like to think he's gazing off into the future.

me holding the first of what would prove to be too many corndogs, I found myself grinning and thinking, This is how I always wished it would be. I watched Todd shake hands and chat with people on the street, and I thought, maybe this is actually going to happen. I listened as dozens of people talked about how they saw things in their lives, and wished that somehow things could be better, and I thought, We're going to win this thing. Kelsie was right. Most of the people we met weren't Democrats, and it didn't seem as if many of them were planning on voting, period, much less in a primary. But they were earnest, and they were honest, and above all, they were *kind*.

They listened while we listened and, holy shit, it felt good.

Maybe we weren't lighting the activist world on fire. Maybe we didn't always (or even mostly) make the right political decisions. Maybe the arrival of a third candidate in the race, a young, charismatic, and well-spoken candidate, was a sign that the voters of the district disagreed with my optimism about the Todd Allen campaign. But none of that mattered; not on our own personal moneyball metric, anyway. That night at Grapefest, I saw an elderly Black man take a reflective swig of a beer and then tell Todd, "Don't worry about all that policy shit, son. You just tell people why you're doing this, just like you told me. You'll do fine." He and Todd chatted for a few more minutes about absolutely nothing at all, just like people do all the time, and before Todd turned to go, the man reminded him, "Be sure to tell people your why."

Was there a gazebo on Main Street in Grapevine, Texas? There sure as shit was. We were going to win this thing. And we were going to do it without a crooked logo.

Someone find me a fucking fedora.

Knock, Knock

If you want to talk about odd tribal rituals and political sacred cows, follow any given candidate or activist organization on the weekends during campaign season and you'll find a doozy. Our campaign had been on a bit of a roll when it came to ignoring political adages and strategies we felt we had no use for, but we weren't entirely immune, which is why I often found myself sitting for hours on end behind the wheel of my Challenger, idling curbside while Todd walked up to a house in the district with a handful of campaign literature and a smile.

Knock, knock.

No answer.

Todd left a flyer on the doorknob and strolled back down toward the car.

"Next one is two houses down," I said, glancing at the voter database on my phone. He nodded and began walking that way as I eased off the brake and the car slowly crawled forward, keeping pace. Now, there are any number of ways to spend a Saturday afternoon if what you really want is a concrete example of time wasted. Junior High track meets. Faculty meetings. T-ball. The sophomore outing of any film series directed by JJ Abrams.[1] Franchise barbecue. I'm sure you have your own personal list, filled with things you'd rather not do for people you'd rather not know.[2] My own list is long and distinguished, but pride of place on that list is occupied by the political sacred cow known as blockwalking.

Modern-day blockwalking, the act of strolling through neighborhoods knocking on doors and hoping to have a heart-to-heart with a voter, was only distantly related to the far better-known economic activity known as streetwalking, if only because the technological tools supporting your average blockwalker were fairly sophisticated. Armed with a mobile device and the right databases, volunteers for a political campaign can see which households on any street in America had voted Democrat in the last election (saving them from inadvertently rousing a Republican), providing a guide to which doors should be knocked.

"Personally, I think this is a waste of time," I often grumbled whenever blockwalking loomed on our schedule.

"I think there are a lot of political experts out there who might disagree with you," Todd would reply. "I don't, but then, I'm not a political expert."

Then I'd sigh and say, "That's what Kelsie keeps telling me."

Then the round of door knocking and disappointment would begin.

Blockwalking was on the short list of things that were commonly acknowledged as activities a political candidate should do in order to win an election.[3] Tell activists that you spent a day knocking on doors and they'd nod approvingly and applaud your grassroots appeal. Tell those same people that you skipped out and instead spent the day comfortably ensconced in an air-conditioned room, using media tools to reach a couple of thousand guaranteed primary voters, and they'd adopt a stern

---

[1]You know it's true; give him the first film and he'll provide an entertaining master class in worldbuilding. Let him dabble in a franchise a second time and you suddenly get Benedict Cumberbatch playing a very British version of a dude supposedly named Khan Noonien-Singh.

[2]Come to think of it, this is actually a better definition of *politics* than anything I've seen in a civics textbook over the years.

[3]The list included purchasing yard signs, courting activist groups, having no job to distract from campaigning, and making at least an hour's worth of cold calls each day to ask strangers for money.

Todd and his stalwart campaign manager in a rare photo showing our exhaustion and exasperation.

expression before telling you that what you really needed to do was get off your ass and go blockwalk.

"Let me just ask you a question," I said, hanging my head out the window.

"Shoot," Todd said. He wiped his forehead with his sleeve. It was a typical Texas fall day, which, in a word, meant it was *hot*.

"Do you, and I mean under any circumstances, ever open your front door if someone knocks on it?"

"Rarely," Todd confirmed without hesitation.

"Follow up question. Do you ever pick up the phone if you don't recognize the number of the caller?"

"No," Todd said. "That's why voicemail is a thing. If it's important, they'll leave a message."

"So blockwalking and phone banking would have zero impact on someone like you?"

"Exactly," Todd said. He gestured and said, "This the house?"

I looked down at my phone, checked the address, and said, "Yep."

"Okay, I'm gonna go knock on this door and wait awkwardly for nothing to happen," Todd said.

I didn't bother to put the Challenger in park; I just put my foot down on the brake and waited as Todd went up to the door, making a small bet with myself whether it would open. If the inhabitants were anything like a Heath Hamrick or a Todd Allen, they wouldn't open the door, even if they were home that day. It was one of the big problems I had with campaigning: so often the activities everyone seemed to think were important would have had zero impact on someone like me. I didn't open my front door. I didn't answer my phone. I didn't look twice at political literature left on my porch (unless to tut-tut at a poorly chosen graphic or bitch about a crooked logo). I didn't seek out a club of people meeting monthly at an area restaurant. I didn't spend a weekend protesting in front of City Hall. And I wasn't friends with anyone who did any of those things. I knew they existed. Hell, I had seen them, shaken their hands, chatted with them at pizza buffets and across a bowl of queso at activist meetings. I just struggled to understand them. My life didn't look like theirs.

It was a bit of a problem, as Kelsie often reminded me.

I have a vivid imagination (after all, I could envision myself as chief of staff to a newly minted congressman, which obviously required a capacity for fantasy that was both wide and wild), but I struggled to understand people who'd cheerfully stand at a door and chat about politics. If someone with political experience is reading this, they probably just snorted and muttered, "Well, that is the problem with the campaign, right there." They wouldn't be wrong.

Knock, knock. No answer.

Todd was back. I glanced at the database. "Four doors down."

"Yup," Todd said, and started to walk.

"I got an email about our yard signs," I mentioned. "It was suggested that we be sure to mention that you were a progressive somewhere on the sign."

Todd shot me a glance. "Don't we already say that we're running as a

Democrat?"

"Yes," I said, "but apparently we need to also mention that you are progressive."

"Okay," Todd said, shaking his head. "So the list of things to put on the sign, so far, is my full name, the district I'm running in, the position I'm running for, my political affiliation, a progressive label, my profession, my sexual orientation, my gender, a notarized college transcript, and . . . what else?"

"I actually think your sign needs to be nothing but a solid block of text laying out your policy positions in language that could in no way be construed as nuanced."

He laughed and walked up to the next door.

Knock, knock.

We had been having the yard sign discussion for a while. It was going to be the single largest campaign expense, so we wanted to get the design right. Fortunately, everyone had opinions about what information needed to be conveyed, and the list of suggestions was not a short one. We took suggestions on designs of every shape and color. We accepted advice on blurbs, slogans, and headings that could fill a billboard, much less a yard sign. We nodded sagely whenever anyone talked about the absolute importance of yard signs in the life of a campaign. The truth, I thought, was that yard signs were important because seeing them out and about in the real world helped your own supporters feel as if they were part of something that was real. No one likes to feel as if they are alone. No one wants to see a dozen signs for Candidate One on their street while they are the only yard sporting a sign for Candidate Two.

No one likes to lose, even in Loserville.

The door Todd had knocked on opened momentarily. Todd had time to utter a phrase or two before the door was shut firmly in his face. He was still wearing a smile as he turned back to the car, but it faded pretty quickly. He was shaking his head a little as he got to the curb.

"I told the guy who I was," Todd said. "He said he was gonna vote for Jan McDowell."

"Then he shut the door in your face?"

"Then he shut the door in my face," Todd confirmed. "Which one next?"

I nodded down the street. "Two houses down, the one with the blue garage door."

Todd nodded, mechanically started walking. "Tell me about that study you were talking about, again—the one about money in politics."

"It's fascinating shit," I said. "Wherever they were from, Stanford, Yale, somewhere like that,[4] they basically said that all the money that was spent on politics, at least on a national level in a general election, was pointless. Ads, yard signs, billboards, canvassing, blockwalking, commercials, it didn't influence how an American would vote."

"How is that possible?" Todd asked.

"Don't ask me, I didn't go to Stanford or Yale."

"So we need to spend money on yard signs because . . . ?"

"Because people want us to," I answered. "Because the more money we spend, and particularly the more money people see us spending, the more people will support you."

"Not my ideas or my policies or even if I'm a decent person," Todd said wonderingly. "Just how much money I spend. What a process."

Up to the next door. *Knock, knock*. Back to the car.

"How long have we been doing this?" Todd asked.

I didn't need to look at the time, but I did. "About an hour. Eric and Mike started a bit earlier in the morning over in Hurst. I think they're wrapping up."

"Okay," Todd said. "I know you've done the research. Tell me how badly we've wasted that hour."

Now, you might think my disdain for retail politics like blockwalking was a bit hypocritical, given my sentiments about the need to reach outside the typical confines of the activist community. You might think I'd *like* the idea of going door to door, having real conversations with real people, especially with my proclivity for *Mr. Smith Goes to Washington*–style politics. You'd be wrong, though, because I had done the research. Turns

---

[4]It was Stanford and Berkley, actually. Kalla, Joshua and Broockman, David E., *The Minimal Persuasive Effects of Campaign Contact in General Elections: Evidence from 49 Field Experiments* (September 25, 2017). American Political Science Review, Stanford University Graduate School of Business Research Paper No. 17-65, Available at SSRN: https://ssrn.com/abstract=3042867.

out that studies had been done on the efficacy of dang near everything involved in the political process, and that included the impact of block-walking. I was actually amazed at how many of the sacred cows of retail politics turned out to be, in one way or another, based on outmoded ideas, unsubstantiated theories, and just plain good old-fashioned nostalgia. When looking backwards meant wearing snappy hats, I was all aboard, but when it meant I was spending a Saturday slowly cruising up and down the streets of Carrollton, I was less enthusiastic.

"Campaigns teach their volunteers to expect perhaps 30 percent of doors will open on any blockwalk, and, on a good day, a blockwalker might have twenty-five actual conversations an hour." I paused. "Most campaigns seem to peg the actual realistic figure at twelve conversations."

Todd didn't look shocked. "So I'm performing below the curve?"

"Substantially," I said dryly. "Apparently you're just not that good at this. This is the door, by the way."

Todd looked up and saw the Trump 2020 flag flying over the garage, shook his head and said, "No, I don't think so. Next?"

"Across the highway. Hop in."

He jumped in, cranked up the AC, and sighed a bit as I maneuvered the car out onto the access road.

"You know," I pointed out, "just one of our better social media posts will see maybe a thousand people engage with it. Maybe four or five thousand people will see it. Takes fifteen minutes to make and post, and we don't have to knock on doors."

"We gotta knock on doors," Todd said.

"It'll take you fifty-four hours to get those same numbers while block-walking," I said.

Todd said, "Fifty-four hours? Really?"

Then the phone rang.

"You have to stop," Kelsie said over the line when I picked up.

"Thank God," I said with relief. I gestured to Todd. "Hey, Kelsie says we can stop knocking on doors."

"No, he has to keep knocking on doors," Kelsie said over the line, no-nonsense. "I meant the campaign has to stop sharing media into the group pages on Facebook."

Todd and I exchanged glances.

"Why is that, Kelsie?" Todd asked.

"We're starting fights," she said. "They don't know how to handle what you're doing. These group pages usually share info about community protests and town halls and an occasional news article. Now, all of sudden the top ten things on the feed are Todd Allen and Todd Allen and Todd Allen. They're calling it spam. The group admins are getting complaints, which means I'm getting complaints."

"That means we're doing something right," Todd said with more good humor than I'd have if I had been walking door-to-door in the Texas heat for an hour.

"No, we're not," Kelsie said. "I just got off the phone with an old PR friend. I asked them to take a look at what we are doing."

"And?" I asked.

"And we got a warning," she said. "We don't look very legit when we go group to group sharing stuff. He recommended that we only post to the campaign account and let other people share our stuff organically. Social media doesn't have a very high return on investment in the long run anyway, and sharing our own material is making the campaign look like amateur hour."

Todd took it in stride.

"Well, I keep saying I'm *not* a politician," he joked.

"Wait," I jumped in. "Are you saying that your friend, who works in public relations, says social media isn't worth it?"

"He's a professional," she said shortly.

"I'm just saying, would he recommend that McDonald's stop putting ads on TV? Rely on organic word of mouth and a quality burger as a business model?"

"They know Todd exists," Kelsie said shortly. "They just don't like what they are seeing."

Todd took a deep breath. "You know . . . I didn't choose to run because there was a lack of good policy ideas among Democrats, Kelsie. I ran because how politics and politicians behave just doesn't make any sense to people like me anymore. I ran because I felt someone from the normal walk of life needed to. Now, I don't want to be a martyr for a lost cause, I really don't, but I'm not going to become something I'm not. I was never going to win a contest of Who's the Better Activist? and that's something voters will either have to accept or, well . . . they'll vote for one of the other guys."

"I understand," Kelsie said. "But the whole point of the campaign is that we don't *want* people to vote for anyone else. These people are ready to vote for a good candidate, and a good candidate can surprise everyone and win in November . . . but that won't happen unless you two realize that I know what I'm talking about, and what I'm talking about right now is a large chunk of primary voters who just don't think you're a good candidate."

Todd said, "I know, Kelsie. I appreciate everything you do."

"You have to give me something to work with," Kelsie added.

"Stick with us idiots a little longer and we'll do our best," Todd promised. "We're gonna get back to knocking on doors, but tell your friend thanks for his advice."

"Which he can keep to himself and/or stuff up his ass," I grumbled after I hung up the phone. Rant mode was activated. "I don't buy it. How can local political groups, theoretically all about local people interacting about local politics, *not* be the place to post about a local politician? They don't care what you think? They don't want a chance to see what you would do on your first day in office?"

Then the phone rang again. It was Kelsie.

Todd shot me a look. "You did make sure to hang up before you suggested that her PR friend could shove his advice up his ass, right?"

"Yep," I said, with more confidence than I felt. Then I answered the phone. "Kelsie, we couldn't possibly have done anything wrong in the last sixty seconds, right?"

"Biggan's raised twenty-five thousand dollars already," she said.

I pulled the car over to the curb and put it in park. "I'm sorry, what?"

"He just posted on Facebook," Kelsie said. "In his campaign's first two weeks they raised over twenty-five thousand dollars in donations." She paused. "It's more money than any candidate in this district has ever raised for a campaign. It's being shared around like crazy. This is all anyone is going to be talking about. If he can raise that much money, people are gonna start asking why Todd or Jan can't. It doesn't look good."

"It isn't good," Todd said grimly. "Who is this guy?"

I already had an answer to that question.

"He's you," I said softly, "if you did things the way Kelsie wanted you to."

Todd didn't respond.

I didn't know a lot at that point about John Biggan, but I still felt as if I had hit the nail on the head (and nothing I learned in the weeks, months, and years since have changed my mind). Biggan and Todd were near mirror images when it came to gender, age, policies, and even profession, with both coming from the world of education. Heck, they both had wives named Lauren. The mirror only began to crack when it came to how they approached politics. Todd was running as the average American outsider while Biggan was running as the ultimate political up-and-comer. From what we had heard, he embraced blockwalking like it was a religious article of faith, spent hours on fundraising calls,[5] cheer-fully courted the leaders of the local activist groups, and ignored social media. In short, he was doing what Kelsie wanted us to do.

"He's doing what a candidate needs to do to win," Kelsie stated. "You two are doing what you *want* to do. That's the difference. And now he's raised twenty-five thousand dollars. And at that first forum next week Todd is going to be asked to explain why he hasn't been able to raise money like John Biggan, the candidate who matters."

Ouch.

After hanging up, Todd looked over at me. "I don't really feel like knocking on any more doors now, do you?"

"I feel like a double quarter pounder and a large order of fries," I said, putting the car back in gear and easing into traffic. I knew there would be a McDonald's nearby; this was America, after all.

---

[5]Todd always struggled with these calls; simply put, he felt he hadn't been raised to ask people for money.

Do Less Better

Tuesday

FROM: kelsie@toddallenforcongress.com
SUBJ: Social Media Use

We need to convince Heath that for our purposes right now email is
more effective at rallying the troops than media posts. Maybe he's not
happy with the email list to date, and we can talk about ways to grow
this list (are we collecting email addresses at doors, coffees, meetings,
and any other interaction with voters responsive to the message?). Social
media should be more for generating interest to go to the site or sign up
for the newsletter, etc.

FROM: toddallen@toddallenforcongress.com
SUBJ: RE: Social Media Use

Not sure he needed convincing on that one. Maybe just a second
voice offering it as an option. Sometimes when you create the menu, buy

the groceries, prepare the meals, serve the meals and clean up, items slip through the cracks.

FROM: kelsie@toddallenforcongress.com
SUBJ: RE:RE: Social Media Use

    Anecdote: do less better. :)

FROM: toddallen@toddallenforcongress.com
SUBJ: RE:RE:RE Social Media Use

    We are trying. :)

FROM: kelsie@toddallenforcongress.com
SUBJ: RE:RE:RE:RE Social Media Use

    I know you are. You're both new to campaigning and doing a damn good job at it.

Thursday

FROM: kelsie@toddallenforcongress.com
SUBJ: RE: Social Media Usage

    Todd,
    I was disappointed to see the campaign ostensibly recruit a friend to post a campaign ad again in Ronnie's Facebook group page, which was also subsequently deleted by the group admin, and I was charged with informing you another time what the group rules are. As I have warned you many times, the campaign's social media tactics are unprofessional, petty, and lack the dignity one would expect from a congres-

sional candidate. For that reason, I don't think you have the maturity or temperament to represent the people of the 24th Congressional District. Effective immediately, I am resigning all associations I have with your campaign, and I will be rescinding all public support and associations as well.

Best of luck.

Questions at the Blue Duck

The parking lot was almost empty by the time I got there. Of course, the Blue Duck Mexican Cantina wasn't exactly lighting up the internet with positive Yelp reviews, so an empty lot on a Thursday night was nothing unusual. I knew what I'd see when I got inside: a few sad and lonely people sitting on faded stools around the bar, watching sports on a single, cracked television screen, and maybe a table or two of diners slowly realizing they'd picked the wrong venue for an exciting night out. The Blue Duck's one virtue (other than a decent basket of fried stuffed jalapeños) was that it was exactly midway between where Todd and I lived, making it a good spot to meet for emergencies like the one awaiting us that Thursday night. It wasn't hard to spot Todd's car, since he had decided to park under the single unbroken streetlamp in the entire lot. Unbroken didn't mean undamaged, however—I brought the Challenger to a stop next to Todd's SUV in a flickering, sputtering halo of dingy light. I figured Todd had chosen the spot for a good reason.

He always did have an eye for the dramatic.

"Doctor," he said curtly, handing me a manila folder. Inside was a single sheet of paper with Kelsie's "resignation" email.

"Jesus," I said. "You brought a print-out?"

He shrugged. "Felt appropriate. Let's get a table."

"Hold on." I was struggling to find a way to ask the question I knew I'd have to ask before the night was out. It wasn't that I couldn't fathom why Kelsie would give the ole *ave atque vale*[1] to the campaign, especially as we shifted our message toward something she didn't necessarily agree with. It was the vitriol and the absolute anger I sensed in that email that made no sense to me. By the time either Todd or I had seen the email and then gone online to find out just what the hell Kelsie was talking about, the offending post had been deleted, leaving us with nothing but questions. I knew one thing for certain: neither Todd nor I had encouraged anyone to go post media on pages that Kelsie had forbidden us to post on, especially after the multiple warnings Kelsie had flung our way. It was a complete fucking mystery, and it was ruining my week.

I was scared it might ruin the campaign, too.

"Look," I told Todd as we stood awkwardly by our cars under that flickering streetlight. "Obviously, we're going to get into this email, and we're gonna figure out how we handle things and what you should write back, but first, there's something I've got to know."

"Okay," Todd said, waiting.

"I've been trying to figure this out, and I just can't. I don't get how we go from *doing a great job* to *fuck you*, and all I can think is . . . well, I gotta ask you a weird question. I think I know the answer, but I gotta ask."

"Shoot," Todd said.

"Okay, well . . . " I finally came out with it. "You didn't, I dunno . . . wave your dick at her or anything?"

Todd laughed.

"I . . . wasn't being funny," I said lamely.

"No, I know. It's just . . . I was going to ask you the same question. Swear to God. I was going to get you a bowl of queso and say, 'Heath,

---

[1] Latin. Hail and Farewell. *Boom*. Education.

you didn't suggest that this campaign would benefit if she'd send you a topless photo or something, did you?' I just couldn't figure out how to bring it up."

"The queso would have been a good start," I confirmed. "Let's go in and get some."

As we headed for the door, I asked, "You think it's sexist that we both jumped to the conclusion that Kelsie was potentially angry at us for sexual harassment?"

"Probably," Todd said. "But we're *benevolently* sexist, remember? And in this case, we can't figure out her sudden shift into anger, and we're grasping at straws."

"Sexist straws," I corrected.

We found a table and spent a good half hour reading through Kelsie's email, line by line. Todd was looking for something he had missed, something that would explain the sudden shift in Kelsie's attitude (at least, as expressed in email) from her messages on Tuesday to her angry resignation on Thursday. I'll admit I was less interested in diving into the reasons for Kelsie's departure than I was into figuring out how her leaving would negatively impact the campaign. Right off the bat, I knew it wouldn't look good—how could it? The female communications director leaving the campaign of a male candidate shortly after the surprise entrance of a third candidate in the race? I knew what people would think. We might as well draft a post for social media now: "The candidate would like to reiterate that no one affiliated with the campaign made crude suggestions or gestures with or about their genitalia to the former communications director."

Without any context, people would draw their own assumptions and conclusions (much as we had), and I was willing to bet hard money that few of them would decide that the break was due to creative differences. What's more, people in the local groups knew Kelsie, and liked her, which automatically placed Todd squarely in the antagonist column. None of that took into account what would happen if Kelsie decided she didn't want to be a silent player in this post-fallout drama. There were already signs that she wasn't just walking off the battlefield with the rest of the Scots; she was gearing up to swing a mean mace with

Longshanks.[2] She had already made a few posts in reply to Allen campaign media being shared on local political pages on Facebook, pointing out that the posts were inappropriate, unprofessional, and unworthy of anyone's time.

"When did she decide to become the Facebook police?" I muttered to myself.

She was angry, that was obvious, and angry people are like snakes: they don't always warn you before they decide to sink their fangs into your shins. Were strategy sessions and campaign discussions about to be leaked to the activist community? The last thing I wanted to worry about was answering a bunch of questions that began, "Kelsie says that you said . . ."

But why was she so angry?

Todd looked at a message on his phone. "It looks like it was Leslie who posted on that activist page and prompted all this."

I was a little surprised. "Leslie? Like . . . the Leslie that teaches with Lauren? The Leslie that hasn't posted anything about the campaign, *ever*? That Leslie?"

"That Leslie," Todd said. "She remembered us asking people to share stuff months ago and just now decided that she wanted to be more involved. She liked the message of the post and wanted to go ahead and start doing more for the campaign by sharing it. It was the RFK graphic, by the way."

"Oh," I said. "That was a good post."

"Yeah. Anyway, that was what set Kelsie off. Leslie shared a post. I didn't know and you didn't know. I think I'll respond to Kelsie by saying that first." He turned his attention back to his phone and spent a minute or two typing while I munched on chips and fried jalapeños. I didn't think Todd's explanation (or his excuse, depending on the point of view) was going to matter, and it definitely wasn't the heart of the conversation we needed to have. Picking up the last of the jalapeños, I looked at Todd and said, "You know she doesn't care who Leslie is or why she posted.

---

[2]Does this make me or Todd the William Wallace in this analogy? And which one of us winds up getting gutted?

This isn't about Leslie."

Todd put down the phone. "You're right."

"This is about Kelsie," I continued. "And it's about us figuring out how someone who said we were doing great suddenly decided to tell us to go fuck ourselves."

Todd tapped the printout in the manila folder. "She didn't actually tell us to go fuck ourselves."

I waved his comment away. "So what are we supposed to take from all this?"

Todd considered for a moment, then snagged a fried jalapeño from the fresh batch the waiter delivered to the table. "I think," he said, "maybe a communications director needs to feel valued for her advice on communications."

"But didn't I lose more arguments than I won with her?" I countered. "We went to bullet points on the website. Every time she asked us to scrub language that she suggested was sexist, we scrubbed it—"

"Even Bobby Kennedy," Todd said.

"Even Bobby Kennedy!" I shot back.

"But she didn't like the moneyball approach," Todd pointed out. "And she wasn't even in the room when we decided we were going to change the campaign's message to We Can Be Better."

I held up a finger. "First, the moneyball approach was not something we came up with out of the blue, it was something your private family life required of the campaign. Second, we did have multiple conversations about our discomfort with the demands of the activist base and portraying the campaign as red-meat-slinging partisan warriors. She told us to get over it; we said no."

"We said no," Todd repeated. "Is that not our answer, right there?"

I popped another jalapeño.

"No, it isn't," I insisted. "That doesn't explain the hostility. I get her frustration with the campaign. But she went from zero to pissed in less time than it takes to tell it, and I don't get it."

Silence fell over the table. A few more jalapeños disappeared. The queso bowl was emptied for a second time. We quietly pondered the unknowable mysteries of the universe. Finally, Todd said, "Okay. The anger is unexplainable to me, and I'm not interested in ordering a third round of jalapeños in order to figure it out. I think Kelsie wanted to help us. I think Kelsie didn't get what she wanted out of the campaign, and I think a lot of that is because we didn't want the campaign to be what she wanted it to be. I'm not bent out of shape about that. I wish we could have ended this with a handshake, and I don't understand why we couldn't. Let's draw a line under it and call it done."

I took a deep breath and said, "You're right. I'm gonna eat the rest of these stuffed jalapeños and then I'm gonna go home and worry about something else until I pass out."

Before we left, Todd wordlessly handed me his phone so I could see what he had written in response to Kelsie. I read:

> *Regarding your departure from the campaign, I wish you nothing but the best. I always appreciated your insight and passion. You were a great sounding board and played an instrumental role in navigating policy so that it was more easily disgusted by folks in the twenty-fourth. I'm sorry to hear you find me and my campaign's maturity and professionalism lacking. . . . Kelsie, you will always have a place within my camp. You were an early soldier in this fight. Keep fighting the good fight, and one day down the road, I hope we can talk politics, family, and the role activist groups are playing in the changing landscape of primary politics.*

"Calm and measured, right?" Todd asked.

I nodded. "Sure, but I think you actually mean digested here."

"What did I say?"

"Disgusted," I pointed out.

"Could go either way," Todd admitted, standing up to leave. "I'll change it before I press send."[3]

We walked out into the night with a lot on our minds (not to mention the grease riding heavily in our stomachs). The primary was no longer a contest between a habitual loser and a newcomer; it was a three-way battle royale and Todd was the one walking into the arena with nothing

---

[3]He didn't.

but a loincloth and a pointed stick. John Biggan had stepped into the race and instantly claimed the mantle of front-runner by producing more cash than I had brought home in my first year as a teacher. The most important campaign event of the year was just a few days away, a forum that would give every activist in the Twenty-Fourth District a venue to watch three candidates tie themselves into knots trying to find different ways to say the same exact things about policy. Our campaign's communications director had resigned in acrimony, somewhat ironically over what I assumed to be a lack of communication. And, not to forget, the candidate's wife was still angry at me for being the living symbol of her husband's selfishness in pursuing a political career.

In other words, we were getting to the part in the movie where the best friend dies tragically to serve as an inspiration to the hero in the third-act climax. That should have worried me, but I had something else on my mind as we walked out into that darkened parking lot. I opened the Challenger door, but paused before ducking inside. There was some-thing I just had to get off my chest before I could call it a night.

"Hey, Todd," I asked hesitantly, "this isn't my fault, is it?"

He looked back at me over the roof of the Challenger. "I was about to ask you the same thing."

Big Enough

They were just beginning to set up the chairs in the auditorium of the Rec Center when Todd, Liz, and I showed up. We were habitual early birds to events during the campaign, and most of the time we'd lend a helping hand, push tables into place, set up folding chairs, and then make ourselves comfortable as the organizers wondered why such notorious assholes were acting like nice guys.[1] Of course, we usually acted like nice guys because we usually were nice guys, a fact that continuously seemed to surprise the people we met in politics, which probably says a lot about politics. It was the night of the first big candidate forum, however, and nerves were running high, so instead of being nice guys, we took a seat in a nearby lounge and tried not to look too worried as we brooded on all the ways we could screw up in the next couple of hours. It was the first time all three candidates were going to be up on a stage together, taking questions from a moderator and giving voters a chance

---

[1]Todd and I once set up the room for a forum hosted by Myra's group. Yes, the Myra of the infamous Article I, Section II phone call. Did she say thank you? I honestly can't remember.

to watch them take fire, speak passionately, and look good doing it.

Liz took a picture with her phone to capture the moment for posterity: Todd looked tense but casual in pressed jeans, a suit coat, and a button-up without a tie, clearly vying for the title of Coolest Teacher in the Room. By contrast, I appeared to have just rolled out of bed and into my campaign uniform—a baby-blue T-Shirt (wrinkled) and a go-to-hell cap (rumpled). In the picture, both of us look lost in deep thoughts of utter significance.

Those thoughts, succinctly summarized, amounted to a rolling repetitive marquee of Holy Shit, Holy Shit, Holy Shit, Holy Shit . . .

Maybe it was just nerves.

Maybe it was just me.

Were we ready for a campaign event important enough that the powers that be decided it needed to be held in a municipal auditorium instead of a building primarily focused on serving fried foods? We'd been practicing for weeks, rolling through potential questions and the best possible answers. We'd identified areas where Todd might get tripped up or get thrown a gotcha. Watch out for a question on your voting record, I had told Todd repeatedly. Be ready for some kind of question that accuses you of being a secret Republican. Try to sound confident, but not insanely naïve when you suggest that money isn't the most important thing in a campaign.

In other words: Don't fuck this up, buttercup.

That's what I thought but not what I said. I was a teacher after all, so I knew when to prep and when to step off the gas before the big test day. Besides, there was an elephant in the room, or at least the building—I had spotted Kelsie's Prius out in the parking lot. She hadn't wasted any time in scraping off the Todd Allen for Congress sticker on the bumper. Her right rear tire was also riding a little low, but that probably wasn't pertinent.

"She really should get that tire checked," I mused aloud as the three of us waited.

Well, I wasn't exactly known for keeping conversations centered on the pertinent or the scintillating. Besides, I'd rather go ahead and grab the bull, elephant, or former communications director by the horns. I

The infamous picture snapped by Liz as Todd and I waited for the candidate forum to start.

had a campaign to run, and Todd had a forum to attend, and neither one of us could afford even an ounce of additional self-doubt. For arrogant assholes, we carried around a surprising amount of self-doubt as is. Luckily, Liz picked up the Kelsie ball and ran with it so I didn't have to. She showed more outright anger at the situation than either Todd or me—she was mad and she wasn't afraid to make her feelings known.

"She sat with us at dinner," Liz said, voice low and dare I say dangerous. "She came to our house. She used our toilet! It was an invasion!"

"I think she even lost her phone in the cushions of the couch that one time," I pointed out.

"How are you so matter-of-fact about all this?" Liz asked incredulously.

I shrugged. "I can throw shit if you want, but they'd probably ask me to leave."

Truth be told, I was still too mystified to be mad. It's hard to be angry when you're confused, a fact of life I've internalized after having children. Many a tantrum has been headed off in the Hamrick household by posing a sudden and perplexing question totally unrelated to the potential meltdown at hand. Anyway, I might not have been spitting nails, but my mind was still all caught up in Kelsie's bizarre actions. I know Todd had professed to being over the Kelsie situation, but I didn't have that luxury. Kelsie was the unexplainable and unpredictable development popping up on U2 photos over Cuba, and either those missiles had to go or there was going to be one really big mushroom cloud hanging roughly over Hurst, Texas. I turned to Todd to mention this handy-dandy Cuban missile crisis metaphor but stopped short. There was something a bit different about him that night that had been bugging me since we walked in, and I suddenly realized what it was.

"You think the people of Metropolis will figure out your secret identity?" I asked.

He looked over at me, a little confused. I gestured at his face.

"When did you start wearing glasses?" I asked.

"I've always had glasses."

"I've never seen you wear them, and I've known you since college."

"Well, I'm wearing them now," Todd said. He leaned forward, quietly added, "I thought they might help me stand out from the other middle-aged white guy on stage."

"Ah," I said. "The one not wearing glasses. Nice."

"I thought so," Todd said, then went back to staring at his notes.

The doors to the civic center opened and John Biggan walked in with his campaign manager, a young man named Miller that I'd seen working for various candidates who had no chance in hell of chalking up a win come November. Miller looked our way and smirked, then turned to Biggan to share something they both apparently found hilarious. Their laughter echoed down the hall, together with a chorus of greetings that met them as they walked into the auditorium. I turned and caught Todd's gaze fixed on the now empty hallway, saw his eyes narrow ever so slightly behind those glasses. I had to admire his control. I wasn't going to emulate it, but I admired it.

"I'm really not liking them," I confessed.

Todd laughed and relaxed into the chair. "Let's go over it one more time."

I nodded, cracked open my notebook, and found the right page. "Well, the gist is that this is a forum, which, next to T-ball, is the most pointless event conceived by the mind of man. There's a moderator that will ask the questions and give each of the three candidates a chance to

My typical pose during the campaign: judgmental.

answer it. It's not a debate: y'all don't get to interact with each other or challenge each other's bullshit. My guess is that most people here are hoping to see one or all of you trip up on language or say something stupid."

"Like when someone throws a chair on *Jerry Springer*," Liz added.

"Exactly like that," I said. "In fact, if shit goes sideways, you might wanna keep the chair thing in your back pocket." I looked back down at my notes. "Now, here's what I think: Jan is going to be Jan. She's consistent and predictable. She's got no passing gear. She'll be the activist up there, the one who's been in line the longest, the one with the progressive bona fides."

"Right," Todd said.

I took a deep breath. "Biggan is gonna be the policy guy."

Todd tensed, like I knew he would. "I know I've asked this before, but why does *he* get to be the policy guy?"

"Because people want him to be," I said. "He keeps saying he's a brain scientist, whatever the fuck that is—people think he's got the high card as far as ideas go."

Todd grumbled a bit at that, and I couldn't blame him. On the same day that Kelsie had decided to resign, another supporter, Patty, had messaged Todd to let him know that she would no longer be supporting him either. The reason, dear Patty informed us, was that she found Biggan's lengthy policy explanations as laid out on his website to be both in-depth and nuanced. She actually used that term, *nuanced*, and it took everything Todd had not to remind Patty that she had been sitting right *there* in the booth, eating bad pizza and nodding right along with Ronnie, Handlebar, and everyone else urging him to replace his own nuanced policies with bullet points.

Regardless, Patty was out, and she added that she'd set up a monthly automatic donation to the John Biggan campaign.

Liz looked worried. "If Todd can't have ideals and he can't have ideas, what does that leave?"

"Stories," I answered.

"Stories?"

"Stories," I repeated, rubbing my hands together. I turned a few pages in my notebook, found the page I wanted, and cleared my throat. "Mr. Allen, how do you feel we should confront the onslaught of gun violence, particularly mass shootings, in this country?"

Todd got into character. He leaned back in his chair and adjusted his glasses. "Well, I'm glad you asked me that, Bob. A few weeks ago my wife Lauren and I got to attend a concert, which is not something we get to do all that often with two kids at home. I should have been pretty happy that I was spending an actual date night out with my wife, but as I walked up, I couldn't help but notice all the apartment buildings overlooking the venue. I couldn't help but think about what I'd do if shots rang out. Escape routes. Keeping Lauren safe. Thoughts like that, thoughts I'm willing to bet most of you have had at a concert, or a football game, or even dropping your kids off at school. Those are the times we live in. Now, we can change it, one issue, one crime, at a time. Rather than focusing our efforts and rhetoric on some big idea of gun control, we need a laser focus. Take bump stocks off the market and we maybe prevent another Vegas. Tighten up oversight and reform the database system and maybe we prevent another Sutherland Springs. We have to start somewhere."

Liz started an appreciative clap.

"Oh, we have more," I said, then turned back to Todd. "Mr. Allen, how would you mend the broken mess of our country's immigration system?"

Todd cleared his throat and leaned forward to look right at Liz. "When you work in an urban school district like I do, immigration reform isn't an abstract concept: it has a face, it has a name, and it sits in the front row of my classroom. Folks, every day, I teach students who were brought here when they were younger. DREAMers. This is their home. This is the only country and culture they have ever known. Now, I think this country should not be in the business of evicting our own. Ever."

"Wow," Liz said. "Hold for the applause."

"Sure, if he doesn't fuck it up," I noted.

Todd echoed, "If I don't fuck it up. What we figured was that every issue has to start with a story, and that's something I know how to do. I'm a storyteller. Heath's a storyteller. One way or another, we've been trying to tell a good story since college. They ask about immigration, they ask about health care, they ask about my voting record, whatever they ask about, I'm going to start with a story and then lead them to my policy position. Everyone up on that stage is gonna have the same policy beliefs anyway, so the least I can do—"

"Is to have a story," Liz finished for him. She looked over at me, and I swear to God it was with pride. I smiled back. There isn't a whole lot that feels out of reach when someone like Liz is proud of you, and that's the truth.

"Your hubby hasn't been wasting *all* his time," Todd said matter-of-factly. Then he sighed and stood up. "Alright. Let's go do this thing."

Liz and I skipped the tables and chairs and went straight to the far end of the room where we sat on the ground with our backs to the wall.

This was my typical post during any campaign event. I sat with my notebook at the ready and my laptop open, mostly to discourage anyone from coming up to start a conversation. I kept the brim of my cap pulled low and waited to see what the night had in store for the Todd Allen for Congress campaign. Beside me, Liz pulled out a big yellow notepad and purple pen, ready to grade the candidate responses and maybe write sarcastic comments in the margins that she could share with me via an elbow nudge and a giggle. Both of us were looking up on stage at the three candidates awkwardly sitting on bar stools, waiting for the moderator to begin.

"Todd does look like the coolest teacher in the room," Liz whispered.

Jan, on the other hand, looked as if she would rather be anywhere else than sitting up on that stage. She looked angry—she always looked angry—and it didn't take a huge mental leap for me to imagine that she was more than a little pissed that two guys she had never heard of before the campaign were swooping in to try to steal her nomination. She wasn't halfway through her introduction before I realized that she wasn't having her best night. Some nights, Jan just sounded like what she was: a grandmother who was passionate about progressive politics. Other nights, she struggled, and her tone and volume fluctuated oddly. This was one of those nights.

And then there was John Biggan.

Todd had been right: where he had gone teacher casual, Biggan had opted for a dark suit and striped tie. He looked a little uncomfortable, perched up there on that bar stool, but I knew it wouldn't last. I'd done my homework. As a youth and through college, Biggan had been in theater productions and stage plays, and I was willing to bet any amount of money that he was at home up on a pedestal with all the lights and eyes focused squarely on centerstage. Of the three candidates, Biggan was the one with the most effortless presence, the smoothest charisma. He was the one that could make the audience laugh and feel relaxed and then switch gears and launch into the intricacies of policy, all without skipping a beat or dropping the ball. Todd's strength, by contrast, came in the Q&A periods, in answering questions and making those one-on-one connections and extemporaneous comments. I had a hunch that once things got off script, Biggan would stumble a bit, and that would be our chance (if, in fact, we had one in hell).

Of course, we had to make it to the Q&A period first, and we had a long way to go.

"Hello," John Biggan said as he took the mic. He went on to introduce himself as John Biggan, a brain scientist, an Eagle Scout, and a candidate for Congress.

Liz nudged me sharply. "What is a brain scientist?" she hissed.

"It's a mystery," I said.

My phone buzzed. I looked down and saw a text message from Lauren, who was watching the live feed of the forum from home, where she was valiantly trying to corral two young kids and write a dissertation.

What the fuck is a brain scientist? the message read.

It's a mystery, I typed back.

Up on stage, Biggan had gone on to explain that he had become an Eagle Scout for a simple reason: he just wanted to help the world and make it better. No, that isn't exactly right—what he said was that he wanted to Make It Better. Before he finished his intro, I had already snapped a pencil in two in sheer frustration. Looking down, I saw that I had scrawled the following in my notebook: *Fucker stole our slogan!*

Now, look, there is nothing new under the political sun. I know that. You show me a snappy slogan, I'll find half a dozen campaigns that have used it or something like it. Todd and I have a running joke that somehow our phones are bugged, and we have spy satellites trained on our homes because every so often we recognize a scene in a movie, a line of dialogue in a book, or an argument in a *Times* editorial, as something we've tossed around before, sometimes years earlier.[2] So, no, I didn't really think the Biggan campaign had snatched our slogan; if they were in the habit of stealing good ideas, or at least workable ones, they would have fixed that crooked logo of theirs.

But as Biggan was mid-introduction I had spotted a familiar face in

---

[2] One example: our campaign volunteer in the snappy suits, Mike, tested the waters for his own run for office a few years later and I designed a logo that took the initial of his last name (A) and weaved it into a star that hearkened back to the insignia on old Air Force jets (Mike was ex-Air Force). Damned if the character of John Walker wasn't wearing that same symbol as Captain America on Disney Plus five years later!

the crowd. Kelsie was standing by a side exit with a few of the usual suspects: Ronnie, Handlebar, Patty, and even Myra. She was nodding as Biggan talked about making the world better, and suddenly I got it. We had wanted Kelsie to be a bridge to the activist community, but what she was, first and foremost . . . was an activist. It was why Biggan's rallying cry of Make It Better, implying not only a desire for progressive change but a willingness, even an eagerness, to take action to make it happen, was resonating with her. It was why Todd's competing vision, We Can Be Better, never had: it was as much about *how* things changed as what changed.

"Huh," I said aloud, thinking that Todd was right. The time had come to close the book on the chapter of the campaign titled "The Kelsie Conundrum." It was political James Joyce. I was never going to understand it anyway.

Then Todd took the microphone to answer his first question. The moderator, a local news anchor, asked him about health care, and Todd smiled. "You know, I've got a story about that."

He was going to be fine.

The forum went well. Todd didn't knock every answer out of the park, but he got over his nervousness quickly and gave the audience something different from what they were getting from the other candidates. It wasn't always good, but it was different. The audience didn't always appreciate or relate to the way he approached policy, but I thought he managed to both hold his own on the details and stand out on a crowded stage. Liz was grading him at a solid B+, and she's a tough grader. Jan was consistently awful, having exactly the kind of bad night I had called for her earlier, and Biggan was a roller coaster. When he was good, he was great, engaging the audience and commanding the stage; when he was bad, he was a substitute teacher realizing he was expected to lecture on Shakespeare when his degree was in Chemistry.

Then the question-and-answer period started, and Todd's star began to shine, just as it always did, and Biggan stumbled a bit more. It made sense: Todd was a teacher, engaging one-on-one with students who needed it, and Biggan was a professor, lecturing on a stage. He'd get a lot better as the campaign went on; I knew he would, an actor improving with every chance to run his lines. But for the moment, Todd was in his element, and I thought he had the advantage. Hopefully I wasn't the only one.

Then Liz elbowed me hard in the ribs again, calling my attention out of the land of political daydreams, and whispered, "Listen!"

So I listened.

John Biggan was announcing something new. He informed the audience that he had just given his two weeks' notice to his job, and starting soon, he'd be able to give 100 percent of his time and efforts to the campaign. He framed it as something that was necessary—hell, expected—of any legitimate candidate: they couldn't expect to run for office and keep a nine-to-five job. The district and the voters, I remember him suggesting, deserved a candidate who could devote every ounce of himself to winning the election.

There was a smattering of applause, maybe even a lot of it. From my seat in the back, I saw some heads nodding, some appreciative murmurs, some enthusiastic supporters offering applause. I also saw something else, the issue I could use to recast the race in Todd's favor without ever having to say a negative word about either of his opponents. As Biggan was proudly bragging about quitting his job in order to devote himself to politics, at least half the room was seeing him as he saw himself—as a selfless crusader who was making a sacrifice in order to give all his attention to the campaign. The other half was thinking what I was thinking: Well, I'm glad you can afford to take six months off, but here in the real world, normal people can't survive when they miss a paycheck.

A tall, stately woman with dark hair stood up and talked about recently losing her job in the high-tech sector at an age when people are usually starting to think about retirement, not starting over. Her name was Sara, and her question was essentially one of desperation, a cry for someone to acknowledge that she and others were in dire straits and needed help. Later in the campaign, Biggan would have handled the question differently. Later, he would have charmed Sara and recognized that she needed support and understanding, not just a policy paper on immigration policies in the high tech industry.

But that was later. That night, Biggan stumbled a bit, or misread the room or the person asking the question, or maybe just made an honest mistake (and God knows Todd and I had made plenty of our own since the campaign started in the spring). What he wound up suggesting or implying to Sara, who we came to find out had multiple degrees in her field, was that she needed opportunities to go back to community college to obtain more education to compete in the modern world.

Biggan's answer absolutely infuriated Sara, and it was not hard to see why. He didn't know it yet, but he'd just defined both campaigns, his and ours—the elitist, wealthy activists and the working-class, pay-check-to-paycheck realists. It was a label he never succeeded in shaking off.

Todd walked up to the edge of the stage. He didn't take the micro-phone. He took off his glasses and looked at Sara. "I'm sorry. I'm sorry that happened to you and I'm sorry you're having to deal with it and I'm sorry nothing I can say tonight is going to fix it. I'm very sorry. I'd love to talk to you more when this event wraps up, okay?" He had no micro-phone, but the audience didn't have any trouble hearing him; he was an ex-coach, remember. Members of that fraternity have the Voice, like that kid in *Dune*.

"Look," he told everyone as he stood at the edge of that stage, "I'm not someone with wealth to burn and time on their hands. I'm just . . . a guy. Just a normal guy who goes to work every day to put food on the table, then goes out to campaign in the few hours he has left in the evening. When I talk about healthcare reform, it is because my wife and I sometimes have to decide if our kid is really sick enough to take to the doctor. When I talk about tax reform, it is because I know what a few hundred dollars a month would mean to my family. And when I talk about running for Congress, about doing this great, big thing that someone like me has no business doing . . . it's because I'm a bit pissed that bigger people aren't doing more."

He seemed to run out of energy and sag a bit. Quietly, he finished, "I wish I was bigger so I could do more for all of us." Then he looked over at Sara. "And I wish I had a better answer for you, Sara. It's my first forum, you know."

There was some applause and some chuckles and some stone-faced silence, but from two spectators at the very back of the room, there was nothing but the highest marks of all: respect. As Todd mingled and the crowds thinned, Liz hugged my arm. "I'm glad you're doing this."

I guess sometimes a cause and a candidate can be big enough.

Highlighted

The secret inner workings of the Todd Allen for Congress campaign could be found in two places, and unfortunately neither of those places were a high-tech vault under the Las Vegas strip. The first was a series of whiteboards in a spare bedroom at my house. I say *spare*, but what I really mean is that it usually housed boxes that had never been unpacked and junk I hadn't gotten around to throwing away yet. I had colonized the room in the name of the Allen campaign back in the spring, which basically meant that I had done my best to clear a path from the door to the wall where I hung up the whiteboards. Aside from the boards, there was my notebook, a collection of doodles, smart-ass comments, and political prognostication where I kept a day-to-day record of Todd's run for office. It still sits on my desk, by the way, the blue cover worn and warped, the pages bulging with inserts and business cards and little scraps of unadulterated political savvy. It's a little bit like that diary from *Indiana Jones*, only you couldn't find the Holy Grail with it, and Hitler never signed it.

Think of it as a rough first draft of what you're reading now.

As the Christmas season began to roll our way, one word kept appearing on those whiteboards and scrawled on the pages of that note-book, often circled, underlined, and dragging along a pack of anxious exclamation marks. That word, boys and girls, was *endorsements*. Typi-cally, they didn't matter just all that much in Loserville because there was usually only one candidate vying for the nomination; the lack of an endorsement only meant that you'd pissed on the fire of the activist leader in charge. The 2018 election, however, was a whole new beast when it came to Loserville, and suddenly there were several candidates clamoring for the honor of getting their ass kicked by the Republicans in November. Endorsements, in other words, mattered.

"I'm not sure how much they matter, though," I said as Todd and I walked through the doors of a club meeting in Dallas County.

"If going through this process has taught us anything," Todd remind-ed me, "it is that we can't be really sure that anything we do matters in the long run." He paused and said hello to the greeter at the doors. "But . . . it can't hurt. Better to have an endorsement and not need it than find out we need it and don't have it."

I grumbled a bit, making a mental note to mark down what he'd said in my notebook.[1] The process for endorsements was remarkably similar for every political group, activist club, association of interested parties, or Democratic organization of name-your-choice-of-hyphenated-Amer-icans. Sometimes Todd would be asked to meet with a small interview committee of club officers/elected officials, but most often the groups wanted a bit more spectacle involved. Usually, that meant the candi-dates would be asked to attend a forum, answer questions submitted by the group members, then stand in a back room and wait anxiously for votes to be counted and an endorsement announced. Then the winner would thank the room and the losers would slink away . . . until the next day, when a different group would hold a different forum for a different endorsement.

I grabbed Todd's arm suddenly.

"What?" he asked.

I couldn't answer right away. My mind was still trying to process what

---

[1] You know . . . for posterity.

my eyes were seeing, a little bit like the bridge officer of the *Titanic* needing some clarification from the crow's nest on what, exactly, they meant when they reported sighting an iceberg ahead. Did that mean a couple of miles off, or did that mean . . . ? Oh. Well, shit.

"I really fucking hate democracy sometimes," I managed to say finally. Todd didn't ask for clarification because by that point he had looked down at the endorsement ballot in my hands and seen for himself exactly where the iceberg was. He didn't say anything for a long while, just stood there looking down at that ballot, making a noise low in his throat that could have been a *Hmmmmmm* or could have been something a lot more primal.

Right there on the ballot, members of the group were asked to check the box by their preferred candidate. Todd was listed right alongside Jan McDowell and John Biggan, but only Jan's name had been highlighted. Looking down at the other races featured on the ballot, I could see that in each race, the organizers had taken a yellow highlighter and marked the name of a preferred candidate.

Goddamn, I thought, they might as well have stood up there and introduced the candidates by saying, "And finally, this is Jan McDowell, the one you'll be voting for if you know what's good for you."

"Well," Todd finally said, "I think I'm ready to answer that question you were asking."

"What question?" I managed to sputter out. I was still fuming.

Todd crumpled up the ballot. "About how much this matters."

The rest of the event was a bit anticlimactic after that. Todd, Jan, and John (whom I had finally decided to mentally grace with his first name) got up in front of everyone, introduced themselves, answered the same policy questions they had answered in forums a dozen times before, tried not to say something stupid, and then thanked everyone for their time. I didn't stick around in the audience to watch the voting happen; instead, I went into the storage area that was being used as a green room, which on nights not hosting Democratic primary events was packed with cleaning supplies and not candidates for public office. Looking around the room, it was easy to see nothing but stereotypes and clichés, which apparently aren't just limited to bad novels and crummy TV shows.

I wondered if every back room at every political event in Loserville, Republican or Democrat, north or south, coast to coast, was a similar, interchangeable collection of standardized political bobbleheads.

"Let's take a little tour around the room," I muttered, trying to keep my voice low.

Todd nodded his assent with a neutral expression.

"First, we have a group that makes up maybe 65 percent of the attendees at any political event," I said. "If you see a person in a suit and tie who doesn't seem that eager to talk to you, you're probably meeting one of the umpteen Judicial Candidates Who Might as Well Have No Name or one of their siblings, the Collective of County Office Candidates. They are either running for a seat that a brain-damaged sea otter would win due to gerrymandering or they're getting set to get trounced by twenty points. Either way, they are here to beef up the audience attendance numbers and eat up at least a half hour of time introducing themselves at each and every meeting."

"Fair," Todd said, starting to smile.

I gestured subtly at someone else. "Okay, then we have the activist. Let me tell you what they believe in: that you are wrong. Doesn't matter what subject, you're wrong, fuck you for existing, and they will find ways that you are not only wrong, but demonstrably racist, sexist, or morally bankrupt. They are the champions of ists and isms. They, too, will lose by twenty points come November, but they don't care about that as much."

Todd couldn't hide it anymore. He was smiling, and now he wanted to get into the game.

"Alright," he said and pointed at someone else. "There's always a Central Casting Guy at these things. Perfect hair. Perfect suit. Smiles constantly. Wife. Two kids. Dog."

"You could be the Central Casting Guy," I said, squinting at him as if I were examining him for minute flaws. "You'd probably need better clothes, though. And a dog."

"Gives me something to work toward," Todd admitted. Then he nodded his head over at a woman who was being trailed by a camera crew. "And then we come to the Attention Junkie. Good looking and knows it.

Sam got bored during one of Todd's speeches and ran up to his daddy, who scooped him up and continued speechifying without missing a beat.

Posts stuff to Instagram that verges on salacious. Has a look on their face as if they have just realized that they can make a pretty decent living being a perpetual candidate."

"Don't forget the Fighter Pilot," I said, and now it was me who was laughing. "Sometimes it's jets, sometimes it's helicopters. Submarines barely acceptable. Sexy because they constantly remind you that they've done really cool shit, and this is a step down. Closely related to the Crimefighter, the crusading ADA or law enforcement officer who is ready to trade a badge for a shot at the ballot."

"And sometimes there are the rare, elusive, but always entertaining Assholes," Todd said with finality. "Among which we would undoubtedly number."

"Only because I never won the Top Gun trophy," I pointed out.

"Among other things," Todd said before another candidate moved our way, and we had to stop entertaining ourselves and start being sociable.

The night ended in a predictable fashion, the highlighted candidates won, and Todd and I went home with nothing to show for it but a few new entries in that notebook of mine. It was one of a hundred similar nights and comparable events, a confused blur of policy questions, glad-handing, tut-tutting, and too much time spent in back rooms mingling with other candidates who were all beginning to get the bags under their eyes that spoke of too many nights at too many forums. In a way, I realized, the other candidates had become our roadies, and we had become theirs. In the back room, everyone lent a hand, everyone offered a drink, everyone bitched about the same things and complained about their schedules, and everyone sympathized. As much as the members of the Back Room Irregulars would snipe and snicker and take a decent shot at stabbing each other in the back when out in the world, they'd take off the masks, put down the knives, and call a truce while backstage.

"You know," Todd said as we walked out that night, "I don't trust these people any further than I could throw them. I don't enjoy spending time with them. We wouldn't be friends in the real world."

"But?" I prompted.

"But, I'll say this: they put their names on the ballot. They're in that room. They stand up and say, 'Okay, world, take your shots.'" He shrugged. "They stand up, is all. Most people don't."

"Most people don't."

I never learned to like most of the people I met in the back rooms of primary politics. Hell, I never learned to like most of the people in the front of those rooms, either, and Todd's opponents and my detractors wasted no time pointing that out. During the campaign, I felt as if the activist community and the political regulars who should have welcomed a couple of teachers into the fold had instead told us we weren't welcome or wanted, and, besides, we were assholes. I lost count of the times someone accused me of a moral or ethical or progressive failure, much less a failure of political strategy.

But even so, I want to make this clear, right now and for all time: Todd was right that night. Yes, I made fun of them, and yes, I could cheerfully chuck the lot of them into the nearest ocean.

But they stood up. They were there. They took the shots. They were on a ballot.

It does matter.

Even to an asshole like me.

All the Best Heath Stories
Involve Vomit

T his, I thought to myself, is awkard as hell. I was wearing a suit
and tie, something I typically did only for job interviews and
funerals, but that wasn't the reason I was uncomfortable. Not the main
reason, anyway. I was sitting at a table at the front of a meeting room
in a Chinese resteraunt with Jan McDowell and John Biggan, who had
just introduced themselves, and someone was handing me a microphone.
Todd was nowhere in sight; he wasn't even in the same state that particular night.

Dig deep, I told myself, wondering how the hell I got into fucked-up
situations like running a congressional campaign that required me to
make occasional public appearances. I took the microphone somewhat
hesitantly and told the crowd, "Hello. I, uh . . . well, I'm going to throw
a bit of a wrench in things here, because, uh . . . I'm not Todd Allen."

There was only the politest of chuckles from the audience.

I cleared my throat and plunged ahead, trying to ignore the glares
from this particular forum's organizer, an activist named Meredith who,

unbeknownst to her, had the most in common with me that evening: neither one of us wanted Heath Hamrick to be on that dais introducing himself. "So . . . my name is Heath Hamrick, and I'm a teacher, just like Todd. I've known him for over fifteen years, I'm his campaign manager, and he's my best friend. He, Lauren, and the kids are in Mississippi tonight, burying a loved one. He wanted me to convey how sorry he is that he could not be here, and how grateful he is that you are allowing me to speak and answer questions for him." I paused. "So . . . thanks. Thanks a lot."

I glanced over at Meredith, thinking how much easier things would have been if she had just told Todd that not only no, but hell no, he couldn't have a surrogate appear at her group's forum. I'd come damn close to getting my wish earlier in the evening, anyway, when I strolled up to Meredith to introduce myself (for about the tenth time during the campaign) and remind her that Todd was out of state and that I was his poor substitute. She'd grimaced and decided that she'd never told Todd that I could speak for him (shock) and the only way she'd allow it to happen was if the other candidates were cool with it.

"Well?" Liz asked expectantly as I strolled back over to the table where we were wrapping up our pre-forum buffet dinner.

"They are cool with it." I slipped into the booth beside her and wondering if the egg-noodle soup was still lukewarm.

I felt a headache coming on—and maybe something more. The world was floating around in front of my eyes as if it had come ever so slightly unmoored from reality. There was a faint ringing in my ears. The lights in the buffet were a little bright, the noise from the diners a little too loud.

Liz noticed, because of course she did. One way or another, she's been watching out for me ever since our first date.

"Hey," she said softly. "You okay? Is it your head?"

I patted her hand. "Just a little nervous about screwing up tonight. Todd doesn't deserve that."

Liz kissed my cheek and took her seat in the audience, front and center (with her yellow pad and purple pen), and I took my own place beside John Biggan up at the front of the room. He watched as I laid out my notes in front of me, a mess of type-written stump answers and handwritten exhortations, warnings, and maybe even some kind of spell to ward off evil spirits and trick questions. His eyebrow arched up ever so slightly. Then he smiled, welcomed me to the table, and wished me good luck. I'll say this about John: just like Todd, he knows the toll it takes to stand in front of people confidently, and he always offered respect where it was due.

His logo was still crooked, though.

Then the nightmare started in earnest, the questions were posed to candidates (and one surrogate), and I spent half my time wondering when Freddy Krueger would emerge from the kitchen in a chef's hat. There were no surprises, no shocking moments, just the usual grab-bag of progressive policies with minute differences of style, rather than substance, bandied about by politicians who were more than used to it by now. For my part, I managed not to throw up or call the moderator a bad name, kept to my script, and tried to remember that I was a teacher who prided himself on being the best damn storyteller in any given building. I'd like to say that I gave Jan and John a run for their money, but then, John, especially, had raised a lot more of it than I had, so he probably didn't have to worry about running after It at all.

And the world was still off-kilter, floating ever so slightly to starboard (if you're nautically inclined).

Then the moderator asked about healthcare, and I found myself telling the room exactly why I looked so pale that night.

"So, you might have noticed that I'm not my usual cheerful self," I told them, and enough of them were familiar with my reputation to fill the room with appreciative laughter. "It's not just that I'm nervous, though I am. I've spent all night hoping I wouldn't screw up because Todd is my friend, and I don't want to let him down. My wife wanted me to stay at home tonight."

I pointed her out to the audience. She blushed, and not just because I had singled her out. She knew where this story was going.

"A few days ago," I told them, "I reached down to unplug my vacuum cleaner from the wall and something weird happened. I got dizzy. I felt sick to my stomach. I had to sit down for a minute. A couple of hours later it happened again. I looked down to take a knife out of a kitchen drawer . . . and suddenly the world just came unglued. They call it vertigo, and it's not just dizziness. Have you ever gone up to the top of a skyscraper and looked down and got that feeling as if you might fall? Yeah, imagine that multiplied a couple of hundred times. Also imagine it not ending, not even when you collapse to the ground and everything you know tells you that you're lying still, but your eyes and something inside your head is screaming that you are falling. That's vertigo, and that's what happened. I fell because I couldn't not fall. I couldn't feel my limbs, and oh, by the way, I was throwing up and I couldn't stop. I thought I was having a stroke. That's when my wife came home and found me lying on the kitchen floor next to the vomit. She was going to call an ambulance."

I paused.

They were listening, and why not? It was a room full of people who were mostly retired, looking down the backside of the hill of life, and I had missed my guess if most of them hadn't experienced a medical emergency that scared the living shit out of them. For that moment, if never again, I was relatable.

Then I told them why she hadn't called an ambulance that day.

I told them about lying there, wondering if I was dying, wondering if all those bowls of queso had finally caught up with me and this was what a heart attack felt like. I told them about how it feels when a part of your body that had previously been totally reliable (not to mention under total control) suddenly decided, Fuck it, time to go nuts. I told them how scared I felt for Liz, who walked in the door and found her brand-new husband lying on the ground covered in vomit, moaning, and crying. I told them what it felt like to have my eyes fiercely shut but nevertheless feel as if everything around me was heaving on a heavy sea and if I didn't catch my balance I'd fall.

But she didn't call the ambulance, and I didn't make her. You want to know why?

The audience at the forum did, even Meredith. Even Jan and John were on tenterhooks.

"We can't afford it," I told them matter-of-factly. "I thought I was having a stroke. Liz thought I might be dying. But . . . we can't . . . afford . . . an ambulance. So Liz asked if I could get to the car so she could drive me to the hospital. And when it became obvious that I couldn't get to my feet, she asked if I could crawl. So that's what I did, folks: I crawled from the kitchen out into the driveway and into my wife's car."

Liz absolutely hates it when I tell this story, so I don't. In fact, this was the one time I told it, and Liz still thinks Todd owes her a pretty big one. I think it is because she's ashamed that she kept her head when someone she loved had lost his. I'm glad she did. She took command in that kitchen, and I realized I might not be dying after all. With that being the case, I had already scared her enough so maybe I needed to reach down deep and see if I could fucking crawl a little. Turns out I could, and I was glad I did, and I was even more thankful that Liz was there, keeping her cool so I could attempt to regain mine.

"I crawled," I told them. "And I bet many of you would, too. Because healthcare in this country is a mess. Our insurance system is broken, and at best only turns catastrophic debt into crippling debt. And if Todd were here, he'd say that this isn't just about insurance: it is about costs. Eighty percent of the cost for research and development of new medicines is paid for by the federal government—by Todd, by my wife Liz, by you, and by me. Yet drug companies are allowed to take that money, develop a new drug, and then patent it. And control the price on it. And here is the kicker: there is legislation, on the books right *now*, that allows the government to step in and set a price cap on those drugs. Todd would ask, 'Why aren't we using it?' He would want you to ask the same thing. And while you were at it, he'd ask why, in the greatest country on Earth, someone would ever lie in their own vomit and decide to crawl to the car because they couldn't afford the ambulance."

I passed the microphone to the next contestant, pleased that I had scored at least one hit that night. I knew audiences. I could read them like a book, and I knew that they were listening that night. What's more, I knew I had them. They agreed 100 percent with everything I said and the way I said it.

Now if only my eyes would stop bouncing when I closed them.

For the curious, I was eventually, after attacks of more lasting severity, diagnosed with Meniere's Disease, a disorder involving the inner ear that isn't very well understood by medical science. It involves a grab bag of fun and delightful symptoms, including attacks of crippling vertigo, severe nausea, exhaustion, tinnitus, and eventual complete loss of hearing in the affected ear (or ears). It is incurable, but there is a treatment: sometimes a surgery of the inner ear, designed to drain excess fluid buildup from the ear into the spinal column, can mitigate the severity of attacks. I'd finally go under the knife about a year after the campaign, and about a month after an attack put me on the bedroom floor, unable to move and pissing into a Gatorade bottle, for about eighteen hours.

You know what is a trigger for Meniere's attacks?

Stress. Alcohol. Salt.

Luckily, none of that was present on the campaign trail.[1]

The nightmare didn't end without reminding me that I was, after all, in enemy territory, and I needed to watch my back. It came with the question I always dreaded, which was a demand from someone in the audience to explain Todd's puny voting record. Myra strikes again.

"You know," I said, meeting the question head-on, "in the last election over 95 percent of Texans didn't vote, but Todd did. He cast a ballot for Hillary Clinton. You might not know that 46.9 percent of Americans didn't vote, period, and that was in an energized election. I know some of you are mad that Todd is doing this without voting more often. You know what I think? I think there are so many Americans out there who aren't awake to politics. Over the last six months, as Todd and I have met with groups like this, we've been surprised how many people have come up and said, 'I was never involved until Donald Trump became president.' They had woken up. We all come to that point where we wake up. For Todd, it was the birth of his second child, and his school asking him to start teaching government, and Donald Trump running for president, all at the same time. It was a wake-up call. Todd's awake now, and he's ready for a fight."

Then Jan McDowell took the microphone. "Well, I'm glad he's finally awake."

---

[1] He said sarcastically.

The room tittered. I fumed as she went on to explain how she had been involved for years, had run against Kenny Marchant in the last election, and how she had paid her dues. The subtext was simple: She was dependable. She was going to show up, win or lose. As for Todd? Well, he isn't here tonight, is he? Maybe he's sleeping.

At least the world was spinning for an understandable reason now: I was angry. I was angry that Jan had taken a shot at Todd while he was burying a family member. I was angry she was taking shots at a surrogate while the candidate was in another fucking state. I was angry that I had set her up for it, lofted it up like a big, fat, lazy softball, just asking to be smashed over the right field fence. I was angry that I didn't know what was wrong with me. I was angry that I couldn't be sure that I wasn't about to collapse in front of everyone, and I was angry that, if I did, I didn't know if I could control myself enough to projectile vomit in Jan's general direction. I was angry that I was so worried about finances that I crawled instead of calling an ambulance. I was angry that my insurance wasn't covering much of my hospital visits.

And I was angry that Todd and I had spent six months of constant campaigning, thinking about policy, thinking about the voters, thinking about what could be done for the district, and all activists cared about was the fifteen collective minutes they thought he should have spent in a voting booth over the years.

For the first time, I didn't want to be better. I wanted to be mad.

I See It, Too

I'll say this for him: for a man who didn't much care to cook, Todd sure had an impressive gas-fed grill. It had that polished chrome look of equipment that was only used once in a blue moon, it was roughly the size of a Boeing 747, and, most importantly, it was mounted on wheels. Traditionally speaking, mobility isn't high on my criteria for outdoor cooking platforms, but when said platform weighs a metric ton and you're the one tasked with moving it across seven or eight suburban blocks, the mobility factor does tend to creep up on the scale of things that matter. The way things worked out, I was pushing and Todd was pulling, and the pavilion we had reserved for an All in for Allen campaign cookout and general day of jubilee was looking as if it might as well have been on the moon instead of a city park near Todd's house.

"Nah, dude," Todd assured me. "It's just a few blocks."

I grumbled something about distance being deceptive when you were the one guiding the rhinoceros instead of the one shoving the big bastard down a neighborhood street. He might have been inclined to argue the point, but he thought better of it after looking over his shoulder and noticing my face reddening with the effort of pushing a grilling behemoth uphill. Instead of pointing out my appalling lack of athletic skill, Todd opted for diplomacy. "Hey, the yard signs look good."

Yeah. Yeah, they did.

There was a stack of about fifty of those signs balanced precariously atop the grill, threatening to tumble to the street if I so much as took my steadying hand away for half a second. They were royal blue and white, nothing fancy or much out of the ordinary for political signs, and they certainly did a respectable job. The only thing wrong with them was that they broke a cardinal rule of marketing and it was mostly my fault: they took what had been a recognizable political brand and turned it on its head. Instead of displaying the stylized dialogue bubble that had been the campaign's logo since I sketched it out on a napkin at a Golden Nugget roulette table, the signs showed the angry, snarling face of a bear.

You read that right: a bear. Snarling. Growling, even.

In any case, upset.

I'm not sure when I first noticed Todd slipping in new stump language that referred to irritated mammals of the fuzzy variety. It might have been while I was cleaning up his answers to a candidate questionnaire for the newspaper, or maybe during one of his typical two-minute elevator pitches at a coffee shop meet and greet. Heck, it's even possible he tested out the bear language during one of our typical early morning, drive-to-work phone calls, and I just wasn't paying that much attention. I'm not sure when it first happened, but once I noticed it, I couldn't help but notice something else: saying it obviously made him happy because he kept saying some version of the same closing lines for the rest of the campaign.

"Look," he'd say, holding up a *Finger of Doom*, Harrison Ford–style. "I'll tell you the truth. I'm sick and tired of waking up every morning feeling as if my representative has kicked me right in the teeth. I'm sick and tired of feeling like my government doesn't know a damn thing about me, or my family, or how working-class Americans live. I'm tired of being told that I've got no place in this process because I hold down a job and raise a family and scrape by month-to-month. You know what people like me are? The American middle class? We're a sleeping bear that has been poked and prodded too long."

That's me doing a lot of the work and Todd smiling at the camera.

Then he'd bring it home.

"Friends," he'd say, "that bear is waking up and is gonna be ready for one hell of a fight. That is why I'm running for Congress: to fight for my family, for your family, for all of us. Thank you."

Then came the applause, which differed from what we usually heard at activist meetings and political get-togethers in one important way: it seemed genuine. For the first time, Todd seemed to be reaching a group of voters that had previously seen him as an amateur political adventurer at best and a Republican-lite political plant at worst.

Bears. I shook my head every time I thought about it, wondering whether finding the right mascot had been the key all along, not to

Todd pretends that he likes grilling.

mention finding the right tone. Todd wasn't saying anything substantially different—his policies hadn't shifted appreciably. He wasn't suddenly extolling the virtues of raising a monument to Vladmir Lenin on the Washington Mall. No, what had changed was how he said those things, and that harder edge seemed to make all the difference.

"Got an email today," Todd said casually as the grill inched its way down the street. "Sounded like the guy was just out of college. Said he was mad he had just now found out there was a strong progressive in the race. Said that, aside from Bernie Sanders in '16, I was going to be the first candidate he felt like he was voting for."

"That's gotta make you feel good," I said, trying not to sound like a winded octogenarian. "You know, if Kelsie had just hung around a month or so longer, I think she'd say you were doing exactly what she always wanted you to."

Todd looked over his shoulder. "Or maybe we should have listened to her a little more and got here a little sooner."

"I don't remember her ever mentioning bears," I grumbled.

It *was* funny, though. Todd was suddenly being viewed as the progressive he always had been, the progressive Kelsie had always said he needed to be, and that I always insisted he was. We hadn't even stopped using the language that had caused such consternation in the activist community: Todd always reminded people that We Can Be Better, he still spoke of the need for civility, conversation, and change. He just did it wearing a bear logo on his shirt and a bite in his voice I hadn't heard since my days in shoulder pads, waiting for the coach to come in to chew the team's ass out for literally and figuratively dropping the ball. To be honest, I was never sure in those closing months whether Todd wanted to pass progressive policies to support the working class, or he was hoping to see the defense get off their ass a little and swarm to the ball before the Bears lost by six touchdowns.

Regardless, he sounded good while saying it, comfortable in his own skin, and the more he said it, the more it called out to the anger in me that had been festering almost since the campaign started. The "Bear Rising" concept hadn't started out as a campaign strategy or a branding exercise or a much-needed rhetorical flourish, it was an honest moment of Todd Allen connecting emotionally with voters; including me, on a level that made sense.

Fuck yeah, I remember thinking, I'm angry. I've been teaching government classes for over a decade, lauding the virtues of our Republic to students, urging them to participate, but, goddamnit, it sure seems as if my government isn't interested in my problems. Where was affordable, quality healthcare when I needed it? Behind a rather hefty credit card payment. Where was financial support for student loans for teachers, or, for that matter, emotional or professional respect? Let me know when you find it. How come I have to worry constantly about what to do if I hear gunshots in the school hallway instead of worrying about how to tutor little Johnny or Jackie? Because, you know, fucking reasons, man.

So, sue me, I finally just asked Todd if he wanted to go ahead and change the logo to reflect his new language, and now we had signs emblazoned with a snarling bear.

"Did you freehand that bear or what?" Todd asked suddenly.

I snickered. "Sure, right after Liz asked me to draw her like one of my French girls. No—I did what I always did, found something that looked right online and did some Photoshop magic."

"What looked right?"

"A panda," I finally admitted.

Todd stopped even pretending to contribute to the transportation of the grill and turned to look at me incredulously. "A fucking panda?"

"Every good idea," I reminded him, "starts as a bad idea. Well, in this case, our bear started out as a panda. Live with it."

"Huh," he said, then put a guiding hand back on the grill. After a moment, he said, "There's the park. Looks like a good turnout, dude."

There were at least twenty people gathered under the pavilion by the time Todd and I arrived with that grill, most of them wearing baby-blue shirts with Todd's name on them. It wasn't a Beto rally by any stretch of the imagination, but then, no one had ever expected it to be. What Todd had wanted was one event, one day, that wasn't about impressing voters and stumping for new supporters; it was about saying thanks to the ones he already had. The campaign staff and volunteers had been invited over for hotdogs and drinks and a little fun in the sun, and if people out there in the Twenty-Fourth District wanted to come along, they could. Meanwhile, they'd find Todd firmly ensconced behind the grill, slapping hotdogs into buns and honestly seeming to enjoy himself. And they'd find me with my phone out, snapping pictures, taking videos, and amassing a collection of media I could use in the homestretch of the campaign.

By December and January, the race had solidified and settled down, though what it had settled into was a mess with no clear frontrunner. The endorsements from local activist groups and political associations had been trickling out, split almost evenly between Jan McDowell and John Biggan, with Todd taking a handful here and there, generally from groups representing marginalized or minority communities. In donations, John was the clear prize winner, raking in more than four times what Todd had. He was courting the activist community hard, block-walking constantly, and ignoring social media almost completely. Jan seemed to be coasting on longevity and familiarity with the base, cashing

Harper coloring in a message in sidewalk chalk: We Can Be Better.

in on the relationships she had established over the years and the fact that she was a permanent Loserville resident while Todd and John were seen as transients. To sum it up: Jan had name recognition, John had money, and Todd had media. None of the campaigns seemed willing or able to encroach upon the strength of the others.

So things were essentially in a holding pattern, waiting on something that would matter in the big picture, something that could shake up the race. There were two endorsements out there that had that potential; one was the coveted nod from the *Dallas Morning News*, which wouldn't even interview the candidates until January (by which time a surprise fourth candidate, Josh Imhoff, who I suspected actually was a plant from the GOP, had joined the race). We couldn't expect that endorsement until the end of January, maybe the beginning of February, and until then all the campaigns were just spinning their wheels and moving from event to event like political zombies moaning for brains or donations, whichever was at hand.

When I looked up from my phone after snapping a picture of Todd's daughter, Harper, scrawling a bright sunflower on the sidewalk in chalk, I noticed that there were quite a few more people under that pavilion, and none of the newcomers were wearing the campaign's baby blue. They were friends of friends, families of volunteers, colleagues of supporters, and, hot damn, people who had just seen the invite on social media and decided to come out and see why a candidate would use a logo better suited for the side of a football helmet (and, if possible, snag a free lunch while at it).

I moved over to where Todd was standing by the grill, watching the people mingle and laugh and converse.

"Dude," he said, almost reverently, gesturing at the gathering. "Would you look at this?"

I saw Liz and Lauren sitting at a picnic table, chatting and laughing as Todd's wife balanced his son Sam on her knee. I saw Leslie, resplendent in her cornflower blue campaign shirt, kneeling beside Harper on the sidewalk, using a thick piece of yellow chalk to scrawl out a reminder that We Can Be Better. I saw several kids I didn't know running around on the grass, playing tag. I saw Eric locked in a deep conversation with Sara and her mother. I saw Mike, for once not clad in a three-piece suit, looking a little uncomfortable in a Todd Allen T-shirt, but nevertheless smiling as he mingled with the curious walking up to the pavilion to see what all the fuss was about. I saw the stack of yard signs with Todd's snarling bear start to dwindle before finally vanishing, and I thought, Wait, didn't we bring out a hundred of these?

"Yeah, dude," I finally said. "Yeah, I see it."

"Me too," Todd said, and neither one of us was talking about anything or anyone under that pavilion. "The door knocking. The call lists. The groups. The interviews. The endorsements. The speeches. The hand shaking. Asking for money I won't get . . . "

He didn't finish the thought or the list. Instead, he bent down to pick up Sam, who had toddled over to him with a laugh for his daddy, and straightened with a sigh that, for the first time in months, wasn't directly attributable to fatigue or mental exhaustion or emotional trauma. It sounded . . . happy.

"I see it," he said again, and my friend was smiling.

Then my phone dinged, and being the social media junkie that I am, I set the golden moment of campaign success aside and looked down, hoping that I wouldn't see a political fire erupting that would necessitate anything more than an email to put out. It was a message from one of my teaching colleagues who had a vague interest in local politics without any intention of volunteering, donating, or maybe even voting, for anyone. The message was short and simple, with a link to a website. Heart racing, I opened the site . . . then reloaded it twice, just to be sure.

Just to be sure.

Then I stepped out to the middle of the pavilion and held up a hand.

"Folks," I said, raising my voice to be heard over the din. "Folks, I have a quick announcement to make."

People turned to look my way, their expressions curious, especially from those wearing baby blue. I had a carefully cultivated reputation for grumpy silence, after all.

"Thanks for coming," I began. "I know Todd appreciates it, and I appreciate it. Hope you enjoy the hot dogs." I looked down at my phone one last time to be sure, then added, "I just wanted to say that today, we can proudly announce that Todd Allen has won the support of the largest labor organization in the country. The Dallas AFL-CIO has endorsed Todd Allen for US Congress."

There was a second of stunned silence, then the cheers and applause erupted, followed by the buzz of excited conversation. There was a lot to be excited about: there were two endorsements that had the potential to shift the momentum of the race, two endorsements that could really matter, and, surprise, surprise, Todd Allen had just won the first. Not Jan McDowell, who was a long-standing member of the activist community with name recognition; not John Biggan, who had raised more money than anyone in the district had ever dreamed and was following the politico playbook page-by-page; but Todd Allen, the teacher and normal guy with a fucking bear on his shirt.

I moved closer to Todd, who was dazed and still holding Sam with a goofy smile frozen on his face. I shook his hand, but I'm not sure he noticed it: he was lost, somewhere, inside his own head, and I knew why.

"Yeah, I see it, too," I said again. "I see it, too."

PART IV

The Distance

The Rabbit Lady

B ack in the Antebellum Era, the political opponents of James K. Polk trumpeted a newspaper article about the travels and travails of an American frontiersman named Roorback that, among other things, accused presidential candidate Polk of branding his slaves.[1] The accusation wasn't true, and the article didn't have the intended effect of preventing Polk's ascension to the White House. But it did coin a charming term we just don't hear much about anymore: *roorbacking*, an unforeseen event emerging before an election to plague a political campaign. You don't hear the term much anymore because a staffer with Ronald Reagan came up with a snappier way to say it, which is why Mr. Roorback and his adventures in the American Southwest are no longer remembered even when we talk about the phenomenon of the October surprise. I preferred the earlier term, if only because it was funny to say, a detail that might snag on a student's memory.

"We've been roorbacked," I said aloud as Liz and I waited for Todd one night in late January, the Challenger's engine idling softly and the

---

[1] The fact that he *owned* people, apparently, wasn't enough.

sound of Miles Davis playing on the radio.

Liz raised an eyebrow.

I took it as an invitation to explain, which is actually more than a history teacher really needs. "Anyway, other than being fun to say," I said after finishing up my little spiel on Mr. Roorback and his impact on presidential politics, "it sums up a political event that comes along and just changes everything about a campaign. Usually something the candidate can't predict. Usually something that sucks real hard."

"Oh," Liz said, then she tried it on for size. "We got roorbacked."

We sat in silence for a moment, then she added, "It does sound funny to say."

"Yeah," I said.

Then I lapsed back into silence, trying to figure out what to say when Todd got to the car. Somehow, I didn't think a history lecture was going to cut the mustard, no matter how funny the word was when you said it aloud (and it was, go ahead and try it). Only a few weeks had passed since that moment when Todd and I had stood gazing around that gazebo in something like contentment, watching supporters chit-chat and munch on hot dogs. Only a few weeks since I had first seen Todd's name on the Dallas AFL-CIO's website. It felt like a big deal. It *was* a big deal. It was a sign that maybe, just maybe, Todd's messaging was getting through all the barriers and pitfalls in the way, and voters were listening.

So, I wondered as I sat there drumming my fingers on the Challenger's steering wheel, how do we get from the heights of that announcement to where we are today, just a few weeks later, with Liz and I down in the dumps and an angry, dejected candidate? How?

When in doubt, look to Marky Mark.

I'd like to think that your average person can prepare for the unexpected unpleasantness of life by immersing themselves in the cinematic *oeuvre* of Mark Wahlberg. Are you being threatened by psychotic trees looking to even up the score on a wasteful society? Check, I've seen that movie. Need a tutorial on staying true to childhood friendships with talking teddy bears, or how to deal with a cruel world that takes away Mila Kunis and replaces her with Amanda Seyfried? Seen it, absorbed it, learned from it. Caught in the freak intersection of three storm systems of hurricane strength while struggling to support yourself as a fisherman in the North Atlantic? Sure, it's a niche audience who take life lessons from *The Perfect Storm*, but I'm one of them, even if I've never set foot on a fishing trawler or dated Diane Lane.

Todd walked out to the car with his face set in a carefully composed mask. He cheerfully greeted Liz and chatted with her about her day as I pulled away from the curb and headed for the highway. We were heading to a late endorsement forum all the way out in Denton, a town that had managed to carve out its own unique pioneer identity long before it was swallowed up by the Dallas/Fort Worth Metroplex. The event being hosted out in Denton was as far afield as we ever went during the campaign, necessitating a drive of about forty-five minutes. I didn't know how long Todd could keep up the chatter about idiot administrators and helicopter parents with Liz, and I knew he didn't want to rehash the painful conversation we'd had that afternoon, so I reached for *The Perfect Storm*.

"Okay," I said, keeping my eyes on the darkening road ahead. "You know the end of *The Perfect Storm*? Everyone's made their peace with each other on the boat, they've got a fortune of fish in the hold, and they are steaming as fast as they can for the edge of the storm?"

"Sure," Todd said.

"There they are, taking waves head on, plowing ahead, and suddenly they see a ray of sunlight that breaks through the clouds and Mark Wahlberg's character goes all wide-eyed and says, 'Skipper, we're gonna make it!'"

I paused to allow Todd a chance to fill in the end of the scene, but he wasn't rising to the bait. Now, I knew he was familiar with the intricacies of *The Perfect Storm*, since one of his favorite time-killer conversational tools, when all other diversions failed, was to ask anyone who cared to listen who would win in a fight between Choose Your Own Character and the storm from *The Perfect Storm*. I'm about 90 percent certain that the very first conversation I ever had with Todd took place as the two of us stood in the back of a drill line during football practice at Trinity University, where Todd grilled me about who would emerge triumphant if Kurt Russell as Snake Plissken from *Escape from L.A.* would fight the storm from *The Perfect Storm* while in the frozen food aisle of a grocery store.[2]

So I knew he knew what the fuck I was talking about; he just didn't want to play along, a sure sign that the day's news had hit him below the emotional belt. But that's not how our friendship works, so I prompted, "You remember how that scene ends, right?"

"Yeah," Todd confirmed.

But then he changed the subject back to Liz's day and the classroom antics of her students. I exchanged glances with Liz, confirmed what she thought by noting her furrowed brow and worried expression. I sighed, concentrated on the road and on the monotonous droning of directions from Google Maps, and wondered how the campaign could have gone from the heights of bagging the AFL-CIO whale at Christmas to where we were that night. The answer, you might imagine, had nothing to do with our geographic location on I-35 somewhere north and west of Lewisville. The answer, truth be told, had come through just that morning, revealed on a web page refreshed for the thousandth time that finally told a different, infuriating tale than the one that came with the 999 clicks before.

The internet is funny that way.

The new year, for the campaign, had been a pretty damn good time. There had been no surprises, no new frustrations, no big swings to the election outlook, just the sense that what we were doing worked (at least for some people) and there was no reason to change. John Biggan was still making more money, still blockwalking and phonebanking, still doing everything by his consultant's playbook (and the smart gambler, I often thought in the deepest recesses of my consciousness, would place all their chips on him). Jan McDowell was still drawing endorsements from the older groups who were predictably sticking by one of their own, while the newer outfits were all-in on John. And, over on our little corner of the campaign, Todd Allen was the choice of those coming to the election via social media or word-of-mouth—not to mention the

---

[2]Snake all the way—he rode the wave.

choice of the Dallas AFL-CIO, an endorsement we trumpeted over and over as we put the holidays behind us and started down the homestretch of campaign season.

I had been in touch with the PR person over at the Dallas AFL-CIO, wanting to coordinate some media responses once the state convention of the AFL-CIO gathered mid-January and rubber-stamped the various chapter-nominated endorsements. That day came and went, and a little cloud appeared on my personal horizon. I reached out to my AFL-CIO contact without any luck. I phoned, I emailed, and I was just about ready to drive down to their headquarters and walk into the nearest office demanding answers that Todd's spider-sense was already giving him a preview of.

"I told you my gut was saying something was wrong," Todd muttered darkly from the passenger seat.

I frowned. I fear Todd's gut the same way some people dread going to the dentist and for the same reason—I've never heard good news while sitting in one of those torture-chamber-style dental chairs, and I've never known Todd's gut to be anything but the most cynical, pessimistic bastard in any room. Todd's gut is the kind of guy who stands up next to their buddy at a wedding and constantly mutters that it's not too late, they can always do a runner out the side door and get back the deposit on the venue.

I've also never known Todd's gut feelings to be wrong, which obviously sucked pretty hard for me.

That morning, his gut's dour grumblings of doom and gloom proved true, as I refreshed the AFL-CIO website and found, where once there had been a proud endorsement of the congressional candidacy of Edward "Todd" Allen, now there was nothing but a solid dash through the column where a name should be. I freaked. I erupted in anger. I cried salty tears of frustration. I wailed and moaned about the bitterness of betrayal. I cursed loud and long. I clicked refresh a dozen more times, I wrote long emails, I left messages that I thought were monuments to restraint but, upon further reflection, were probably about as tactful as a grizzly bear nosing through a campsite looking for treats. I delicately insinuated that I thought that it was pretty fucked up that the Dallas

AFL-CIO was screwing over a *teacher* without the courtesy of a reason. Then I did it again, without the delicacy.

All for naught.

Six weeks before the election, the Dallas AFL-CIO rescinded Todd's endorsement without so much of a word of explanation. The largest labor union in the nation had rescinded an endorsement of the only member of a union in the race, and they did it without a murmur of justification.

"Which no one's gonna need," Todd said quietly. He got quiet when angry. "All John or Jan or any of their friends in the groups have to do is ask what happened to that AFL-CIO thing we were so proud of. And everyone out there is gonna make up their own answer. And they will." He leaned back into the passenger seat and muttered, "They've fucked us."

Yeah. They did.

"We got roorbacked," I said.

Todd didn't even ask what I was talking about.

"I wish we had a villain in all this," Todd muttered. "Someone to . . . be mad at."

"Well," I said as I spotted our exit, "I don't need a villain to be mad."

"I just want to know *why* this happened," Todd said finally. "I just want to know *why*."

I wished that I could provide the answer, but I had none to give as we pulled into the parking lot of a Denton-area Chinese buffet in a strip mall. It was a bit of an odd event that awaited us: Todd and the other candidates, across a range of offices, were invited into a back room to be interviewed by a panel of activists. Those proceedings, unusually, were closed—meaning Liz and I had a solid hour or more to settle back into worn red faux-leather booths, pick our way through a wilted salad (Liz) and stress-eat lo mein and Mongolian beef (me). I was on my second or third trip to the buffet bar when I found myself standing next to a gray-haired woman with a kind smile. Something about that smile, or maybe it was the bifocals that made her look a bit like Mrs. Claus, made it seem like a good idea for an introvert like me to actually venture a comment to a stranger. Maybe it was just because I was emotionally wrecked, physically and mentally drained, and eating calories in bulk.

Or maybe someone, somewhere, knew that I needed to meet this lady at that particular moment. Things happen for a reason, Todd and I often said. Faith in the face of doubt.

I gestured to the bin full of fried chicken wings. "I know it's probably sacrilege, but the best thing at any Chinese buffet is the wings."

"Sounds like you've had extensive knowledge of Chinese buffets," she replied with a laugh. She gestured at the bin. "They are all yours!"

I laughed out a thank you. "I've been around my share of buffet tables. Umm . . . my buddy is running for Congress, and I'm basically all the help he has, so I've done a lot of these meetings. They never throw them at a gym, I've noticed. Anyway. . . I might as well have a doctorate in fried food studies."

She leaned forward to grasp my arm lightly. "Oh, is your friend Todd Allen?"

"Yeah. How'd you know that?" I asked curiously.

She smiled. "It's on your shirt."

I laughed. "I guess it is."

She looked at me and said sincerely, "I think he's doing *such* a good job."

Well, that was unexpected.

No, really. I've received compliments on Todd's behalf during the campaign, I've taken up donations and collected petition signatures, but I had never, until that moment, run into someone who didn't seem to have a political point to make or ax to grind. Apparently, she just honestly thought Todd was doing a good job, which, by extension, meant that she thought that I was doing a good job. And, right there by the chicken wings and the batch of french fries no one ever eats, because a stranger with a kind face said something nice to me on the worst day of the campaign, I damn near started to cry. I didn't, but it was an effort, and it didn't go unnoticed, because the lady with the smile and the compliments became concerned. "Are you alright?"

"Yeah," I said haltingly. "It's, uh . . . it's just been a long couple of months."

Then, on a whim, or maybe because on some level I sensed that I needed help, I asked her if she'd care to have dinner with me and my wife as we waited on the endorsement interviews to come to an end. Of course she said yes, because eating with strange couples you find at Chinese buffets in a state of emotional distress is just part of being on the campaign trail.

And that is how I met the Rabbit Lady.

Turns out she was also a candidate for public office, running for a county-level position in Denton in an unopposed primary. She worked in a law office, but her passion was clearly for her work running a rescue shelter for rabbits both domestic and wild, something she had been doing for a couple of decades and gained a lot of notoriety for. I think she was even featured in *Playboy* at one point (the *articles*, people). "She's like something out of Hollywood back in the thirties," Liz whispered to me at one point, and by then I knew what she meant—the Rabbit Lady was a class act in every possible way.

She was also an activist. The experience of the campaign had taught me what that meant: we were enemies, the British and the French, Indiana Jones and the Nazis, Mario and those weird mushroom things. Except, we weren't because the Rabbit Lady was, well . . . the Rabbit Lady. One of a kind.

We *did* talk about what she liked about Todd and his campaign, by the way, but not as much as you might think. In fact, we hardly talked about politics at all as I remember. Liz later said that it was the only time during the entire election season when someone seemed to see her for herself and not as just an instrument of the campaign or a cog in the Todd Allen machine. She and Liz spent a lot of time talking about teaching—what Liz liked about it, what the challenges were, what kept her going, questions that I wished more school administrators thought to ask. The Rabbit Lady wasn't just marking time until the event was over; it might sound silly, but she made us feel like *we* were the event.

She even got me talking about my own teaching, and a project that my students were going to be doing soon. I have a habit of doing big, ungainly, nearly unmanageable things, as I'm sure you've guessed by now, and in my classroom one of those things was an annual historical role-playing project. Some years I'd get kids in a room that looked like it hadn't been renovated since the sixties and we'd spend thirteen hours pretending we were in the Kennedy Administration during the Cuban Missile Crisis (I have a pretty awful Boston accent, it turns out, but that didn't stop Kevin Costner). Sometimes we'd be in Mission Control during the Moon Landings, or hauling cannons as part of George Washington's army. That year, we were planning on kids portraying passengers on the last night of the maiden voyage of the *RMS Titanic*.

"There are so many little details to work in," I told the Rabbit Lady.

"I'll bet," she said.

"You know," I said, "I found something interesting as I was doing research for this. What is the one thing you always hear about the *Titanic* story, the one thing that could have saved lives?"

"More lifeboats," the Rabbit Lady answered promptly. "They didn't have enough lifeboats, right? Not even close."

"Right," I confirmed. "They had what the law required plus a little extra, but that still didn't account for more than about half the passengers. They could have had more, the designers had even planned for more, but the decision was made that more boats would take up too much deck space and annoy passengers." I paused and took a drink of flat soda. "But it turns out that doesn't matter at all. No amount of lifeboats would have saved those people."

"But . . . if they had more . . . ?"

"The limiting factor was time," I said, totally into my subject now. I was a history teacher, after all. "Time. The ship sank in about two hours. They barely had enough time to launch the lifeboats they had, and not even all of those. They didn't have time to launch more, even if they had them. It didn't matter at all."

I sat back, suddenly melancholy, and repeated, "It didn't matter at all . . ."

"Not exactly the story we've been told, is it?" the Rabbit Lady said.

"No," I muttered. "Kinda like politics. Getting involved. It's not . . . not what Aaron Sorkin and Jimmy Stewart told me it would be."

"Maybe I should have a word with them," the Rabbit Lady suggested gently, and we all laughed a little.

And that's when it all came out. I told her how excited I had been back in the spring, even if I tried to play it cool and convince Todd that actually winning wasn't really a possibility. I told her about how proud I was of what Todd had done, what we were all doing: we weren't just talking, we were running, doing exactly what the Founders envisioned. It was like something out of those textbooks I taught from, an example of civic engagement that I thought was really kinda extraordinary. We were just teachers, Todd was just a teacher, which, of course, meant that he worked long days for little pay and less respect, and he did it because he gave a shit about the world around him. He tutored kids who needed it. He held hands through tough assignments and rough times. He bought more than one lunch for more than one kid who couldn't afford it. And he taught. Goddamnit, he taught. He brought the concepts the Founders had enshrined in the Constitution to life and made it matter, and when kids left his class, they at least knew what their country was supposed to be.

"I thought people would love the idea of what he was doing," I admitted to the Rabbit Lady. "I thought . . . here was a guy who was an amazing teacher, a husband, and a father, and he's making this huge sacrifice of time and money that he doesn't have because he thinks he should. I thought people would understand."

"But they didn't?" the Rabbit Lady asked.

I looked up at her, and if I wasn't tearing up, it was only because I was scared that once I started it would get ugly in a hurry. "They hate him," I said frankly. "They hate *us*. We showed up and they didn't welcome us at all, the activists, the groups. They just say we haven't done enough. We didn't blockwalk enough. We didn't vote enough. We didn't spend enough time marching, or protesting, or . . . sitting at buffets like this one. None of the time and effort he's spending now matters to them. And I don't know why."

I was looking down at the table, now, because it was easier. Because I didn't want to see the Rabbit Lady frown and disagree with me. Because just one more disappointment, just one more, on that day, and I probably would have grabbed Todd and told him that we were done—or at least I was. I looked down at that table and said, "All we've been told, from the beginning, was that we weren't welcome. I don't know how to square that with what I teach kids about elections and campaigns. I don't know what to teach them anymore. I don't know what to think."

After a long moment, the Rabbit Lady said, "Well, honey, first you have to realize that it was never about the lifeboats."

I looked up into her eyes, and the kindness was still there. "I'm sorry," she said simply, as if she could apologize for the process, the activists, the disappointment, the AFL-CIO, all of it.

And, in that moment, it turned out she could. "Tell Todd, for what it is worth, that he has my vote."

"I will."

"And, honey, everything you've done, or said . . . it all matters."

Todd didn't get the endorsement of that Denton group that night, but he got the Rabbit Lady's vote. I introduced them as soon as he stepped out of the back room, then moved outside to wait and think as they talked. Out into the cold night air, where I could take the little nugget of something new that I had learned and examine it without the smell of frying oil and wantons. While Liz waited in the Challenger with the heater running and Todd discovered that there was at least one activist who was inspired by what he was doing, I stood out in the chill of that Denton night and took out my new discovery to examine it a little closer. It was nothing fancy, nothing complex, just a simple fact that glittered more than gold and meant more than any endorsement.

It was the realization that there was one person in politics who was a decent human being.

Right then and there, that realization meant more to me than anything in the world.

When Todd walked out to join me, he had a little smile on his face. Before I could ask him about his conversation with the Rabbit Lady, my own discovery of the political Ark of the Covenant, or even about the group endorsement he'd just spent an hour trying and failing to win, Todd looked up at the clear sky, the bright moon. "God, it's a nice night."

It actually was.

Then he added, "That scene, from *The Perfect Storm*—There they are, powering through the waves, going for broke to escape the storm, they see that glimmer of light, and everyone watching thinks 'Holy shit, those guys are gonna make it.' Even though they know, they *know* how the movie ends. But for that one moment, they forget and convince themselves that maybe they survive. Maybe. Then the light gets covered up by a cloud and Clooney says something like, 'She's not gonna let us out.'"

"Yeah," I said softly.

"Yeah," Todd echoed, still looking up at the sky. He sniffed and declared a fact, a realization: "We can't win, can we?"

"No," I responded quietly. "No, I don't think so."

He finally looked away from the sky and put a hand on my shoulder. "That's not actually the end of the scene, you know."

"What isn't?" I asked, confused.

"*The Perfect Storm*," Todd said. "That scene doesn't end with the storm swallowing up the light and everything going to hell. It actually ends with George Clooney turning the ship around to head *back* into the storm."

"Yeah, it does," I said. "I guess I forgot about that part."

"Me too," Todd said. He took a deep breath. "I think we've got two choices: accept the inevitable, just hide away and wait for election day, or we can keep fighting and keep throwing punches until the end." He paused. "What do you think?"

He didn't need me to tell him what to do; I already knew. I'd known since two idiots made an overnight dash for fame and fortune in a long drive to California. I knew he wasn't going to quit. But, at that moment, I think what he needed me to say was that he wouldn't be alone in that ring, that I would finish the fight with him.

I didn't hesitate.

"Turn the boat around," I told him.

"Yeah," Todd said with a smile. "We finish this on our own terms. We say what we've gotta say. And we tell the fucking storm to Bring It On."

A cynical person might wonder why Todd and I chose to mix cinematic allusions from *Rocky* and Marky Mark together in one of the most meaningful moments of the campaign. Such people probably didn't vote for us, and are all the poorer for it. Also, *fuck* those people: this is who we are, how we think, how we talk, and how we live. This is us, Todd and Heath, and how we faced what was coming. Take it or leave it.

I nodded.

"Okay, Skipper," I said. "Let's go the distance."

That Scene from *Heat*

It took until the week before Election Day for me to figure out the most important secret about the political process that a neophyte campaign manager could learn. It turns out that the most effective way to survive, possibly even enjoy, a meeting of political activists or a candidate meet and greet is simple: just don't be there. In the building, obviously, just not in the actual room where the candidates are introducing themselves for the hundredth time. That night, for that event, I decided that the last thing Todd needed was to look up and see me sitting along the back wall, doing my best not to look disappointed. He didn't need me there for emotional support or to rush to his defense or even to collect signatures; after all, we were long past all that. So instead of giving myself a cramp by crouching in a catcher's squat against a wall, I took a table in the restaurant, ordered some nachos and a margarita, and settled back to enjoy the good life.

And it *was* good. I could even see a football game on a television over the bar.

I spent my time doodling numbers in my notebook. As a history teacher, I was not overly fond of numbers, doodled or otherwise, and I had a long-standing argument with a friend and math teacher about how unfair it was that mathematics had started colonizing letters, which I felt was unfair. That night, however, was an exception, because despite our conversation outside of that Chinese-food buffet in Denton, I was trying to convince myself that Todd Allen could win. I just needed to find the numbers to prove it, first to myself, then to Todd and, more importantly, Todd's gut instinct. I was looking at voting trends in the district, making what I hoped were educated guesses on vote totals and who might vote for whom. A picture started to emerge that I thought offered some hope.

Sure, Jan had the support of most of the activist and political clubs, but what did that really mean? How many of those people were there? In more than six months, I had seen, what, maybe a hundred different individuals? Two hundred, at most? Let's even be generous and give the groups voting power equivalent to their social media follower counts. How many voters was that as a percentage of the primary voting population? And Jan was splitting that number with John, who was running a campaign aimed squarely at those same voters.

Which way would new voters go? I asked myself. Where would they discover information about candidates? On what would they make their decisions? Word of mouth? Activist recommendations and endorsements? Or . . . social media content?

I was seeing a path to victory. Maybe.

Then a shadow fell across the page. Looking up, I saw something entirely unexpected and unwelcome: instead of the waiter dropping by with a fresh basket of chips and a refilled mug of margarita, I saw John Biggan's young campaign manager, Miller, grinning and sticking out a hand. I took it reflexively as he said, "Hi, I don't think we've ever officially met. I'm Miller, with John's campaign."

I shook his hand. "Well, we have exchanged a glare or two in every Mexican restaurant or Chinese buffet in the district, so . . . that counts, right?"

I'm an introvert, so I was hoping it counted, and also that Miller would pick up on the subtitles running at the bottom of the screen, which read, Hey, I'd really like to not talk to you. Not everyone watches movies with the subtitles, unfortunately, so after I gave him my name, he gestured at the seat across from me. "Do you mind if I sit with you tonight?"

Oh, God, please don't, I thought.

I didn't say that, however, just nodded as he sat down with his Diet Coke.

I made an effort. I motioned to the nachos. "These are community nachos, by the way. Open to the table. Help yourself."

That was my way of playing nice.

He sat down and for a moment there was awkward silence because of course there was. Neither one of us had shown the slightest inclination of shooting the shit or passing the time of day for six months, so it wasn't as if we had a storehouse of useful chitchat to make now. He took a chip, ate it slowly. I took a chip, ate it slowly. We watched each other chew.[1]

"So," he ventured, "just about over, isn't it?"

"Yep," I said, and the ball was back in his court.

He ate another chip, then took the plunge.

"How do you think it's gonna turn out?" he asked, smiling.

I shrugged. "Well, I hear that Gene McCarthy is doing well with the college kids, but I think they'll come around."

He just looked at me.

Don't they teach anything in government courses anymore? I thought to myself, then decided that his efforts at conversation, polite conversation even, merited more than me being a smart-ass. "I think it'll go to a runoff," I offered, and felt pretty good about myself for contributing to the dialogue.

He nodded. "That's what we think, too. No one will get that fifty plus one and we'll have a runoff." He paused, stirred the ice in his glass with his straw, then added, "Jan's got one of the runoff spots sewed up."

"Sure," I said. "*Dallas Morning News* endorsement pretty much guaranteed that, didn't it?"

---

[1] Humans look weird when they eat, did you know that? Seriously, we're odd looking.

"Yeah," Miller said, leaning forward, eager to talk shop. "I was surprised by that endorsement. My guy walked out thinking it was all his."

"Mine too," I admitted.

When the *Dallas Morning News* had come out recommending Jan McDowell, Todd and I weren't too shocked or too rocked by it. The AFL-CIO, if nothing else, had prepared us for disappointment in that respect. Still, the manner of the endorsement had led to a nice drive-to-work bitch session, mostly because the representatives of the Editorial Board had only mentioned a single policy of Jan's that impressed them: her support for STEM education. Now, despite the fact that I had heard Jan speak literally countless times and never heard her talk about public education, there was another reason the endorsement annoyed me. How, I wondered, was it possible that, with two actual fucking educators in the room, the Editorial Board has decided that the one without teaching experience was the one with an education policy worth talking about?

But it didn't annoy me for long. Todd and I had reached a level of calm acceptance where it came to the campaign. Maybe we had just been hit enough times that we were numb to it, and that numbness actually helped us get past the frustration and keep punching, harder and faster, like a boxer who had broken a hand and couldn't even feel the pain anymore (I'm 90 percent certain I've seen that in a *Rocky* movie). Todd was as relaxed and confident during those last weeks as I had ever seen him, smoothly charismatic during a speech and as personable as ever, if not more so, as he worked a room. The pressure was off, there were no more endorsements to win, no more donors to court, no more strategies to try, nothing but the will of the voters come March and, until then, the chance to stand up and speak in front of a captive audience.

He spoke, and he did it with a smile.

I was so proud of him. How often in life can you say you've ever been proud, truly proud, of a friend? Well, I can say it: I was proud of him. Going the fucking distance.

"You know, the runoff doesn't have to necessarily include Jan," Miller suggested, interrupting my thoughts. He was still leaning forward, his voice pitched low, and I thought, Ah, so here's the real conversation. "You didn't get back to us in December when we reached out to you about ballot access."

"It was a cryptic message, Miller," I reminded him. "A message you sent on Christmas Eve, actually. I figured you'd get back to me if it was important."

"We've hired a lawyer," he said, still almost whispering. "There's something wrong with Jan's petition signatures."

"For ballot access?"

He nodded. "The lawyer thinks that not all of them are genuine. Lots of duplicates, questionable addresses, non-district residents, stuff like that. Not enough valid signatures there to get on the ballot. And if she's not on the ballot . . . "

I reached for a chip. "Okay, so what are you waiting for?"

He smiled ever so slightly. "We thought it would be good for there to be a united front from all the candidates. Todd should join the suit, maybe even kick in some dough to pay for it."

Then he leaned back, still smiling, and the rest of the conversation took place without a word being said aloud, just two guys staring at each other over a plate of rapidly dwindling nachos.

Why would we do something like that? I wondered.

Because we think you are fucking idiots, his smile answered.

Because y'all think we are fucking idiots, I answered for myself, shaking my head. You think we don't realize that launching a lawsuit to get Jan McDowell off the ballot will piss off her supporters, which is a large part of the activist community? You think I don't know that, with her off the ballot, the anger will be directed at Todd, who they love to hate, and the clear beneficiary becomes John Biggan? I am naïve, I may even be politically incompetent, but I'm not brain-dead.

Finally, I broke the silence. "Well, why don't you grab Todd when this shindig is over and see what he thinks?"

I had learned at least this much about politics: never say no, never say yes, and, if you can help it, never say anything.

He made a gesture as if it was all no big deal. "Sure, I'll see what he thinks."

Then I asked the kind of question one politico shouldn't ask of another: a real one. "So, hey," I said, "I've been wondering what John said to the AFL-CIO to get them to rescind Todd's endorsement."

Miller's face colored just a bit. This was a conversation he didn't really want to have, but I was forcing it on him, and now he was having to decide how peaceful our little dinner table truce really was. "Oh," he said, trying to sound nonchalant, "I don't know much about it, really. We did make the point that it didn't seem fair that John never got to address the committee for that one. He was in Hawai'i with his family."

"On vacation," I added through gritted teeth. I remembered the photos on social media. Beautiful place, Hawai'i. Maybe one day I'll go there, I thought, if, of course, I can avoid the cops and get some pretty good plastic surgery after I commit bloody fucking murder right here over the chips and queso.

I had always had the suspicion that there was something just a bit sketchy, a bit shameful, about the AFL-CIO endorsement and its sudden disappearance, as if pulling it was something they weren't really proud of. Miller didn't have to get too detailed in his reply; his smirk was enough to let me know where the pressure had come from. The truth, I realized, was that we had played politics as a clean game, and it wasn't, and I was sitting at a table with living proof of that.

"Hey, your turn to clear up something," Miller said, still smirking a bit. "What's the next animal y'all are going to use as a mascot?"

Because I'm generally a non-confrontational person, I didn't make any rude suggestions at the moment. Back in the fall, shortly after John entered the race and announced his first huge fundraising haul, I had cut an ad for Todd that referred to our campaign as an underdog. It was a good ad, and I ran with that theme for a week or so on social media, building upon the class dichotomy that emerged after the forum. It was really the first stirring of what would become our Bear Rising approach. Apparently, the addition of a bear to the milieu had caused some merriment among those who ran under the banner of a crooked logo.

"Well," I said carefully, "I think the image of a Republican elephant getting devoured by a shark carried by a blue wave could be appealing."

He laughed.

I couldn't resist. This time it was me who leaned forward and lowered his voice. "Miller, when all is said and done on election day and if you've lost, what are you gonna do the day after?"

He looked confused, hesitant, and suspicious. Carefully, he said, "I really don't know. Someone will be running and need my help, so I suppose I'll be working somewhere to beat the GOP in November."

I wasn't surprised by his answer, but I'm sure he was surprised by mine. I said, "You know what I'll do? I think I'll take my wife out to dinner. Somewhere Italian, because I've had enough Mexican and Chinese food to last a lifetime, and also because I'm a sucker for carbs. We'll talk about the baby due in July and maybe finally decide on a name. Maybe not. Maybe we won't have to decide on anything. Maybe we'll just talk. About her students, mine. About administrators acting stupid or parents making impossible demands. Maybe just about whether we need that second boat of alfredo sauce, and we will. Then we'll go home."

I leaned back. "That's what my day after will look like. A great day."

"I hope you get the chance to enjoy it," Miller said, and I heard the edge to it.

"I will enjoy it," I said, meaning it.

That confused him again. He smiled and nodded and said something pleasant, but our conversation was essentially over, and we both knew it. I gestured at the space in front of me where I had pushed away an empty plate of nachos. "I'm going to go ahead and order a slice of *tres leches* now."

As a goodbye, it wasn't half bad. I'm an introvert, remember.

As he walked back into the meeting room, I glanced back down at my notebook. The numbers written there made sense, they could be real, they could be the story of what was coming. Or, conversely, they could just be numbers. I didn't know, but did it matter? The only numbers that were going to matter were the ones that would show up on my computer screen on the night of the election, and those numbers wouldn't need much interpretation. Meanwhile, why worry?

I ate my cake.

The Letter

The last strains of Tom T. Hall's "That's How I Got to Memphis" were fading away on the radio as Todd and I pulled up to a random polling place on election day. The parking lot was mostly empty, as you might expect of a municipal building of questionable necessity on a Tuesday morning; primary elections were never really barn burners when it came to turnout. I parked the Challenger beside the largest political sign in the lot, the royal blue and white behemoth that urged people to vote for Todd Allen or, and my design was only meant to subliminally suggest this, they'd risk getting mauled by an angry bear. It was the only sign our campaign had at that particular location (the budget for ursine-themed political adverts wasn't inexhaustible), but it was striking, nevertheless, even when surrounded by a literal forest of colorful examples from every other candidate under the sun. I spotted dozens of purple yard signs supporting Jan and an equal number bearing the name of John Biggan before I stopped counting or caring.

A voter walked into the building, eyes on her phone, never once look-ing at any of the signs. Then another, also looking at her phone. Then a third, who didn't even have the excuse of a phone: he walked into the building briskly, looking straight ahead, hands in his pockets.

I grunted. "I wonder how much wasted money we're looking at out there, just for this one location?"

Todd chuckled and looked up from his own phone. "If nothing else, this experience has taught me that there is no limit to the amount of money people will waste if it makes them feel good."

Then he sighed, and I could follow his gaze and guess why. Just outside the boundary lines required by law, a group of activists that we knew only too well (and yet, hardly at all) were camped out in lawn chairs under giant umbrellas. Any minute now, Todd would have to get out of the car and go shoot the shit with them for a while, greet voters, smile and laugh and shake hands and, in my wildest dreams, point to his sign while delicately suggesting that we had a bear on call and we'd neglected to feed it for the last week. Then we'd get in the car, drive to the next location, and do it again, then again, then again, over and over until the polls closed.

So, naturally, Todd sighed. "I don't think I want to."

"Greet poll watchers and voters?" I asked.

"Win," Todd corrected after a moment's pause. "I was talking to my dad last night, and the last thing he did was wish me luck. I didn't know how to tell him that I really didn't want it."

It was a stunning admission, especially for two competitive guys like us, but I wasn't surprised at all. It was the kind of thing we'd probably never talk about aloud to anyone, because who would understand how it felt to do something like this, what it cost, when you were just two classroom teachers doing their absolute best and realizing it probably wouldn't be enough? It wasn't about giving up, or conceding defeat, or even being lazy; it was about the trauma of six months of the completely unexpected coming to a probable end.

We sat in silence for a moment, then Todd turned to me. "You know I didn't put in for a substitute for tomorrow? As far as the school is con-cerned, the day after the election I'll be standing in that classroom, just

We couldn't afford many signs, but we could afford big signs, and I like to think it was a good strategy.

like I did yesterday. Teaching government."

"Me neither," I confirmed, smiling a little. It *was* funny: two teachers had spent months running for Congress, all while still spending nine or more hours of each day lecturing on the virtues of democracy, and now . . . neither of them had any plans to do anything but head back to the classroom the day after it all ended. It was, if nothing else, exactly on brand for Todd Allen, the guy who had been selling himself since the beginning as just an average, everyday American trying to do something extraordinary.

It wasn't a hard sell: he *was* that guy.

And he deserved a day off.

"Dude," I said. "You don't need to get out of this car today. You don't have to justify today to anyone. If you don't shake hands and kiss babies today, and you lose, who gives a shit? And if you don't shake hands or kiss babies today and you win, then *fuck you, you sonsofbitches*, we won."

I paused. "Either way, this is *your* day. I don't want to jinx it, but . . . we're only going to do this once. In our entire lives, this is the only time we'll do this. We did it, though. *You* did it. You ran for US Congress. You walked into a voting booth and put a check by your name. Those people walking in right now, they are gonna look down and see your name because you worked your ass off to put it there. So today, if you want to fuck off, drive around, listen to music, and drink a fucking milkshake, let's drive around, listen to music, and drink fucking milkshakes."

"Yeah, we better go," he said without a moment's hesitation.

"Hell yeah." I reached for the keys and gunned the engine to life.

We decided we'd keep to our basic plan for the day, touring each polling place, but without any pressure to actually campaign, glad-hand, or do anything other than appreciate the fact that people were walking in to cast votes on a ballot with Todd's name on it. We'd grab some milkshakes, bitch about politics and activists, then head to my house to await the election results over a beer or two. Eric and Mike had urged us to consider having a watch party that evening, like the other candidates, but neither Todd or myself were all that eager to share the moment of almost-certain defeat (or unbelievable triumph) with a larger audience. People had been watching Todd for six months and more. The least I could do was make sure that, for this one day, he had an opportunity to face the results on his own terms.

"Like in *Predator*," I explained to Todd as we pulled out of the Whataburger drive-through.

"You lost me," Todd said.

"The Indian dude in *Predator*," I clarified. "He just up and decides, fuck it, I'm facing this space ghost thing on my own terms, right here on this fucking log, and I'm gonna do it with nothing but a bare chest and this machete."

"Then he gets gutted, right?"

"Well," I said, ". . . they leave that up to the imagination. Happens off-screen. Just like us watching the results tonight."

I'll be honest: I was feeling good that day. I hadn't felt that good in a long, long time, almost buoyant, absolutely free of concerns, like that guy off of *Office Space*, but without the hypnotism or flair. It wasn't even

Look, we have flyers and signs and a logo and everything.

necessarily because I thought we were about to lose, because I am an optimist, remember? I had those numbers in my notebook and I was half-convinced that our social media game had reached all the new voters pouring into polling places, and at 7:00 p.m. we'd hear that the Mid-Cities wanted to send a teacher to Congress. I knew Todd was in a different place. He didn't have the faith in the magical powers of my notebook that I did. His gut, his dreaded intestinally based intuition, had been telling him for some time that not only was he not going to make a runoff, but that there wasn't going to be a runoff, *period*. He was dead certain that Jan McDowell was going to come out of this primary as the clear winner.

I couldn't see it. I just couldn't see the district, including all those new voters, deciding that Jan McDowell was the best candidate to take out an entrenched Republican with a deep war chest. John Biggan, certainly, yes, I absolutely could see that happening. But Jan?

"Hey, speak of the devil," I said, pointing out the window. At a local library, John and Miller were planted out on the sidewalk, smiling so much that I wanted to stop and ask them if they had some kind of medical condition and if it was catching. To the very end, John was doing *exactly* what he needed to do, and should do, if you wanted to win an election. He had courted the important activist leaders, he had hired a consultant, he had raised an astounding amount of money for a district in Loserville, he had quit his job to campaign full-time, he had block-walked and blockwalked and blockwalked, and now he was greeting voters, vying for every last possible vote. He was Todd's mirror image, the one who did things the way they were supposed to be done; Todd did things the way they had to be done for an everyday guy just trying to make it from day to day without getting fired, divorced, or imprisoned.

I was okay with that. Plus, I had a milkshake and Miller didn't, so, you know, who really won, in the end?

I reached down and found a song on my phone. The sound of the Avett Brothers crooning "Head Full of Doubt" began to fill the car.

Todd smiled knowingly. "Ah, yes, where it all started." He sipped on his milkshake. "I love that line: *Decide what to be and go be it.*"

I pulled into a back corner of the library's parking lot and we sat for a moment, watching John Biggan work the voters, watching other candidates appear and do the same, all while we finished milkshakes and I polished off a large order of fries. A thought struck me, which I immediately voiced: "Back in the beginning, if you had asked me how election day would look, I would have described, I dunno . . . something a lot more chaotic. Something like you'd see in a movie about Eisenhower's headquarters during D-Day. We'd be in a bare-walled strip mall office, streamers running wall-to-wall, campaign signs leaning up against corners, five or six people constantly on telephones, maybe a map of the district or a whiteboard with someone constantly updating numbers . . ."

I trailed off, then added, "I never really pictured it being just the two of us sitting in a car with milkshakes."

Todd set his empty cup down, said, "I dunno, dude . . . even if we won in a landslide, I kinda think it would always end up with the two of us sitting in a car with some milkshakes."

"And if we don't win in a landslide? If we lose?"

"I'm cool with that too," Todd said. "These last few weeks, I've tried to focus on why I wanted to do this in the first place. And I remembered it was never about winning. I mean, in the movie in my head, sure, but in reality, it was also about taking a risk, and proving that regular folks could make a difference." He reached for his own notebook, which he habitually brought to every campaign event and which I had never seen him actually open. He plucked out a loose sheet of well-wrinkled and worn paper torn from a personalized pad labeled *From the Desk of Mr. Allen*. On it were a few hastily scrawled sentences. I'd seen it before. I knew what it said. I'd even made one of Todd's most successful video ads based on what was written there.

But it had been a long, long time since I had thought about what it actually meant.

"I was rummaging through all the campaign material last night, and right on top was this guy," Todd said holding it up. "I must've read it a hundred times last night."

I took the paper and remembered when I'd seen it for the first time. It had been back in the spring, on the day Todd showed up at my house with a milkshake and a decision: he was going to run for US Congress. There was a line in a song he couldn't shake, *decide what to be and go be it*. As he sat in his empty classroom, staring at the posters of influential people and documents he believed in and taught, something clicked, and he wrote out exactly why he was making the decision to throw himself into a campaign for public office. We'd always just called it "The Letter":

> *I don't want to look back on my life and wonder about the shots I didn't take. What legacy will I leave for my children? Will they know their dad took his shots, fought the fight, and proved despite the odds, risk is worth experience? I want Harper and Sam, twenty or thirty years from now, to take chances, because their dad took chances. I still believe in America. I still believe a teacher can challenge a millionaire Washington elite and win. If nothing else my children will know their dad believed the impossible was possible. That it's not too late for us. That people, character, and truth still matter.*

After a moment, I handed The Letter back to him, said, "Okay, I'm a

FROM THE DESK OF
Mr. Allen

I don't want to look back on my life and wonder about the shots I didn't take. What legacy will I leave for my children? Will they know their dad took his shots, fought the fight, and proved despite the odds, risk is worth experience? I want Harper and Sam, twenty or thirty years from now, to take chances because their dad took chances. I still believe in America. I still believe a teacher can challenge a millionaire, washington elite, and win. If nothing else, my children will know their dad believed the "impossible" was possible, that's its not too late for us, and that people and character and truth still matter.

Todd's inspiration and most passionate supporters: Sam and Harper!

believer. Even after six months of excruciating bullshit and a steady diet of daily dick punches, I still think it was worth it. It matters."

"It matters," Todd echoed. Then he said, "You know, we started talking about running for Congress because we felt like we needed to. To prove something. To do something. To live with ourselves. Fuck, I dunno, maybe because we like long odds and we like the attention and we thought we'd get our fill of both. None of that was enough, though. I didn't decide to run until I thought of my kids. I thought of what running would mean for Harper and Sam."

Todd paused for a second, searching for the right words. "I mean, I know they barely understand what's going on right now. All they probably know for certain is their dad has been gone a lot. But back in April, I just thought . . . Man, I want them to know that when things got dark out there, their dad did *something*. I wanted them to know that chasing big, bold ideas is okay. Taking chances is okay. This impossible thing we did, this big, bold, impossible thing . . ."

"It was worth a shot," I said softly.

"Yeah," He looked at me and nodded. "It was worth a shot. One day, when they are older and understand what this was all about, I hope they know that I tried and that, when the time comes, they can try, too. Because risk is worth experience, and nobody can tell you it's too big, or too much."

Heavy moment. It was a shame to ruin it with a smart-ass comment, but we are who we are. I took a last swig of my Dr. Pepper milkshake, which Whataburger really should sell year-round, cracked a grin, and said, "So you're saying you just wanna go the distance, am I right?"

Todd understood. What's more, he understood that I understood.

"God damn it," he said with a smile and a sigh. "Let's get some lunch, I feel like we need some tacos, probably some queso."

"Torchy's?" I asked.[1]

No hesitation. "Fuck, yes."

---

[1] The queso is out of this world. Take my word for it.

What Kind of Day Has It Been

Todd was on the shitter when the first election results came in on March 6, 2018.

U. S. Representative District 24

Jan McDowell	*14,626*	*52.47%*
John Biggan	*5,998*	*21.52%*
Edward "Todd" Allen	*5,574*	*20.00%*
Josh Imhoff	*1,678*	*6.02%*

We didn't say very much after seeing those numbers roll across my laptop screen. Todd went home without ever finishing his beer. For my part, I had a snack and then headed up to my office to fulfill my last obligation to the Allen for Congress campaign. I found my copy of *Legends of the Fall* on the shelf and prepared the campaign's final statement for social media. I posted it without asking permission, but I didn't think Todd would mind. It was a short video clip of the last few seconds of the film, when the grizzled hero, Tristan Ludlow, meets his end, knife in hand, locked in combat with an even more grizzled antagonist: an actual grizzly bear.

The copy attached to the post was simple.

I wrote: "It was a good death."

Forget It, Jake
(A Kind of Epilogue, I Guess)

A lot of water has flowed under the bridge since the spring of 2018. The world has turned a few times. Shit has gone down. Donald Trump lost an election, threw a hissy fit, bullied elections officials, and inspired an armed insurrection that stormed the Capitol Building, and the only surprising thing about any of it was that none of it was surprising at all. A pandemic brought the world to the brink of something out of a Stephen King novel. Schools shut down, the economy shuddered and nearly collapsed, and somehow the takeaway Americans ran with was that teachers were to blame for all of it. The Supreme Court decided that decades of precedent in *Roe v. Wade*, not to mention the fundamental right women have over their own biology, could be tossed overboard for legal reasons that amounted to Because We Can. School boards became politicized and then weaponized. Books were banned. LGTBQ students were ridiculed, harassed, and discriminated against, and laws were passed saying that all of it was pretty much okay as long as you lived in Texas. It became unpopular and then dangerous to discuss issues like race, slavery, or the Holocaust in public schools, all while questions of race, policing, discrimination, and our shared history were spilling out into the streets.

And there was a pretty damn good *Top Gun* movie that came out somewhere in there.

For the Allen and Hamrick families, life had continued on without too much muss or fuss. Todd and Lauren continued to raise their two beautiful kids, and Liz and I welcomed two of our own into the world. The former congressional candidate and his former campaign manager went back to doing what they did best. We stood up in class, we taught, we lectured on the intricacies of American government to high school seniors, and if either of us thought that we had a little more insight into the reality of that government after a run for office, we kept it to ourselves and kept our jobs. Todd moved out of the classroom in 2022 and into a leadership position as an assistant principal. Come early October of that year, as election season reached a fever pitch, he finally got to enjoy a much-needed Saturday without a single school function needing administrator oversight, meaning he finally got to stick around the house in jogging shorts and an old T-shirt, watching *John Wick* on HBO and thinking about nothing in particular.

Then the doorbell rang.

Lauren answered the door, and Todd didn't think too much about it until he realized that a few minutes had passed and he could hear Lauren *still* conversing with whoever had appeared at the front door. He decided that he had seen *John Wick* enough times that he could afford to step away from the television for a bit just to see what was up.

What he found at the front door was his wife in pleasant conversation with two other women, both of them holding pamphlets for political candidates in their hands. Well, it was that time of year, and there were certainly several school board races that were drumming up controversy.

Then Todd recognized one of the blockwalkers.

It was the Green Dress Lady.

Fixing a smile on his face, he walked up to the door and said cheerfully, "Well, hello, there." The Green Dress Lady looked up at him, and he saw a flicker of confusion and hesitation on her face at the familiar nature of the greeting. She covered it quickly, gave him an equally pleasant hello and how-are-you, but the cat was out of the bag. Todd guessed the awful truth: She doesn't know who I am, he thought.

"Todd Allen," he said as he walked up and took a pamphlet. "We met about five years ago. I was running for Congress, remember?"

Hesitation.

"As a Democrat?" she asked.

"Yeah," Todd confirmed.

The Green Dress Lady shook her head with a little smile on her face. "I'm sorry, I'm not sure that I remember. We . . . we might not have met."

"We met," Todd assured her. "I don't think you voted for me."

Then he looked down at the flyer. "You can tell these folks they've got my vote. The other guys are nuts."

"They sure are," the Green Dress Lady agreed, laughing a little.

Then they were gone, the door was closed, and Lauren was looking at Todd with wide eyes. "Are you kidding me?" she said incredulously, then started laughing. Then Todd joined in. It's entirely possible his earliest campaign nemesis heard that laughter as she and her companion walked down the driveway to the sidewalk, already looking up the next door they needed to knock on.

I'd like to think they could. I'm a bit vindictive that way.

So how do we get from the disappointment of losing a primary in the spring of 2018 to that day almost four years later when Todd met the Green Dress Lady at his door and realized that she either didn't remember him or wanted to pretend that she didn't? How did two teachers assimilate the lessons of a long, expensive, time-consuming march through the American political process? Quite frankly, it began by not talking about it at all. I don't think I spoke to Todd for at least two weeks after the election. It wasn't anything personal, it was just that both of us were devoting all of our time to the cause of repairing our lives, fixing the holes in relationships with family, friends, and professions that giving ourselves over to a political campaign had caused. I went from

The Bear Rising logo on our big signs.

worrying about how well-prepared Todd was for an endorsement forum for the Dallas County Stonewall Democrats to stressing out over how well prepared my students were for their end-of-course exams. Actually, that's not quite right—Todd and I never forgot we were teachers, and our kids did as well or better that year we spent chasing an impossible dream than they did in years prior. For all of our faults as politicians, and we had plenty, everything we did was done in addition to being first-rate educators. I'd like to see some of our more persistent detractors try pulling that off.

Anyway, we slipped back into our lives, and for a long time it was disturbing how easy it was. How could something we had spent so much time doing, and put so much of ourselves into, be so easily forgotten and set aside? Hell, we never even talked much about the results in those first weeks. Todd was right. The day after the election, the day after he lost, we both were back in classrooms as if nothing had happened. At some point on the day after the election, Todd found himself reaching a pausing point in his lecture, taking a breath, and realizing, Holy shit, it's only Wednesday.

We didn't just need a weekend; we needed a vacation.

But by the summer, it was becoming more and more important to me to understand what had happened during that campaign, to figure out what it had all meant. I wanted meaning. I wanted closure. I wanted answers. Todd and I started to pick up on our morning phone calls again, and when we weren't wondering what absolutely fucked up thing the American president was going to do or say next, we were analyzing the campaign, the results, and our mental health (not necessarily in that order). We came up with bullshit theories. We threw out bullshit ideas. And, somewhere in there, we started talking about writing a book.

This book.

"Hey," Liz said as she read through the first draft. "What do you mean when you say this is a *mostly* true story?"

"You were there, you know this stuff happened," I said.

"Then why do you say it's *mostly* true?" she persisted.

"It's true!" I insisted. "Mostly."

Full disclosure: this stuff happened. Except for those who ran for public office and those in marriages to the coauthors, names have been changed to protect the innocent and the assholes alike. There was an additional reason for the obfuscation: many of the characters in this book are actually *composites* of several different people who wandered in and out of our lives during the campaign. The timeline of events has been compressed, here or there. And, as I'm sure you noticed, dialogue has been reconstructed and presented in a narrative format. We wrote it that way for a reason: this is a book about people, and people talk. We wrote it as a narrative because it is a story.

So, this story is true. It happened. Even the weirdest bits.

Especially the weirdest bits.

People sometimes ask what we would do differently if we had the chance to go back in time and do it all over again. I counter, "What would we do differently, or what would we do differently if we wanted to win?" Those are two different questions. If you picked up this book because someone told you it was an entertaining read, or because you were a frustrated American looking to make some sense out of politics, what you're probably hoping to hear is something that would have resulted in a more storybook ending, something a lot more like *Rocky IV* than *Rocky*. Looking back, I don't know that there was ever a moment when Todd Allen could have won the Cold War with a single punch, but I can imagine how things might have played out to provide what my childhood heroes Wayne and Garth might have called a Mega Happy Ending.

It would begin with one person with clout, one donor or activist leader, who made it clear in July that Todd Allen was something special. Instead of leaving the campaign, Kelsie stayed on board, succeeding in bringing the groups around to an idea of an Allen candidacy. Instead of entering the race, John Biggan decides that he needs to get involved by *joining* the Allen campaign, bringing his ability to work phones, raise money, and court activists to bear for (ha, ha) the candidate with a bear in his logo. Todd wins the primary, maybe not handily, but he wins, and then he takes on Kenny Marchant in November, who treats him almost exactly like he treated Jan McDowell in real life. In other words, Marchant virtually ignores the race, and instead of beating Jan by a shockingly small margin of three points (when he had beat her by double digits two years earlier), Todd makes up that vote gap and wins. Suddenly, he's a politician who has done the impossible, so he gets a lot of news coverage, he rubs shoulders with AOC and Adam Schiff, he winds up meeting Jon Stewart at some rally and delivering a heart-felt plea for the man to please get back on the air because America needs him. Because he has some media love, he's able to bring attention to the education system in this country, and to immigration reform, and to the need for some kind of fucking gun control already.

Does he win re-election in 2020? I think so, because instead of the race being between an ultra-liberal and a blond-haired, blue-eyed Trump supporter, it becomes a race between a guy urging Americans to recognize that We Can Be Better against a woman who was utterly batshit crazy. So I think he wins, which means he and I are probably at the US Capitol on January 6, 2021, when Trump's little insurrection plays out. A scary thought.

And then? Does he run again in '22, our hypothetical two-term Congressman? No, not after the GOP gerrymandered the district into an absolute grand-slam certainty for the Republican candidate for the next decade. What does Todd Allen do? Does he get a call to maybe run for something else, something a little bigger?

Anyway, there you have it: the Mega Happy Ending, the ending Netflix will probably go with if they decide to adapt this book into a series or something.[1]

Now, if you're a young college student and hopeful political operative, then you're probably more interested in practicalities, in which case I can give you some pretty good advice: whatever we did in the book, maybe do the opposite. You couldn't go far wrong in looking up one of Todd's primary opponents, John Biggan, and picking his brain for a while. John did everything right, by the book, and with efficiency, and his campaign was a model of how someone new to the system could excel. I have a lot of admiration for John, and if this book sends a few potential disciples his way or encourages him to take another run at things, all the better.

Of course, John did everything right . . . and lost.

John blockwalked, he raised gobs of money, he worked the phones, he bent the knee to activist leadership, and, when the votes were counted, he got just about the same amount of votes as Todd Allen, a candidate who did absolutely none of those things even remotely well, if at all. The Allen campaign was sincere, we had a great story and a great media game, and that got us 20 percent of the vote count. All of John's work, his money, his blockwalking, got him 21 percent of the vote. It's tempting to think that those researchers from Stanford and Berkley got it right and that the sacred cows of politics, including yard signs and phone-banking, don't do shit. It's also tempting to think that if Todd and I had been different people, and were willing or able to do the things that John did, and combined it with our media game, then Todd Allen might have

---

[1] Wink, wink, nudge, nudge, come on, Sorkin!

won. But that ignores the fact that neither Todd nor John came even close to denying the winner, Jan McDowell, an outright victory.

Someone theorized that Jan got a big bump because it was the Year of the Woman and female candidates across the board saw vote increases. I think that's too easy. Todd's gut says that her name recognition won the day. I think that's too easy, too (with all due respect to Todd's intuition, which, I might have mentioned, I dread). Jan didn't just win: she kicked the living shit out of two candidates boasting a lot of advantages. Then she went on to shock the district by making up a gap of damn near twenty points and nearly unseating Kenny Marchant in November 2018. She announced her candidacy for 2020 the very next day. She was poised to finish the fight. She had momentum. She had proved herself to the world. She was ready to *win*.

But that wasn't the message the world took from the 2018 election cycle. The message the world took was that District 24 in Texas was no longer a political Loserville. It was *in* play. It was serious. And Jan suddenly found herself with more knives in her back then Caesar.

Of everyone portrayed in this book, the only one whose portrayal I feel bad about is Jan. There's nothing for it, considering it's from my point of view at that point in my life, a time in which I saw Jan as nothing but a bad candidate with a squeaky voice, little charisma, and no media presence. What I learned in the years afterward was that Jan was, if nothing else, fucking persistent. She was absolutely a fighter; it came off as being mean during the '18 primary, but, hey, fights are mean things. Jan had flaws as a candidate, huge ones, but you know, she was also hardworking, willing to listen and engage with new ideas, passionate about policy, and absolutely sincere about wanting to work for the people. I was infuriated when the district suddenly emerged from Loserville and voters, including the activist groups so willing to endorse her in 2018, sold her down the river. She came in a distant third in the 2020 primary behind a woman who lived over a hundred miles away and another who was planning on running farther to the left than AOC.

But here's the rub, folks: while Todd and I hope you've enjoyed what is, at heart, a buddy comedy about real, average, normal, ordinary, everyday Americans trying to get involved in politics, there is a deeper takeaway. Deeper, even, than my frustration with a primary system set up to prevent real, average, normal, ordinary, everyday Americans from being welcomed to the process. The true takeaway is that this nation has become, by and large, a Loserville, a place where the only election that matters is the primary election, and for those in the minority party, the impact is staggering. Loserville is a state of mind, and I'm not sure anyone has ever quite delved into what that entails. I don't say that purely because the denizens of Loserville rejected Todd and his campaign (mistakes were made, after all), but because they also rejected John Biggan, who did everything he was supposed to. They rejected Jan McDowell, who fought so hard for two election cycles to close a vote gap of truly astounding proportions. Why?

What is going on in Loserville? What is in the water? And what does it mean for America?

I mentioned earlier that District Twenty-Four was, predictably, gerrymandered after the 2020 election to make it a safe, ruby-red district for the foreseeable future. The Democrat in '22 would lose by double digits and the Republican wouldn't need to spend a dime. This wasn't political prognostication, it was absolute certainty, and everyone knew it. Despite that certainty, and despite the fact that the groups and voters had turned on her as soon as they thought they could actually win in '20, the Democrat who stepped up to run for US Congress in CD-24 in 2022 was none other than Jan McDowell.

Who lost. By over 53,000 votes.

Forget it, Jake. It's Loserville.

About the Authors

Todd Allen and Heath Hamrick are award-winning high school teachers, creative consultants, and just possibly the most naïve, idealistic, and clueless political neophytes in the long history of American politics. Both Todd and Heath graduated from Trinity University in San Antonio with degrees in political science, and by 2004 both were in Texas classrooms, facing the surprising knowledge that they were born educators. In 2018, Todd Allen ran for US Congress in Texas CD-24 as a Democrat, with Heath as his campaign manager, media guru, and wartime consigliere who dispensed the kind of idealistic advice that only works on television shows scripted by Aaron Sorkin. Todd serves as an educational administrator, while Heath works as an educational and media consultant.